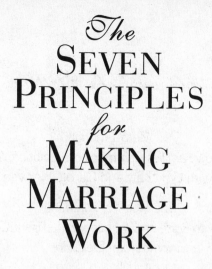

The
SEVEN
PRINCIPLES
for
MAKING
MARRIAGE
WORK

Also by John Gottman

Meta-Emotion:
How Families Communicate Emotionally
with Lynn Katz and Carole Hooven

The Heart of Parenting:
How to Raise an Emotionally Intelligent Child
with Joan DeClaire

The Analysis of Change

Why Marriages Succeed or Fail
with Nan Silver

What Predicts Divorce?

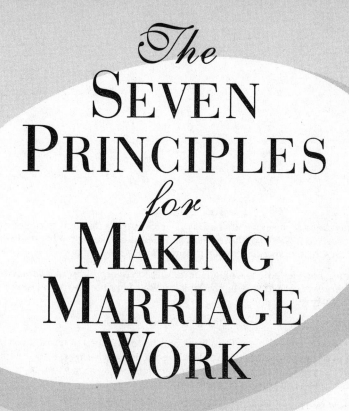

The SEVEN PRINCIPLES *for* MAKING MARRIAGE WORK

John M. Gottman, Ph.D.,
and Nan Silver

THREE RIVERS PRESS • NEW YORK

The anecdotes in this book are based on Dr. Gottman's research. Some of the couples are composites of those who volunteered to take part in his studies. In all cases, names and identifying information have been changed.

Grateful acknowledgment is made for permission to reprint from *After the Honeymoon* copyright © 1988 by Daniel B. Wile. Reprinted by permission of John Wiley & Sons, Inc.

Published by Three Rivers Press, New York, New York.
Member of the Crown Publishing Group.

Random House, Inc. New York, Toronto, London, Sydney, Auckland
www.randomhouse.com

Three Rivers Press is a registered trademark and the Three Rivers Press colophon is a trademark of Random House, Inc.

Originally published in hardcover by Crown Publishers in 1999

Printed in the United States of America

Design by HROBERTS DESIGN

Library of Congress Cataloging-in-Publication Data
Gottman, John Mordechai.
    The seven principles for making marriage work / John Gottman and Nan Silver.
    1. Marriage.   2. Married people—Psychology.   3. Communication in marriage.   4. Man-woman relationships.   I. Silver, Nan.   II. Title.
HQ734.G7136   1999
306.81—dc21   98-45407

ISBN 0-609-80579-7

30 29 28 27 26 25

To Julie Gottman, who gives collaboration a new meaning, and to the core of my team: Sybil Carrere, Sharon Fentiman, and Cathryn Swanson. They made it all possible and helped make the journey itself delightful, like eating pastries and drinking coffee together in a sidewalk café.

J.G.

To Arthur, my beloved and my friend

N.S.

Acknowledgments

First and foremost, I need to acknowledge the brave gift that several thousand volunteer research couples have contributed to my understanding. Their willingness to reveal the most private aspects of their personal lives has opened a hitherto closed door that has made it possible to construct these Seven Principles for making marriages work.

This book was based on research that received continuous support from the National Institute of Mental Health, the Behavioral Science Research Branch. Of great assistance was the dedicated guidance of Molly Oliveri, Della Hahn, and Joy Schulterbrandt.

This book was also made possible by a number of important collaborations that have been a joyful part of my life. These include the main collaboration that has graced my life for the past nineteen years with Professor Robert Levenson of the University of California. Also important to me has been my collaboration with Neil Jacobson of the University of Washington and my work with Dr. Laura Carstensen of Stanford University.

I have been blessed with rich associations inside my laboratory. The cornerstones have been Sharon Fentiman, whose elegance greatly improves my life and keeps me from chaos; Dr. Sybil Carrere, who runs my lab and is a terrific colleague; and Cathryn Swanson, my programmer and data analyst. Not only are they friends and intellectual companions, but they help make coming to work a pleasant experience. I also wish to acknowledge the contributions and stimulation of Lynn Katz.

My wife, Julie Schwartz Gottman, provided love, friendship, motivation, intellectual camaraderie, support, and conceptual organization. She has also been my teacher and guide in practicing psychotherapy. She made doing the couples' and parents' workshops an exciting creative experience. While we are busy with our full-time jobs, Etana Dykan capably runs our Seattle Marital and Family Institute with great spirit and attention to detail, and she also helps facilitate our communication. Her amazingly creative brother, Shai Steinberg, has also been a tremendous asset in many areas of our work. Linda Wright helps us keep the couples' enterprise very warm and human—she is unusually gifted in talking to desperate couples. Peter Langsam has been our faithful consultant and partner throughout, helping us with wise counsel, elemental guidance, and business sense.

I have recently been blessed with excellent students and staff, including Kim Buehlman, Jim Coan, Melissa Hawkins, Carole Hooven, Vanessa Kahen, Lynn Katz, Michael Lorber, Kim McCoy, Janni Morford, Sonny Ruckstahl, Regina Rushe, Kimberly Ryan, Alyson Shapiro, Tim Stickle, and Beverly Wilson.

I need to acknowledge the intellectual heritage upon which I draw. As Newton once wrote, "If I have seen further . . . it is by standing upon the shoulders of giants." For me these shoulders include the work of Les Greenberg and Susan Johnson on emotionally focused marital therapy; Bob Weiss's scholarly work on many concepts, including sentiment overrides; Cliff Notarius's work on many concepts, including couple efficacy; Howard Markman's faith in preventive intervention; Dick Stuart's great contributions, including his approach to behavior exchange; Jerry Lewis's work focusing on the balance of autonomy and connectedness in marriage; and the persistent work of my colleague Neil Jacobson, who is the gold standard for marital therapy research. I am also indebted to Jacobson's recent work with Andy Christensen, on acceptance in marital therapy. I also wish to acknowledge the contributions of Peggy Papp and Pepper Schwartz and their feminist approach to gender differences and egalitarian marriage, as well as the work of Ronald Levant and Alan Booth on men in families.

I must also mention Dan Wile's work on marital therapy, with its superb focus on process. I love Wile's writing and thinking. They are entirely consistent with many of my research findings. I think that

Wile is a genius and the greatest living marital therapist. I am blessed to have been able to exchange ideas with him.

I wish to acknowledge the work of Irvin Yalom and Victor Frankl on existential psychotherapy. Yalom has provided a great faith in the therapeutic process itself and in the human force toward growth. Frankl holds a special place in my heart. He and my beloved cousin Kurt Ladner were both residents and survivors of the Dachau concentration camp. Both found meaning in the context of intense suffering, tyranny, and dehumanization. I hope to bring their existential search for meaning into the marital context. Doing so can turn conflict into a new experience of revealing and honoring life dreams, finding shared meaning, and reaffirming the marital friendship.

I have come to the conclusion that many insightful writers in the marital field are basically correct. I hope my contribution will be to honor them all, adding a bit of precision and integration to the struggle to understand what makes close relationships work.

J.G.

Contents

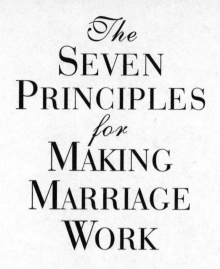

The
SEVEN
PRINCIPLES
for
MAKING
MARRIAGE
WORK

1

Inside the Seattle Love Lab:
The Truth about
Happy Marriages

*I*t's a surprisingly cloudless Seattle morning as newlyweds Mark and Janice Gordon sit down to breakfast.
Outside the apartment's picture window, the waters
of Montlake cut a deep-blue swath, while runners jog and geese wad-
dle along the lakeside park. Mark and Janice are enjoying the view as
they munch on their French toast and share the Sunday paper. Later
Mark will probably switch on the football game while Janice chats
over the phone with her mom in St. Louis.

All seems ordinary enough inside this studio apartment—until
you notice the three video cameras bolted to the wall, the micro-
phones clipped talk-show style to Mark's and Janice's collars, and
the Holter monitors strapped around their chests. Mark and Janice's lovely studio with a view is really not their apartment at all. It's
a laboratory at the University of Washington in Seattle, where for sixteen years I have spearheaded the most extensive and innovative
research ever into marriage and divorce.

As part of one of these studies, Mark and Janice (as well as forty-
nine other randomly selected couples) volunteered to stay overnight in our fabricated apartment, affectionately known as the Love

Lab. Their instructions were to act as naturally as possible, despite my team of scientists observing them from behind the one-way kitchen mirror, the cameras recording their every word and facial expression, and the sensors tracking bodily signs of stress or relaxation, such as how quickly their hearts pound. (To preserve basic privacy, the couples were monitored only from nine A.M. to nine P.M. and never while in the bathroom.) The apartment comes equipped with a fold-out sofa, a working kitchen, a phone, TV, VCR, and CD player. Couples were told to bring their groceries, their newspapers, their laptops, needlepoint, hand weights, even their pets— whatever they would need to experience a typical weekend.

My goal has been nothing more ambitious than to uncover the truth about marriage—to finally answer the questions that have puzzled people for so long: Why is marriage so tough at times? Why do some lifelong relationships click, while others just tick away like a time bomb? And how can you prevent a marriage from going bad—or rescue one that already has?

Predicting Divorce with 91 Percent Accuracy

After years of research I can finally answer these questions. In fact, I am now able to predict whether a couple will stay happily together or lose their way. I can make this prediction after listening to the couple interact in our Love Lab for as little as five minutes! My accuracy rate in these predictions averages 91 percent over three separate studies. In other words, in 91 percent of the cases where I have predicted that a couple's marriage would eventually fail or succeed, time has proven me right. These predictions are not based on my intuition or preconceived notions of what marriage "should" be, but on the data I've accumulated over years of study.

At first you might be tempted to shrug off my research results as just another in a long line of newfangled theories. It's certainly easy to be cynical when someone tells you they've figured out what really makes marriages last and can show you how to rescue or divorce-proof your own. Plenty of people consider themselves to be experts on marriage—and are more than happy to give you their opinion of how to form a more perfect union.

But that's the key word—*opinion*. Before the breakthroughs my research provided, point of view was pretty much all that anyone trying to help couples had to go on. And that includes just about every qualified, talented, and well-trained marriage counselor out there. Usually a responsible therapist's approach to helping couples is based on his or her professional training and experience, intuition, family history, perhaps even religious conviction. But the one thing it's not based on is hard scientific evidence. Because until now there really hasn't been any rigorous scientific data about why some marriages succeed and others flop.

For all of the attention my ability to predict divorce has earned me, the most rewarding findings to come out of my studies are the Seven Principles that will *prevent* a marriage from breaking up.

EMOTIONALLY INTELLIGENT MARRIAGES

What can make a marriage work is surprisingly simple. Happily married couples aren't smarter, richer, or more psychologically astute than others. But in their day-to-day lives, they have hit upon a dynamic that keeps their negative thoughts and feelings about each other (which all couples have) from overwhelming their positive ones. They have what I call an emotionally intelligent marriage.

I can predict whether a couple will divorce after watching and listening to them for just five minutes.

Recently, emotional intelligence has become widely recognized as an important predictor of a child's success later in life. The more in touch with emotions and the better able a child is to understand and get along with others, the sunnier that child's future, whatever his or her academic IQ. The same is true for relationships between spouses. The more emotionally intelligent a couple—the better able they are to understand, honor, and respect each other and their marriage—the more likely that they will indeed live happily ever after. Just as parents can teach their children emotional intelligence, this is also a skill that a couple can be taught. As simple as it sounds, it can keep husband and wife on the positive side of the divorce odds.

WHY SAVE YOUR MARRIAGE?

Speaking of those odds, the divorce statistics remain dire. The chance of a first marriage ending in divorce over a forty-year period is 67 percent. Half of all divorces will occur in the first seven years. Some studies find the divorce rate for second marriages is as much as 10 percent higher than for first-timers. The chance of getting divorced remains so high that it makes sense for all married couples—including those who are currently satisfied with their relationship—to put extra effort into their marriages to keep them strong.

One of the saddest reasons a marriage dies is that neither spouse recognizes its value until it is too late. Only after the papers have been signed, the furniture divided, and separate apartments rented do the exes realize how much they really gave up when they gave up on each other. Too often a good marriage is taken for granted rather than given the nurturing and respect it deserves and desperately needs. Some people may think that getting divorced or languishing in an unhappy marriage is no big deal—they may even consider it trendy. But there's now plenty of evidence documenting just how harmful this can be for all involved.

Thanks to the work of researchers like Lois Verbrugge and James House, both of the University of Michigan, we now know that an unhappy marriage can increase your chances of getting sick by roughly 35 percent and even shorten your life by an average of four years. The flip side: People who are happily married live longer, healthier lives than either divorced people or those who are unhappily married. Scientists know for certain that these differences exist, but we are not yet sure why.

Part of the answer may simply be that in an unhappy marriage people experience chronic, diffuse physiological arousal—in other words, they feel physically stressed and usually emotionally stressed as well. This puts added wear and tear on the body and mind, which can present itself in any number of physical ailments, including high blood pressure and heart disease, and in a host of psychological ones, including anxiety, depression, suicide, violence, psychosis, homicide, and substance abuse.

Not surprisingly, happily married couples have a far lower rate of such maladies. They also tend to be more health-conscious than others. Researchers theorize that this is because spouses keep after each other to have regular checkups, take medicine, eat nutritiously, and so on.

People who stay married live four years longer than people who don't.

Recently my laboratory uncovered some exciting, preliminary evidence that a good marriage may also keep you healthier by directly benefiting your immune system, which spearheads the body's defenses against illness. Researchers have known for about a decade that divorce can depress the immune system's function. Theoretically this lowering in the system's ability to fight foreign invaders could leave you open to more infectious diseases and cancers. Now we have found that the opposite may also be true. Not only do happily married people avoid this drop in immune function, but their immune systems may even be getting an extra boost.

When we tested the immune system responses of the fifty couples who stayed overnight in the Love Lab, we found a striking difference between those who were very satisfied with their marriages and those whose emotional response to each other was neutral or who were unhappy. Specifically, we used blood samples from each subject to test the response of certain of their white blood cells— the immune system's major defense weapons. In general, happily married men and women showed a greater proliferation of these white blood cells when exposed to foreign invaders than did the other subjects.

We also tested the effectiveness of other immune system warriors—the natural killer cells, which, true to their name, destroy body cells that have been damaged or altered (such as infected or cancerous ones) and are known to limit the growth of tumor cells. Again, subjects who were satisfied with their marriage had more effective natural killer cells than did the others.

It will take more study before scientists can confirm that this boost in the immune system is one of the mechanisms by which a good marriage benefits your health and longevity. But what's most important is that we know for certain that a good marriage does. In fact, I often think that if fitness buffs spent just 10 percent of their weekly workout time—say, twenty minutes a day—working on their marriage instead of their bodies, they would get three times the health benefits they derive from climbing the StairMaster!

When a marriage goes sour, husband and wife are not the only ones to suffer—the children do, too. In a study I conducted of sixty-three preschoolers, those being raised in homes where there was great marital hostility had chronically elevated levels of stress hormones compared with the other children studied. We don't know what the long-term repercussions of this stress will be for their health. But we do know that this biological indication of extreme stress was echoed in their behavior. We followed them through age fifteen and found that, compared with other children their age, these kids suffered far more from truancy, depression, peer rejection, behavioral problems (especially aggression), low achievement at school, and even school failure.

One important message of these findings is that it is *not* wise to stay in a bad marriage for the sake of your children. It is clearly harmful to raise kids in a home that is subsumed by hostility between the parents. A peaceful divorce is better than a warlike marriage. Unfortunately, divorces are rarely peaceful. The mutual hostility between the parents usually continues after the breakup. For that reason, children of divorce often fare just as poorly as those caught in the crossfire of a miserable marriage.

INNOVATIVE RESEARCH, REVOLUTIONARY FINDINGS

When it comes to saving a marriage, the stakes are high for every-body in the family. And yet despite the documented importance of marital satisfaction, the amount of scientifically sound research into keeping marriages stable and happy is shockingly small. When I first began researching marriage in 1972, you could probably have held all of the "good" scientific data on marriage in one hand. By "good" I mean findings that were collected using scientific methods as rigor-ous as those used by medical science. For example, many studies of marital happiness were conducted solely by having husbands and wives fill out questionnaires. This approach is called the self-report method, and although it has its uses, it is also quite limited. How do you know a wife is happy just because she checks the "happy" box on some form? Women in physically abusive relationships, for exam-ple, score very high on questionnaires about marital satisfaction. Only if the woman feels safe and is interviewed one on one does she reveal her agony.

To address this paucity of good research, my colleagues and I have supplemented traditional approaches to studying marriage with many innovative, more extensive methods. We are now follow-ing seven hundred couples in seven different studies. We have not just studied newlyweds but long-term couples who were first assessed while in their forties or sixties. We have also studied cou-ples just becoming parents and couples interacting with their babies, their preschoolers, and their teenagers.

As part of this research, I have interviewed couples about the history of their marriage, their philosophy about marriage, how they viewed their parents' marriages. I have videotaped them talk-ing to each other about how their day went, discussing areas of con-tinuing disagreement in their marriage, and also conversing about joyful topics. And to get a physiological read of how stressed or relaxed they were feeling, I measured their heart rate, blood flow, sweat output, blood pressure, and immune function moment by moment. In all of these studies, I'd play back the tapes to the cou-ples and ask them for an insiders' perspective of what they were thinking and feeling when, say, their heart rate or blood pressure suddenly surged during a marital discussion. And I've kept track of the couples, checking in with them at least every year to see how their relationship is faring.

So far my colleagues and I are the only researchers to conduct such an exhaustive observation and analysis of married couples. Our data offer the first real glimpse of the inner workings—the *anatomy*—of marriage. The results of these studies, *not* my own opinions, form the basis of my Seven Principles for making marriage work. These principles, in turn, are the cornerstones of a remarkably effective short-term therapy for couples that I have developed along with my wife, clinical psychologist Julie Gottman, Ph.D. This therapy, and some briefer workshops that follow the same principles, are intended for couples who find that their marriage is in trouble or just want to ensure it stays strong.

Our approach contrasts dramatically with the standard one offered by most marriage therapists. This is because as my research began to uncover the true story of marriage, I had to throw out some long-hallowed beliefs about marriage and divorce.

WHY MOST MARRIAGE THERAPY FAILS

If you've had or are having troubles in your relationship, you've probably gotten lots of advice. Sometimes it seems like everybody who's ever been married or knows anyone who's ever been married thinks he holds the secret to guaranteeing endless love. But most of these notions, whether intoned by a psychologist on TV or by a wise manicurist at the local mall, are wrong. Many such theories, even those initially espoused by talented theorists, have been long discredited—or deserve to be. But they have become so firmly entrenched in the popular culture that you'd never know it.

Perhaps the biggest myth of all is that communication—and more specifically, learning to resolve your conflicts—is the royal road to romance and an enduring, happy marriage. Whatever a marriage therapist's theoretical orientation, whether you opt for short-term therapy, long-term therapy, or a three-minute radio consultation with your local Frasier, the message you'll get is pretty uniform: Learn to communicate better. The sweeping popularity of this approach is easy to understand. When most couples find themselves in a conflict (whether it gets played out as a short spat, an all-out screaming match, or stony silence), they each gird themselves to win the fight. They become so focused on how hurt they feel, on proving that they're right and their spouse is wrong, or on keeping up a cold shoulder, that the lines of communication between the two may be overcome by static or shut down altogether. So it seems to make sense that calmly and lovingly listening to each other's perspective would lead couples to find compromise solutions and regain their marital composure.

The most common technique recommended for resolving conflict—used in one guise or another by most marital therapists—is called active listening. For example, a therapist might urge you to try some form of the listener-speaker exchange. Let's say Judy is upset that Bob works late most nights. The therapist asks Judy to state her complaints as "I" statements that focus on what she's feeling rather than hurling accusations at Bob. Judy will say, "I feel lonely and overwhelmed when I'm home alone with the kids night after night while you're working late," rather than, "It's so selfish of you to always work late and expect me to take care of the kids by myself."

Then Bob is asked to paraphrase both the content and the feelings of Judy's message, and to check with her if he's got it right. (This shows he is actively listening to her.) He is also asked to validate her feelings—to let her know he considers them legitimate, that he respects and empathizes with her even if he doesn't share her perspective. He might say: "It must be hard for you to watch the kids by yourself when I'm working late." Bob is being asked to suspend judgment, not argue for his point of view, and to respond nondefensively. "I hear you" is a common active-listening buzz word. Thanks to Bill Clinton, "I feel your pain" may now be the most notorious.

By forcing couples to see their differences from each other's perspective, problem solving is supposed to take place without anger. This approach is often recommended whatever the specific issue—whether your conflict concerns the size of your grocery bill or major differences in your lifelong goals. Conflict resolution is touted not only as a cure-all for troubled marriages but as a tonic that can prevent good marriages from faltering.

Where did this approach come from? The pioneers of marital therapy adapted it from techniques used by the renowned psychotherapist Carl Rogers for *individual* psychotherapy. Rogerian psychotherapy had its heyday in the 1960s and is still practiced in varying degrees by psychotherapists today. His approach entails responding in a nonjudgmental and accepting manner to all feelings and thoughts the patient expresses. For example, if the patient says, "I just hate my wife, she's such a nagging bitch," the therapist nods and says something like "I hear you saying that your wife nags you and you hate that." The goal is to create an empathetic environment so the patient feels safe exploring his inner thoughts and emotions and confiding in the therapist.

Since marriage is also, ideally, a relationship in which people feel safe being themselves, it might seem to make sense to train couples to practice this sort of unconditional understanding. Conflict resolution is certainly easier if each party expresses empathy for the other's perspective.

The problem is that it doesn't work. A Munich-based marital therapy study conducted by Dr. Kurt Hahlweg and associates found that even after employing active listening techniques the typical couple was still distressed. Those few couples who did benefit relapsed within a year.

The wide range of marital therapies based on conflict resolution share a very high relapse rate. In fact, the best of this type of marital therapy, conducted by Neil Jacobson, Ph.D., of the University of Washington, has only a 35 percent success rate. In other words, his own studies show that only 35 percent of couples see a meaningful improvement in their marriages as a result of the therapy. A year later, less than half of that group—or just 18 percent of all couples who entered therapy—retain these benefits. When *Consumer Reports* surveyed a large sample of its members on their experience with all kinds of psychotherapists, most got very high customer satisfaction marks—except for marital therapists, who got very poor ratings. This survey may not qualify as rigorous scientific research, but it confirms what most professionals in this field know: In the long run, current approaches to marital therapy do not benefit the majority of couples.

When you really think about it, it's not difficult to see why active listening so often fails. Bob might do his best to listen thoughtfully to Judy's complaints. But he is not a therapist listening to a patient whine about a third party. The person his wife is trashing behind all of those "I" statements is *him.* There are some people who can be magnanimous in the face of such criticism—the Dalai Lama comes to mind. But it's unlikely that you or your spouse is married to one of them. (Even in Rogerian therapy, when the client starts complaining about the therapist, the therapist switches from empathy to other therapeutic approaches.) Active listening asks couples to perform Olympic-level emotional gymnastics when their relationship can barely walk.

If you think validation and active listening will make conflict resolution easier for you and your spouse, by all means use it. There are circumstances where it can certainly come in handy. But here's the catch: Even if it does make your fights "better" or less frequent, it alone cannot save your marriage.

Even happily married couples can have screaming matches—loud arguments don't necessarily harm a marriage.

After studying some 650 couples and tracking the fate of their marriages for up to fourteen years, we now understand that this approach to counseling doesn't work, *not just* because it's nearly impossible for most couples to do well, but more importantly because *successful conflict resolution isn't what makes marriages succeed.* One of the most startling findings of our research is that most couples who have maintained happy marriages rarely do anything that even partly resembles active listening when they're upset.

Consider one couple we studied, Belle and Charlie. After more than forty-five years of marriage, Belle informed Charlie that she wished they had never had children. This clearly rankled him. What followed was a conversation that broke all the active listening rules. This discussion doesn't include a lot of validation or empathy—they both jump right in, arguing their point.

CHARLIE: You think you would have been better off if I had backed you in not having children?

BELLE: Having children was such an insult to me, Charlie.

CHARLIE: No. Hold on a minute.

BELLE: To reduce me to such a level!

CHARLIE: I'm not redu—

BELLE: I wanted so much to share a life with you. Instead I ended up a drudge.

CHARLIE: Now wait a minute, hold on. I don't think not having children is that simple. I think that there's a lot biologically that you're ignoring.

BELLE: Look at all the wonderful marriages that have been childless.

CHARLIE: Who?

BELLE: The Duke and Duchess of Windsor!

CHARLIE (*deep sigh*): Please!

BELLE: He was the king! He married a valuable woman. They had a very happy marriage.

CHARLIE: I don't think that's a fair example. First of all, she was forty. That makes a difference.

BELLE: She never had children. And he fell in love with her not because she was going to reproduce.

CHARLIE: But the fact is, Belle, that there is a real strong biological urge to have children.

BELLE: That's an insult to think that I'm regulated by biology.

CHARLIE: I can't help it!

BELLE: Well, anyway, I think we would have had a ball without children.

CHARLIE: Well, I think we had a ball with the kids, too.

BELLE: I didn't have that much of a ball.

Charlie and Belle may not sound like June and Ward Cleaver, but they have been happily married for over forty-five years. They both say they are extremely satisfied with their marriage and devoted to each other.

No doubt they have been having similar in-your-face discussions for years. They don't end off angrily, either. They go on to discuss why Belle feels this way about motherhood. Her major regret is that she wasn't more available to spend time with Charlie. She wishes she hadn't always been so cranky and tired. There's a lot of affection and laughter as they hash this out. Neither of their heart rates or blood pressures indicate distress. The bottom line of what Belle is saying is that she loves Charlie so much, she wishes she had had more time with him. Clearly, there's something very positive going on between them that overrides their argumentative style. Whatever that "something" is, marriage counseling, with its emphasis on "good" fighting, doesn't begin to help other couples tap into it.

Exploding More Myths about Marriage

The notion that you can save your marriage just by learning to communicate more sensitively is probably the most widely held misconception about happy marriages—but it's hardly the only one. Over the years I've found many other myths that are not only false but potentially destructive to a marriage because they can lead couples down the wrong path or, worse, convince them that their marriage is a hopeless case. Among these common myths:

Neuroses or personality problems ruin marriages. You might assume that people with hang-ups would be ill suited for marriage. But research has found only the weakest connection between run-of-the-mill neuroses and failing at love. The reason: We all have our crazy buttons—issues we're not totally rational about. But they don't necessarily interfere with marriage. The key to a happy marriage isn't having a "normal" personality but finding someone with whom you mesh. For example, Sam has a problem dealing with authority—he hates having a boss. If he were married to an authoritarian woman who tended to give commands and tried to tell him what to do, the result would be disastrous. But instead he is married to Megan, who treats him like a partner and doesn't try to boss him around. They've been happily married for ten years.

Contrast them with another couple who do run into marital problems. Jill has a deep-seated fear of abandonment due to her parents' divorcing when she was very young. Her husband, Wayne, who is truly devoted to her, is a debonair ladies' man who flirts shamelessly at parties. When she complains, he points out that he is 100 percent faithful to her and insists she lighten up and let him enjoy this harmless pleasure. But the threat Jill perceives from his flirtations—and his unwillingness to stop—drives them to separate and eventually divorce.

The point is that neuroses don't have to ruin a marriage. What matters is how you deal with them. If you can accommodate each other's strange side and handle it with caring, affection, and respect, your marriage can thrive.

Common interests keep you together. That all depends on how you interact while pursuing those interests. One husband and wife who love kayaking may glide smoothly down the water, laughing, talking, and concentrating together. Their love of kayaking enriches and deepens their fondness and interest in each other. Another couple may equally share a love of kayaking but not the same mutual respect. Their travels may be punctuated with "That's not the way to do a J-stroke, you idiot!" or irritated silences. It's hard to see how pursuing their common interest is in the best interest of their marriage.

You scratch my back and . . . Some researchers believe that what distinguishes good marriages from failing ones is that in good marriages spouses respond in kind to positive overtures from the other. In other words, they meet a smile with a smile, a kiss with a kiss. When one helps the other with a chore, the other intentionally reciprocates, and so on. In essence, the couple function with an unwritten agreement to offer recompense for each kind word or deed. In bad marriages this contract has broken down, so that anger and resentment fill the air. By making the floundering couple aware of the need for some such "contract," the theory goes, their interactions could be repaired.

But it's really the *unhappy* marriage where this quid pro quo operates, where each feels the need to keep a running tally of who has done what for whom. Happy spouses do not keep tabs on whether their mate is washing the dishes as a payback because they cooked dinner. They just do it because they generally feel positive about their spouse and their relationship. If you find yourself keeping score about some issue with your spouse, that suggests it's an area of tension in your marriage.

Avoiding conflict will ruin your marriage. "Tell it like it is" has become a pervasive attitude. But honesty is not best for all marriages. Plenty of lifelong relationships happily survive even though the couple tend to shove things under the rug. Take Allan and Betty. When Allan gets annoyed at Betty, he turns on ESPN. When Betty is upset with him, she heads for the mall. Then they regroup and go on as if nothing happened. Never in forty years of marriage have they sat down to have a "dialogue" about their relationship. Neither of them could tell you what a "validating" statement is. Yet they will tell you honestly that they are both very satisfied with their marriage and that they love each other deeply, hold the same values, love to fish and travel together, and wish for their children as happy a married life as they have shared.

Couples simply have different styles of conflict. Some avoid fights at all costs, some fight a lot, and some are able to "talk out" their differences and find a compromise without ever raising their voices. No one style is necessarily better than the other—*as long as the style works for both people.* Couples can run into trouble if one partner always wants to talk out a conflict while the other just wants to watch the playoffs.

Affairs are the root cause of divorce. In most cases it's the other way around. Problems in the marriage that send the couple on a trajectory to divorce also send one (or both) of them looking for intimate connection outside the marriage. Most marital therapists who write about extramarital affairs find that these trysts are usually not about sex but about seeking friendship, support, understanding, respect, attention, caring, and concern—the kind of things that marriage is supposed to offer. In probably the most reliable survey ever done on divorce, by Lynn Gigy, Ph.D., and Joan Kelly, Ph.D., from the Divorce Mediation Project in Corte Madera, California, 80 percent of divorced men and women said their marriage broke up because they gradually grew apart and lost a sense of closeness, or because they did not feel loved and appreciated. Only 20 to 27 percent of couples said an extramarital affair was even partially to blame.

Men are not biologically "built" for marriage. A corollary to the notion that affairs cause divorce, this theory holds that men are philanderers by nature and are therefore ill suited for monogamy. It's supposedly the law of the jungle—the male of the species looks to create as many offspring as possible, so his allegiance to any one mate remains superficial. Meanwhile the female, given the large task of tending to the young, looks for a single mate who will provide well for her and her children.

But whatever natural laws other species follow, among humans the frequency of extramarital affairs does not depend on gender so much as on opportunity. Now that so many women work outside the home, the rate of extramarital affairs by women has skyrocketed. According to Annette Lawson, Ph.D., of the University of California, Berkeley's Institute of Human Development, since women have entered the workplace in massive numbers, the number of extramarital affairs of young women now slightly exceeds those of men.

Men and women are from different planets. According to a rash of best-selling books, men and women can't get along because males are "from Mars" and females "from Venus." However, successful marriages also comprise respective "aliens." Gender differences may contribute to marital problems, but they don't cause them.

The determining factor in whether wives feel satisfied with the sex, romance, and passion in their marriage is, by 70 percent, the quality of the couple's friendship. For men, the determining factor is, by 70 percent, the quality of the couple's friendship. So men and women come from the same planet after all.

I could go on and on. The point is not just that there are plenty of myths out there about marriage, but that the false information they offer can be disheartening to couples who are desperately trying to make their marriage work. If these myths imply one thing, it's that marriage is an extremely complex, imposing institution that most of us just aren't good enough for. I'm not suggesting that marriage is easy. We all know it takes courage, determination, and resiliency to maintain a long-lasting relationship. But once you understand what really makes a marriage tick, saving or safeguarding your own will become simpler.

WHAT *DOES* MAKE MARRIAGE WORK?

The advice I used to give couples earlier in my career was pretty much what you'd hear from virtually any marital therapist—the same old pointers about conflict resolution and communication skills. But after looking squarely at my own data, I had to face the harsh facts: Getting couples to disagree more "nicely" might reduce their stress levels while they argued, but frequently it wasn't enough to pump life back into their marriages.

The right course for these couples became clear only after I analyzed the interactions of couples whose marriages sailed smoothly through troubled waters. Why was it that these marriages worked so well? Were these couples more intelligent, more stable, or simply more fortunate than the others? Could whatever they had be taught to other couples?

It soon became apparent that these happy marriages were never perfect unions. Some couples who said they were very satisfied with each other still had significant differences in temperament, in interests, in family values. Conflict was not infrequent. They argued, just as the unhappy couples did, over money, jobs, kids, housekeeping, sex, and in-laws. The mystery was how they so adroitly navigated their way through these difficulties and kept their marriages happy and stable.

It took studying hundreds of couples until I finally uncovered the secrets of these emotionally intelligent marriages. No two marriages are the same, but the more closely I looked at happy marriages the clearer it became that they were alike in seven telltale ways. Happily married couples may not be aware that they follow these Seven Principles, but they all do. Unhappy marriages always came up short in at least one of these seven areas—and usually in many of them. By mastering these Seven Principles, you can ensure that your own marriage will thrive. You'll learn to identify which of these components are weak spots, or potential weak spots, in your marriage, and to focus your attention where your marriage most needs it. In the chapters ahead we'll fill you in on all the secrets to maintaining (or regaining) a happy marriage, and hold your hand as you apply the techniques to your own marriage.

THE EVIDENCE, PLEASE

How can I be so confident that doing this will benefit your marriage? Because unlike other approaches to helping couples, mine is based on knowing what makes marriages succeed rather than on what makes them fail. I don't have to guess anymore about why some couples stay so happily married. I *know* why. I have documented just what makes happily married couples different from everybody else.

I am confident that the Seven Principles work not just because my data suggest they should, but because the hundreds of couples who've attended our workshops so far have confirmed to me that they do. Almost all of these couples came to us because their marriage was in deep distress—some were on the verge of divorce. Many were skeptical that a simple two-day workshop based on the Seven Principles could turn their relationship around. Fortunately their skepticism was unfounded. Our findings indicate that these workshops have made a profound and powerful difference in these couples' lives.

Couples who attend my workshop have a relapse rate that's about *half* that from standard marital therapy.

When it comes to judging the effectiveness of marital therapy, nine months seems to be the magic number. Usually by then the couples who are going to relapse after therapy already have. Those who retain the benefits of therapy through the first nine months tend to continue them long-term. So we put our workshops to the test by doing an extensive nine-month follow-up of 640 couples. I'm happy to report an astoundingly low relapse rate. The nationwide relapse rate for standard marital therapy is 30 to 50 percent. Our rate is 20 percent. We found that at the beginning of our workshops, 27 percent of couples were at very high risk for divorce. At our three-month follow-up that proportion was 6.7 percent and at nine months it was 0 percent. But even couples who were not at high risk for divorce were significantly helped by the workshops.

FRIENDSHIP VERSUS FIGHTING

At the heart of my program is the simple truth that happy marriages are based on a deep friendship. By this I mean a mutual respect for and enjoyment of each other's company. These couples tend to know each other intimately—they are well versed in each other's likes, dislikes, personality quirks, hopes, and dreams. They have an abiding regard for each other and express this fondness not just in the big ways but in little ways day in and day out.

Take the case of hardworking Nathaniel, who runs his own import business and works very long hours. In another marriage, his schedule might be a major liability. But he and his wife Olivia have found ways to stay connected. They talk frequently on the phone during the day. When she has a doctor's appointment, he remembers to call to see how it went. When he has a meeting with an important client, she'll check in to see how it fared. When they have chicken for dinner, she gives him both drumsticks because she knows he likes them best. When he makes blueberry pancakes for the kids Saturday morning, he'll leave the blueberries out of hers because he knows she doesn't like them. Although he's not religious, he accompanies her to church each Sunday because it's important to her. And although she's not crazy about spending a lot of time with their relatives, she has pursued a friendship with Nathaniel's mother and sisters because family matters so much to him.

If all of this sounds humdrum and unromantic, it's anything but. Through small but important ways Olivia and Nathaniel are maintaining the friendship that is the foundation of their love. As a result they have a marriage that is far more passionate than do couples who punctuate their lives together with romantic vacations and lavish anniversary gifts but have fallen out of touch in their daily lives.

Friendship fuels the flames of romance because it offers the best protection against feeling adversarial toward your spouse. Because Nathaniel and Olivia have kept their friendship strong despite the inevitable disagreements and irritations of married life, they are experiencing what is known technically as "positive sentiment override." This means that their positive thoughts about each other and their marriage are so pervasive that they tend to supersede their negative feelings. It takes a much more significant conflict for them to lose their equilibrium as a couple than it would otherwise. Their positivity causes them to feel optimistic about each other and their marriage, to assume positive things about their lives together, and to give each other the benefit of the doubt.

Here's a simple example. Olivia and Nathaniel are getting ready to host a dinner party. Nathaniel calls, "Where are the napkins?" and Olivia yells back edgily, "They're in the *cupboard!*" Because their marriage is founded on a firm friendship, most likely he'll shrug off her tone of voice and focus instead on the information Olivia has given him—that the napkins are in the cupboard. He attributes her anger to some fleeting problem that has nothing to do with him— like she can't get the cork out of the wine bottle. However, if their marriage were troubled, he would be more likely to sulk or yell back, "Never mind, *you* get them!"

One way of looking at this positive override is similar to the "set point" approach to weight loss. According to this popular theory, the body has a "set" weight that it tries to maintain. Thanks to homeostasis, no matter how much or how little you diet, your body has a strong tendency to hover at that weight. Only by resetting your body's metabolism (say, by exercising regularly) can dieting really help you lose pounds for good. In a marriage, positivity and negativity operate similarly. Once your marriage gets "set" at a certain degree of positivity, it will take far more negativity to harm your relationship than if your "set point" were lower. And if your relationship becomes overwhelmingly negative, it will be more difficult to repair it.

Most marriages start off with such a high, positive set point that it's hard for either partner to imagine their relationship derailing. But far too often this blissful state doesn't last. Over time anger, irritation, and resentment can build to the point that the friendship becomes more and more of an abstraction. The couple may pay lip service to it, but it is no longer their daily reality. Eventually they end up in "*negative* sentiment override." Everything gets interpreted more and more negatively. Words said in a neutral tone of voice are taken personally. The wife says, "You're not supposed to run the microwave without any food in it." The husband sees this as an attack, so he says something like, "Don't tell me what to do. I'm the one who read the manual!" Another battle begins.

Once you reach this point, getting back to the fundamental bond that united you in the first place can seem as difficult as backpedaling while whitewater rafting. But my Seven Principles will show you how to strengthen your friendship even if you feel awash in negativity. As you learn about these principles, you will come to have a deeper understanding of the role of friendship in any marriage, and you will develop the skills to retain or revive your own.

A HAPPY COUPLE'S SECRET WEAPON

Rediscovering or reinvigorating friendship doesn't prevent couples from arguing. Instead, it gives them a secret weapon that prevents quarrels from getting out of hand. For example, here's what happens when Olivia and Nathaniel argue. As they plan to move from the city to the suburbs, tensions between them are high. Although they see eye to eye on which house to buy and how to decorate it, they are locking horns over buying a new car. Olivia thinks they should join the suburban masses and get a minivan. To Nathaniel nothing could be drearier—he wants a Jeep. The more they talk about it, the higher the decibel level gets. If you were a fly on the wall of their bedroom, you would have serious doubts about their future together. Then all of a sudden, Olivia puts her hands on her hips and, in perfect imitation of their four-year-old son, sticks out her tongue. Since Nathaniel knows that she's about to do this, he sticks out his tongue first. Then they both start laughing. As always, this silly contest defuses the tension between them.

In our research we actually have a technical name for what Olivia and Nathaniel did. Probably unwittingly, they used a *repair attempt*. This name refers to any statement or action—silly or otherwise—that prevents negativity from escalating out of control. Repair attempts are the secret weapon of emotionally intelligent couples—even though many of these couples aren't aware that they are doing something so powerful. When a couple have a strong friendship, they naturally become experts at sending each other repair attempts and at correctly reading those sent their way. But when couples are in negative override, even a repair statement as blunt as "Hey, I'm sorry" will have a low success rate.

The success or failure of a couple's repair attempts is one of the primary factors in whether their marriage flourishes or flounders. And again, what determines the success of their repair attempts is the strength of their marital friendship. If this sounds simplistic or obvious, you'll find in the pages ahead that it is not. Strengthening your marital friendship isn't as basic as just being "nice." Even if you feel that your friendship is already quite solid, you may be surprised to find there is room to strengthen it all the more. Most of the couples who take our workshop are relieved to hear that almost everybody messes up during marital conflict. What matters is whether the repairs are successful.

THE PURPOSE OF MARRIAGE

In the strongest marriages, husband and wife share a deep sense of meaning. They don't just "get along"—they also support each other's hopes and aspirations and build a sense of purpose into their lives together. That is really what I mean when I talk about honoring and respecting each other.

Very often a marriage's failure to do this is what causes husband and wife to find themselves in endless, useless rounds of argument or to feel isolated and lonely in their marriage. After watching countless videotapes of couples fighting, I can guarantee you that most quarrels are really not about whether the toilet lid is up or down or whose turn it is to take out the trash. There are deeper, hidden issues that fuel these superficial conflicts and make them far more intense and hurtful than they would otherwise be.

Once you understand this, you will be ready to accept one of the most surprising truths about marriage: *Most marital arguments cannot be resolved.* Couples spend year after year trying to change each other's mind—but it can't be done. This is because most of their disagreements are rooted in fundamental differences of lifestyle, personality, or values. By fighting over these differences, all they succeed in doing is wasting their time and harming their marriage.

This doesn't mean there's nothing you can do if your relationship has been overrun by conflict. But it does mean that the typical conflict-resolution advice won't help. Instead, you need to understand the bottom-line difference that is causing the conflict between you—and to learn how to live with it by honoring and respecting each other. Only then will you be able to build shared meaning and a sense of purpose into your marriage.

It used to be that couples could achieve this goal only through their own insight, instinct, or blessed luck. But now my Seven Principles make the secrets of marital success available to *all* couples. No matter what the current state of your relationship, following these Seven Principles can lead to dramatic, positive change.

The first step toward improving or enhancing your marriage is to understand what happens when my Seven Principles are *not* followed. This has been well documented by my extensive research into couples who were not able to save their marriages. Learning about the failures can prevent your marriage from making the same mistakes—or rescue it if it already has. Once you come to understand why some marriages fail and how the Seven Principles could prevent such tragedies, you'll be on the way to improving your own marriage forever.

2

How I Predict Divorce

Dara and Oliver sit face to face in the Love Lab. Both in their late twenties, they have volunteered to take part in my study of newlyweds. In this extensive research, 130 couples have agreed to put their marriages not only under the microscope but in front of the camera as well. Dara and Oliver are among the fifty who were observed during an overnight stay at the Love Lab "apartment." My ability to predict divorce is based in part on my analysis of these couples and their interactions.

Dara and Oliver say their lives are hectic but happy. She attends nursing school at night, and he works long hours as a computer programmer. Like many couples, including those who remain content as well as those who eventually divorce, Dara and Oliver acknowledge that their marriage isn't perfect. But they say they love each other and are committed to staying together. They positively beam when they talk about the life they plan to build.

I ask them to spend fifteen minutes in the lab trying to resolve an ongoing disagreement they are having while I videotape them. As they speak, sensors attached to their bodies gauge their stress levels based on various measurements of their circulatory system, such as how quickly their hearts beat.

I expect that their discussion will be at least somewhat negative. After all, I have asked them to quarrel. While some couples are capable of resolving disagreements with understanding words and smiles, more often there's tension. Dara and Oliver are no exception. Dara thinks Oliver doesn't do his share of the housekeeping, and he thinks she nags him too much, which makes him less motivated to do more.

After listening to them talk about this problem, I sadly predict to my colleagues that Dara and Oliver will see their marital happiness dwindle. And sure enough, four years later they report they are on the verge of divorce. Although they still live together, they are leading lonely lives. They have become like ghosts, haunting the marriage that once made them both feel so alive.

I predict their marriage will falter not because they argue—after all, I asked them to. Anger between husband and wife doesn't itself predict marital meltdown. Other couples in the newlywed study argue far more during the fifteen minutes of videotaping than do Dara and Oliver. Yet I predict that many of these couples will remain happily married—and they do. The clues to Dara and Oliver's future breakup are in the *way* they argue.

THE FIRST SIGN: HARSH STARTUP

The most obvious indicator that this discussion (and this marriage) is not going to go well is the way it begins. Dara immediately becomes negative and accusatory. When Oliver broaches the subject of housework, she's ready to be sarcastic. "Or lack thereof," she says. Oliver tries to lighten things up by cracking a joke: "Or the book we were talking about writing: Men are pigs." Dara sits pokerfaced. They talk a bit more, trying to devise a plan to make sure Oliver does his share, and then Dara says, "I mean, I'd like to see it resolved, but it doesn't seem like it is. I mean, I've tried making up lists, and that doesn't work. And I've tried letting you do it on your own, and nothing got done for a month." Now she's blaming Oliver. In essence, she's saying the problem isn't the housekeeping, it's him.

When a discussion leads off this way—with criticism and/or sarcasm, a form of contempt—it has begun with a "harsh startup." Although Dara talks to Oliver in a very soft, quiet voice, there's a load of negative power in her words. After hearing the first minute or so of their conversation, it's no surprise to me that by the end Dara and Oliver haven't resolved their differences at all. The research shows that if your discussion begins with a harsh startup, it will inevitably end on a negative note, even if there are a lot of attempts to "make nice" in between. Statistics tell the story: 96 percent of the time you can predict the outcome of a conversation based on the *first three minutes* of the fifteen-minute interaction! A harsh startup simply dooms you to failure. So if you begin a discussion that way, you might as well pull the plug, take a breather, and start over.

THE SECOND SIGN: THE FOUR HORSEMEN

Dara's harsh startup sounds the warning bell that she and Oliver may be having serious difficulty. Now, as their discussion unfolds, I continue to look out for particular types of negative interactions. Certain kinds of negativity, if allowed to run rampant, are so lethal to a relationship that I call them the Four Horsemen of the Apocalypse. Usually these four horsemen clip-clop into the heart of a marriage in the following order: criticism, contempt, defensiveness, and stonewalling.

Horseman 1: Criticism. You will always have some complaints about the person you live with. But there's a world of difference between a complaint and a criticism. A complaint only addresses the specific action at which your spouse failed. A criticism is more global—it adds on some negative words about your mate's character or personality. "I'm really angry that you didn't sweep the kitchen floor last night. We agreed that we'd take turns doing it" is a complaint. "Why are you so forgetful? I hate having to always sweep the kitchen floor when it's your turn. You just don't care" is a criticism. A complaint focuses on a specific behavior, but a criticism ups the ante by throwing in blame and general character assassination. Here's a recipe: To turn any complaint into a criticism, just add my favorite line: "What is wrong with you?"

Usually a harsh startup comes in the guise of criticism. You can see how quickly complaint turns into criticism when Dara begins to talk. Listen again to what she says:

DARA: I mean, I'd like to see it resolved, but it doesn't seem like it is. *(Simple complaint)* I mean, I've tried making up lists and that doesn't work. And I've tried letting you do it on your own, and nothing got done for a month. *(Criticism. She's implying the problem is his fault. Even if it is, blaming him will only make it worse.)*

Here are some other examples that show the difference between complaint and criticism.

Complaint. There's no gas in the car. Why didn't you fill it up like you said you would?

Criticism. Why can't you ever remember anything? I told you a thousand times to fill up the tank, and you didn't.

Complaint. You should have told me earlier that you're too tired to make love. I'm really disappointed, and I feel embarrassed.

Criticism. Why are you always so selfish? It was really nasty of you to lead me on. You should have told me earlier that you were too tired to make love.

Complaint. You were supposed to check with me before inviting anyone over for dinner. I wanted to spend time alone with you tonight.

Criticism. Why do you keep putting your friends ahead of me? I always come last on your list. We were supposed to have dinner alone tonight.

If you hear echoes of yourself or your spouse in these criticisms, you have plenty of company. The first horseman is very common in relationships. So if you find that you and your spouse are critical of each other, don't assume you're headed for divorce court. The problem with criticism is that when it becomes pervasive, it paves the way for the other, far deadlier horsemen.

Horseman 2: Contempt. Dara doesn't stop at criticizing Oliver. Soon she's literally sneering. When he suggests that they keep a list of his chores on the refrigerator to help him remember, she says, "Do you think you work really well with lists?" Next, Oliver tells her that he needs fifteen minutes to relax when he gets home before starting to do chores. "So if I leave you alone for fifteen minutes, then you think you'll be motivated to jump up and do something?" she asks him.

"Maybe. We haven't tried it, have we?" Oliver asks.

Dara has an opportunity here to soften up, but instead she comes back with sarcasm. "I think you do a pretty good job of coming home and lying around or disappearing into the bathroom," she says. And then she adds challengingly, "So you think that's the cure-all, to give you fifteen minutes?"

This sarcasm and cynicism are types of contempt. So are name-calling, eye-rolling, sneering, mockery, and hostile humor. In whatever form, contempt—the worst of the four horsemen—is poisonous to a relationship because it conveys disgust. It's virtually impossible to resolve a problem when your partner is getting the message you're disgusted with him or her. Inevitably, contempt leads to more conflict rather than to reconciliation.

Peter, the manager of a shoe store, was a master at contempt, at least when it came to his wife. Listen to what happens when he and Cynthia try to discuss their disparate views about spending money. He says, "Just look at the difference in our vehicles and our clothes. I think that says a lot for who we are and what we value. I mean, you tease me about washing my truck, and you go and pay to have somebody wash your car. We're paying through the nose for your car, and you can't be bothered to wash it. I think that's outrageous. I think that's probably the most spoiled thing that you do." This is a textbook example of contempt. He's not merely pointing out that they spend their money differently. He is accusing his wife of a moral deficiency—of being spoiled.

Cynthia responds by telling him that it's physically difficult for her to wash her car herself. Peter dismisses this explanation and continues to take the high moral ground. "I take care of my truck because if you take care of it, it'll last longer. I don't come from the mentality of 'Ah, just go out and buy a new one' that you seem to."

Still hoping to get Peter on her side, Cynthia says, "If you could help me to wash my car, I'd really love that. I'd really appreciate it." But instead of grabbing this chance at reconciliation, Peter wants to do battle.

"How many times have you helped me wash my truck?" he counters.

Cynthia tries again to reconcile. "I will help you wash your truck if you will help me wash my car."

But Peter's goal is not to resolve this issue but to dress her down. So he says, "That's not my question. How many times have you helped me?"

"Never," says Cynthia.

"See?" says Peter. "That's where I think you have a little responsibility, too. It's like, you know, if your dad bought you a house, would you expect him to come over and paint it for you, too?"

"Well, will you always help me wash my car if I always help you wash your truck?"

"I'm not sure that I'd want ya to help me," Peter says, laughing.

"Well, will you always help me wash my car, then?" Cynthia asks.

"I will help you when I can. I won't give you a blanket guarantee for life. What are you gonna do, sue me?" asks Peter. And he laughs again.

Listening to this discussion, it becomes clear that Peter's main purpose is to demean his wife. His contempt comes in the guise of assuming the high moral ground, as when he says: "I think that says a lot for who we are and what we value," or "I don't come from the mentality of 'just go out and buy a new one.'"

Couples who are contemptuous of each other are more likely to suffer from infectious illnesses (colds, flu, and so on) than other people.

Contempt is fueled by long-simmering negative thoughts about the partner. You're more likely to have such thoughts if your differences are not resolved. No doubt, the first time Peter and Cynthia argued about money, he wasn't so disrespectful. He probably offered a simple complaint like "I think you should wash your own car. It costs too much to always have someone else wash it." But as they kept disagreeing about this, his complaints turned to global criticisms, such as: "You always spend too much money." And when the conflict continued, he felt more and more disgusted and fed up with Cynthia, a change that affected what he said when they argued.

Belligerence, a close cousin to contempt, is just as deadly to a relationship. It is a form of aggressive anger because it contains a threat or provocation. When a wife complains that her husband doesn't come home from work in time for dinner, a belligerent response would be "Well, what are you going to do about it?" When Peter says to Cynthia, "What are you going to do, sue me?" he thinks he's making a joke, but he's really being belligerent.

Horseman 3: Defensiveness. It's no surprise, considering how nasty her husband is being, that Cynthia defends herself. She points out that she doesn't get her car washed as often as he thinks. She explains that it's more difficult physically for her to wash her car herself than it is for him to wash his truck.

Although it's understandable that Cynthia would defend herself, research shows that this approach rarely has the desired effect. The attacking spouse does not back down or apologize. This is because defensiveness is really a way of blaming your partner.

You're saying, in effect, "The problem isn't *me,* it's *you.*" Defensiveness just escalates the conflict, which is why it's so deadly. When Cynthia tells Peter how hard it is for her to wash her car, he doesn't say, "Oh, now I understand." He ignores her excuse—he doesn't even acknowledge what she's said. He climbs farther up his high moral ground, telling her how well he takes care of his vehicle and implying that she's spoiled for not doing the same. Cynthia can't win—and neither can their marriage.

Criticism, Contempt, and Defensiveness don't always gallop into a home in strict order. They function more like a relay match—handing the baton off to each other over and over again, if the couple can't put a stop to it. You can see this happening as Oliver and Dara continue their discussion about cleaning their house. Although they seem to be seeking a solution, Dara becomes increasingly contemptuous—mocking Oliver in the guise of questioning him and tearing down every plan he devises. The more defensive he becomes, the more she attacks him. Her body language signals condescension. She speaks softly, her elbows resting on the table, her intertwined fingers cradling her chin. Like a law professor or a judge, she peppers him with questions just to see him squirm.

DARA: So you think that's the cure-all, to give you fifteen minutes? *(sneering)*

OLIVER: No, I don't think that's the cure-all. I think, combined with writing up a list of weekly tasks that have to get done. Why not put it on a calendar? Hey, I'll see it right then and there.

DARA: Just like when I write stuff in your Day-Timer it gets done? *(mocking him; more contempt)*

OLIVER: I don't always have a chance to look at my Day-Timer during the day. *(defensive)*

DARA: So you think you'll look at a calendar, then?

OLIVER: Yeah. At any point in time, if I'm not up to speed, you should ask me about it. But when that happens now, it's not you asking, it's you telling me, "You haven't done this and you haven't done that." Instead say, "Is there any reason why you haven't done this or that?" Like, I mean, when I stayed up and did your résumé that one night. Stuff like that happens all the time, and you just don't take that into account at all. *(defensive)*

DARA: And I don't just all of a sudden do things for you, either? *(defensive)*

OLIVER: No, you do. . . . I think you need to relax a little bit.

DARA *(sarcastic)*: Hmm. Well, that sounds like we solved a lot.

Obviously, Dara and Oliver have resolved nothing, thanks to the prevalence of criticism, contempt, and defensiveness.

Horseman 4: Stonewalling. In marriages like Dara and Oliver's, where discussions begin with a harsh startup, where criticism and contempt lead to defensiveness, which leads to more contempt and more defensiveness, eventually one partner tunes out. This heralds the arrival of the fourth horseman.

Think of the husband who comes home from work, gets met with a barrage of criticism from his wife, and hides behind the newspaper. The less responsive he is, the more she yells. Eventually he gets up and leaves the room. Rather than confronting his wife, he disengages. By turning away from her, he is avoiding a fight, but he is also avoiding his marriage. He has become a stonewaller. Although both husbands and wives can be stonewallers, this behavior is far more common among men, for reasons we'll see later.

During a typical conversation between two people, the listener gives all kinds of cues to the speaker that he's paying attention. He may use eye contact, nod his head, say something like "Yeah" or "Uh-huh." But a stonewaller doesn't give you this sort of casual feedback. He tends to look away or down without uttering a sound. He sits like an impassive stone wall. The stonewaller acts as though he couldn't care less about what you're saying, if he even hears it.

Stonewalling usually arrives later in the course of a marriage than the other three horsemen. That's why it's less common among newlywed husbands such as Oliver than among couples who have been in a negative spiral for a while. It takes time for the negativity

created by the first three horsemen to become overwhelming
enough that stonewalling becomes an understandable "out." That's
the stance that Mack takes when he and his wife Rita argue about
each other's behavior at parties. She says the problem is that he
drinks too much. He thinks the bigger problem is her reaction: She
embarrasses him by yelling at him in front of his friends. Here they
are, already in the middle of an argument:

RITA: Now I've become the problem, again. I started off with the
    complaint, but now I am the problem. That always seems to
    happen.
MACK: Yeah, I do that, I know. *(Pause.)* But your tantrums and child-
    ishness are an embarrassment to me and my friends.
RITA: If you would control your drinking at parties, puleese . . .
MACK: *(Looks down, avoids eye contact, says nothing—he's stone-
    walling.)*
RITA: Because I think *(laughs)* for the most part, we get along pretty
    well, really *(laughs)*.
MACK: *(Continues to stonewall. Remains silent, makes no eye con-
    tact, head nods, facial movements, or vocalizations.)*
RITA: Don't you think?
MACK: *(No response.)*
RITA: Mack? Hello?

THE THIRD SIGN: FLOODING

It may seem to Rita that her complaints have no effect on Mack. But
nothing could be further from the truth. Usually people stonewall
as a protection against feeling *flooded*. Flooding means that your
spouse's negativity—whether in the guise of criticism or contempt
or even defensiveness—is so overwhelming, and so sudden, that it
leaves you shell-shocked. You feel so defenseless against this sniper
attack that you learn to do anything to avoid a replay. The more
often you feel flooded by your spouse's criticism or contempt, the

more hypervigilant you are for cues that your spouse is about to "blow" again. All you can think about is protecting yourself from the turbulence your spouse's onslaught causes. And the way to do that is to disengage emotionally from the relationship. No wonder Mack and Rita are now divorced.

Another husband, Paul, was quite up front about why he stone-walls when his wife, Amy, gets negative. In the following discussion he articulates what all stonewallers are feeling.

AMY: When I get mad, that's when you should step in and try to make it better. But when you just stop talking, it means, 'I no longer care about how you feel.' That just makes me feel one inch tall. Like my opinion or feelings have absolutely no bearing on you. And that's not the way a marriage should be.

PAUL: What I'm saying is, if you wanna have a serious conversation, you're gonna do it without yelling and screaming all the time. You start saying things that are hurtful.

AMY: Well, when I'm hurt, mad, and I wanna hurt you, I start saying things. And that's when we should both stop. I should say, "I'm sorry." And you should say, "I know that you wanna talk about this. And I really should make an effort to talk instead of just ignoring you."

PAUL: I'll talk when—

AMY: It fits your purpose.

PAUL: No, when you're not yelling and screaming and jumping up and down stomping.

Amy kept telling Paul how it made her feel when he shut down. But she did not seem to hear him tell her *why* he shuts down: He can't handle her hostility. This couple later divorced.

A marriage's meltdown can be predicted, then, by habitual harsh startup and frequent flooding brought on by the relentless presence of the four horsemen during disagreements. Although each of these factors alone can predict a divorce, they usually coexist in an unhappy marriage.

THE FOURTH SIGN: BODY LANGUAGE

Even if I could not hear the conversation between Mack the stonewaller and his wife, Rita, I would be able to predict their divorce simply by looking at his physiological readings. When we monitor couples for bodily changes during a tense discussion, we can see just how physically distressing flooding is. One of the most apparent of these physical reactions is that the heart speeds up—pounding away at more than 100 beats per minute—even as high as 165. (In contrast, a typical heart rate for a man who is about 30 is 76, and for a woman the same age, 82.) Hormonal changes occur, too, including the secretion of adrenaline, which kicks in the "fight or flight response." Blood pressure also mounts. These changes are so dramatic that if one partner is frequently flooded during marital discussions, it's easy to predict that they will divorce.

Recurring episodes of flooding lead to divorce for two reasons. First, they signal that at least one partner feels severe emotional distress when dealing with the other. Second, the *physical* sensations of feeling flooded—the increased heart rate, sweating, and so on—make it virtually impossible to have a productive, problem-solving discussion. When your body goes into overdrive during an argument, it is responding to a very primitive alarm system we inherited from our prehistoric ancestors. All those distressful reactions, like a pounding heart and sweating, occur because on a fundamental level your body perceives your current situation as dangerous. Even though we live in the age of in vitro conception, organ transplants, and gene mapping, from an evolutionary standpoint not much time has passed since we were cave dwellers. So the human body has not refined its fear reactions—it responds the same way, whether you're facing a saber-toothed tiger or a contemptuous spouse demanding to know why you can never remember to put the toilet seat back down.

When a pounding heart and all the other physical stress reactions happen in the midst of a discussion with your mate, the consequences are disastrous. Your ability to process information is reduced, meaning it's harder to pay attention to what your partner is saying. Creative problem solving goes out the window. You're left with the most reflexive, least intellectually sophisticated responses in your repertoire: to fight (act critical, contemptuous, or defensive) or flee (stonewall). Any chance of resolving the issue is gone. Most likely, the discussion will just worsen the situation.

MEN AND WOMEN REALLY ARE DIFFERENT

In 85 percent of marriages, the stonewaller is the husband. This is not because of some lack on the man's part. The reason lies in our evolutionary heritage. Anthropological evidence suggests that we evolved from hominids whose lives were circumscribed by very rigid gender roles, since these were advantageous to survival in a harsh environment. The females specialized in nurturing children while the males specialized in cooperative hunting.

As any nursing mother can tell you, the amount of milk you produce is affected by how relaxed you feel, which is related to the release of the hormone oxytocin in the brain. So natural selection would favor a female who could quickly soothe herself and calm down after feeling stressed. Her ability to remain composed could enhance her children's chances of survival by optimizing the amount of nutrition they received. But in the male natural selection would reward the opposite response. For these early cooperative hunters, maintaining vigilance was a key survival skill. So males whose adrenaline kicked in quite readily and who did not calm down so easily were more likely to survive and procreate.

To this day, the male cardiovascular system remains more reactive than the female and slower to recover from stress. For example, if a man and woman suddenly hear a very loud, brief sound, like a blowout, most likely his heart will beat faster than hers and stay accelerated for longer, according to research by Robert Levenson, Ph.D., and his student Loren Carter at the University of California at Berkeley. The same goes for their blood pressure—his will become more elevated and stay higher longer. Psychologist Dolf Zillman, Ph.D., at the University of Alabama has found that when male subjects are deliberately treated rudely and then told to relax for twenty minutes, their blood pressure surges and stays elevated until they get to retaliate. But when women face the same treatment, they are able to calm down during those twenty minutes. (Interestingly, a woman's blood pressure tends to rise again if she is pressured into retaliating!) Since marital confrontation that activates vigilance takes a greater physical toll on the male, it's no surprise that men are more likely than women to attempt to avoid it.

It's a biological fact: Men are more easily overwhelmed by marital conflict than are their wives.

This gender difference in how physiologically reactive our bodies are also influences what men and women tend to think about when they experience marital stress. As part of some experiments, we ask couples to watch themselves arguing on tape and then tell us what they were thinking when our sensors detected they were flooded. Their answers suggest that men have a greater tendency to have negative thoughts that maintain their distress, while women are more likely to think soothing thoughts that help them calm down and be conciliatory. Men, generally, either think about how righteous and indignant they feel ("I'm going to get even," "I don't have to take this"), which tends to lead to contempt or belligerence. Or they think about themselves as an innocent victim of their wife's wrath or complaint ("Why is she always blaming me?"), which leads to defensiveness.

Obviously, these rules don't hold for every male and every female. But after twenty-five years of research, I have noted that the majority of couples do follow these gender differences in physiological and psychological reactions to stress. Because of these dissimilarities, most marriages (including healthy, happy ones) follow a comparable pattern of conflict in which the wife, who is constitutionally better able to handle the stress, brings up sensitive issues. The husband, who is not as able to cope with it, will attempt to avoid getting into the subject. He may become defensive and stonewall. Or he may even become belligerent or contemptuous in an attempt to silence her.

Just because your marriage follows this pattern, it's not a given that a divorce is in the offing. In fact, you'll find examples of all four horsemen and even occasional flooding in stable marriages. But when the four horsemen take up *permanent* residence, when either partner begins to feel flooded routinely, the relationship is in serious trouble. Frequently feeling flooded leads almost inevitably to distancing yourself from your spouse. That in turn leads you to feel lonely. Without help, the couple will end up divorced or living in a dead marriage, in which they maintain separate, parallel lives in the same home. They may go through the motions of togetherness—attending their children's plays, hosting dinner parties, taking family vacations. But emotionally they no longer feel connected to each other. They have given up.

THE FIFTH SIGN: FAILED REPAIR ATTEMPTS

It takes time for the four horsemen and the flooding that comes in their wake to overrun a marriage. And yet divorce can so often be predicted by listening to a single conversation between newlyweds. How can this be? The answer is that by analyzing any disagreement a couple has, you get a good sense of the pattern they tend to follow. A crucial part of that pattern is whether their repair attempts succeed or fail. Repair attempts, as I described on page 22, are efforts the couple makes ("Let's take a break," "Wait, I need to calm down") to deescalate the tension during a touchy discussion—to put on the brakes so flooding is prevented.

Repair attempts save marriages not just because they decrease emotional tension between spouses, but because by lowering the stress level they also prevent your heart from racing and making you feel flooded. When the four horsemen rule a couple's communication, repair attempts often don't even get noticed. Especially when you're feeling flooded, you're not able to hear a verbal white flag.

In unhappy marriages a feedback loop develops between the four horsemen and the failure of repair attempts. The more contemptuous and defensive the couple is with each other, the more flooding occurs, and the harder it is to hear and respond to a repair. And since the repair is not heard, the contempt and defensiveness just get heightened, making flooding more pronounced, which makes it more difficult to hear the next repair attempt, until finally one partner withdraws.

That's why I can predict a divorce by hearing only one discussion between a husband and wife. The failure of repair attempts is an accurate marker for an unhappy future. The presence of the four horsemen alone predicts divorce with only an 82 percent accuracy. But when you add in the failure of repair attempts, the accuracy rate reaches into the 90s. This is because some couples who trot out the four horsemen when they argue are also successful at repairing the harm the horsemen cause. Usually in this situation—when the four horsemen are present but the couple's repair attempts are successful—the result is a stable, happy marriage. In fact, 84 percent of the newlyweds who were high on the four horsemen but repaired effectively were in stable, happy marriages six years later. But if there are no repair attempts—or if the attempts are not able to be heard— the marriage is in serious danger.

I can tell 96 percent of the time whether a marital discussion will resolve a conflict, after the first three minutes of that discussion.

In emotionally intelligent marriages I hear a wide range of successful repair attempts. Each person has his or her own approach. Olivia and Nathaniel stick out their tongues; other couples laugh or smile or say they're sorry. Even an irritated "Hey, stop yelling at me," or "You're getting off the topic" can defuse a tense situation. All such repair attempts keep a marriage stable because they prevent the four horsemen from moving in for good.

Whether a repair succeeds or fails has very little to do with how eloquent it is and everything to do with the state of the marriage. One happily married couple who taught me this lesson were Hal and Jodie. Because of the nature of his research, Hal, a chemist, would often find out at the last minute that he wouldn't be able to get home for dinner. Although Jodie knew Hal couldn't control his hours, the dinner situation frustrated her. When they discussed the problem in our lab, she pointed out to him that the kids always refused to eat dinner till he got home, so they were often having their dinner very late, which she didn't like. So Hal suggested that she give them a snack to tide them over. Incredulous, Jodie snapped at him: "What do you think I have been doing all along?"

Hal realized that he had screwed up. He had displayed a significant lack of awareness about what went on in his own home and, worse, had insulted his wife's intelligence. In an unhappy marriage this could easily be the grounds for some major league sniping. I waited to see what would happen next. Since all other evidence suggested they were happily married, I anticipated that Hal would use some very skillfully wrought repair attempt. But Hal just gave Jodie a really goofy smile. Jodie burst out laughing, and they went on with their discussion.

Hal's quick grin worked because their marriage was working. But when Oliver tried to soften up Dara by chuckling during their conversation about housekeeping, he got nowhere. In marriages in which the four horsemen have moved in for good, even the most articulate, sensitive, well-targeted repair attempt is likely to fail abysmally.

Ironically, we see more repair attempts between troubled couples than between those whose marriages are going smoothly. The more repair attempts fail, the more these couples keep trying. It can be poignant to hear one member of a couple offer up one repair attempt after another, all to no avail. What makes the difference? What predicts that repair attempts will work? Later we'll see that it is the quality of the friendship between husband and wife and, as I described in Chapter One, "positive sentiment override."

THE SIXTH SIGN: BAD MEMORIES

When a relationship gets subsumed in negativity, it's not only the couple's present and future life together that are put at risk. Their past is in danger, too. When I interview couples, I usually ask about the history of their marriage. I have found over and over that couples who are deeply entrenched in a negative view of their spouse and their marriage often rewrite their past. When I ask them about their early courtship, their wedding, their first year together, I can predict their chances of divorce, even if I'm not privy to their current feelings.

Most couples enter marriage with high hopes and great expectations. In a happy marriage couples tend to look back on their early days fondly. Even if the wedding didn't go off perfectly, they tend to remember the highlights rather than the low points. The same goes for each other. They remember how positive they felt early on, how excited they were when they met, and how much admiration they had for each other. When they talk about the tough times they've had, they glorify the struggles they've been through, drawing strength from the adversity they weathered together.

But when a marriage is not going well, history gets rewritten—for the worse. Now she recalls that he was thirty minutes late getting to the ceremony. Or he focuses on all that time she spent talking to his best man at the rehearsal dinner—or "flirting" with his friend, as it seems to him now. Another sad sign is when you find the past difficult to remember—it has become so unimportant or painful that you've let it fade away.

Peter and Cynthia didn't always spend their days arguing about car washing and other money matters. No doubt if you looked at their photo album, you would find plenty of happy pictures from their early days together. But those pictures have long faded from their minds. When asked to describe the early days, they do a good job of telling the facts of their courtship and marriage, but nothing more. Cynthia recounts that they met at a record store where she was the cashier. She got his name and number from his charge card receipt and called him up to see if he liked the CDs he had bought. Their first date followed.

Cynthia says that she was attracted to Peter at first because he was going to college and was interesting to talk to and nice-looking. "I think it was the fact that I had a charge card," Peter slips in, a snide reference to their current fights over money. He himself seems to have a hard time remembering what attracted him to her when they first met. He says, "Uh . . . *(long pause)* I honestly don't know. I never tried to pin it down to one thing. I think for me that would be pretty dangerous."

When they're asked about the kinds of activities they enjoyed back then, they have a hard time remembering. "Didn't we go on picnics or something?" Cynthia asks him, and he shrugs. The same blank feeling is there when they discuss their decision to marry. "I thought it would solidify the relationship. It seemed like a logical progression—that's basically the main reason," says Peter. He recalls that he proposed to her at a restaurant by tying the ring to a white ribbon wrapped around a bunch of white roses. That sounds promising, until he adds with a sad chuckle: "I'll never forget this. She saw the ring. She started shaking a little bit, and she looked and she asked me, 'I suppose you want an answer?' That's kind of not the reaction I was looking for." He turns to his wife. "You weren't smiling or laughing or anything when you said it—you were just deadpan, like, 'You idiot.'"

"Oh nooo," Cynthia says limply.

The picture doesn't get any better. Peter had pneumonia and a temperature of 103 at their wedding. His main memory, other than feeling sick, was being in the limo afterward with Cynthia and his best man. His friend turned on the stereo, and the Mötley Crüe song "Same Old Ball and Chain" came blasting out. Cynthia remembers feeling hurt because many guests left right after dinner. Peter recalls that everyone kept banging on their glasses with spoons to make him and Cynthia kiss. "I was getting really annoyed," he recalls. To sum up their wedding day, he says, "It was your basic tragedy." Cynthia smiles wanly in agreement.

The reason Peter and Cynthia have such distorted memories is that the negativity between them has become so intense, it's as if it's cast in stone. When the four horsemen overrun a home, impairing the communication, the negativity mushrooms to such a degree that everything a spouse does—or ever did—is recast in a negative light.

In a happy marriage, if the husband promises to pick up the wife's dry cleaning but forgets, she is likely to think, "Oh well, he's been under a lot of stress lately and needs more sleep." She considers his lapse to be fleeting and caused by a specific situation. In an unhappy marriage the same circumstance is likely to lead to a thought like "He's just always so inconsiderate and selfish." By the same token, in a happy marriage a loving gesture, like a wife greeting her husband with a passionate kiss at the end of the workday, is seen as a sign that the spouse is loving and considerate. But in an unhappy marriage the same action will lead the husband to think, "What does she want out of me?"

This distorted perception explains why one husband we studied, Mitch, saw ulterior motives whenever his wife, Leslie, bought him a gift, hugged him, or even called him on the phone. Over time he had rewritten his view of their marriage, creating a very negative script. Whenever a conflict arose, he was all set to feel self-righteous and indignant. His negative thoughts about Leslie helped maintain his distress. He'd get flooded as soon as they had a confrontation. Negative expectations of her and their relationship became the norm. Eventually they divorced.

THE END DRAWS NEAR

When a marriage gets to the point where the couple have rewritten their history, when their minds and bodies make it virtually impossible to communicate and repair their current problems, it is almost bound to fail. They find themselves constantly on red alert. Because they always expect to do combat, the marriage becomes a torment. The understandable result: They withdraw from the relationship.

Sometimes a couple at this end stage of marriage will come for counseling. On the surface it may seem like nothing much is wrong. They don't argue or act contemptuous or stonewall. They don't do much of anything. They talk calmly and distantly about their relationship and their conflicts. An inexperienced therapist could easily assume that their problems don't run very deep. But actually one or both of them has already disengaged emotionally from the marriage.

Some people leave a marriage literally, by divorcing. Others do so by leading parallel lives together. Whichever the route, there are four final stages that signal the death knell of a relationship.

1. You see your marital problems as severe.
2. Talking things over seems useless. You try to solve problems on your own.
3. You start leading parallel lives.
4. Loneliness sets in.

When a couple gets to the last stage, one or both partners may have an affair. But an affair is usually a *symptom* of a dying marriage, not the cause. The end of that marriage could have been predicted long before either spouse strayed. Too often, couples begin to seek help for their marriage after they've already hit troubled waters. The warning signs were almost always there early on if they had known what to look for. You can see the seeds of trouble in (1) what couples actually say to each other (the prevalence of harsh startup, the four horsemen, and the unwillingness to accept influence), (2) the failure of their repair attempts, (3) physiological reactions (flooding), or (4) pervasive negative thoughts about their marriage. *Any* of these signs suggests that emotional separation, and in most cases divorce, may only be a matter of time.

But It's Not Over Till It's Over

As bleak as this sounds, I am convinced that far more marriages could be saved than currently are. Even a marriage that is about to hit bottom can be revived with the right kind of help. Sadly, most marriages at this stage get the *wrong* kind. Well-meaning therapists will deluge the couple with advice about negotiating their differences and improving their communication. At one time I would have done the same. At first, when I figured out how to predict divorce, I thought I had found the key to saving marriages. All that was necessary, I presumed, was to teach people how to argue without being overridden by the four horsemen and without getting flooded. Then their repair attempts would succeed, and they could work out their differences.

But like so many experts before me, I was wrong. I was not able to crack the code to saving marriages until I started to analyze what went *right* in happy marriages. After intensely studying happily married couples for as long as sixteen years, I now know that the key to reviving or divorce-proofing a relationship is not in how you handle disagreements but in how you are with each other when you're not fighting. So although my Seven Principles will also guide you in coping with conflict, the foundation of my approach is to strengthen the friendship that is at the heart of any marriage.

3
Principle 1: Enhance Your Love Maps

*R*ory was a pediatrician who ran an intensive care unit for babies. He was beloved at the hospital, where everybody called him Dr. Rory. He was a reserved man but capable of great warmth, humor, and charm. He was also a workaholic who slept in the hospital an average of twenty nights a month. He didn't know the names of his children's friends, or even the name of the family dog. When he was asked where the back door to the house was, he turned to ask his wife, Lisa.

His wife was upset with how little she saw of Rory and how emotionally unconnected to her he seemed to be. She frequently tried to make little gestures to show him she cared, but her attempts just annoyed him. She was left with the sense that he simply didn't value her or their marriage.

To this day I'm struck by the story of this couple. Here was an intellectually gifted man who didn't even know the name of the family dog or how to find the back door! Of the many problems their relationship faced, perhaps the most fundamental was Rory's shocking lack of knowledge about his home life. He had become so caught up in his work that little space was left over in his brain for the basics of his wife's world.

As bizarre as Rory's rampant ignorance may sound, I have found that many married couples fall into a similar (if less dramatic) habit of inattention to the details of their spouse's life. One or both partners may have only the sketchiest sense of the other's joys, likes, dislikes, fears, stresses. The husband may love modern art, but his wife couldn't tell you why or who his favorite artist is. He doesn't remember the names of her friends or the coworker she fears is constantly trying to undermine her.

In contrast, emotionally intelligent couples are intimately familiar with each other's world. I call this having a richly detailed *love map*—my term for that part of your brain where you store all the relevant information about your partner's life. Another way of saying this is that these couples have made plenty of cognitive room for their marriage. They remember the major events in each other's history, and they keep updating their information as the facts and feelings of their spouse's world change. When she orders him a salad, she knows to ask for his dressing on the side. If she works late, he'll tape her favorite TV show because he knows which one it is and when it's on. He could tell you how she's feeling about her boss, and exactly how to get to her office from the elevator. He knows that religion is important to her but that deep down she has doubts. She knows that he fears being too much like his father and considers himself a "free spirit." They know each other's goals in life, each other's worries, each other's hopes.

Without such a love map, you can't really know your spouse. And if you don't really know someone, how can you truly love them? No wonder the biblical term for sexual love is to "know."

IN KNOWLEDGE THERE IS STRENGTH

From knowledge springs not only love but the fortitude to weather marital storms. Couples who have detailed love maps of each other's world are far better prepared to cope with stressful events and conflict. Take, for example, one of the major causes of marital dissatisfaction and divorce: the birth of the first baby. Sixty-seven percent of couples in our newlywed study underwent a precipitous drop in marital satisfaction the first time they became parents. But the remaining 33 percent did not experience this drop—in fact, about half of them saw their marriages improve.

What separated these two groups? You guessed it: The couples whose marriages thrived after the birth had detailed love maps from the get-go, according to a study of fifty couples by my student Alyson Shapiro. These love maps protected their marriages in the wake of this dramatic upheaval. Because husband and wife were already in the habit of keeping up to date and were intently aware of what each other was feeling and thinking, they weren't thrown off course. But if you don't start off with a deep knowledge of each other, it's easy for your marriage to lose its way when your lives shift so suddenly and dramatically.

Maggie and Ken knew each other only a short time when they married and decided to have a family. But what their relationship lacked in longevity, they made up for in intimacy. They were in touch not just with the outlines of each other's lives—their favorite hobbies, sports, and so on—but with each other's deepest longings, beliefs, and fears. No matter how busy they were, they made each other their priority—always making sure they had time to catch up on each other's day. And at least once a week they'd go out for dinner and just talk—sometimes about politics, sometimes about the weather, sometimes about their own marriage.

When their daughter Alice was born, Maggie decided to give up her job as a computer scientist to stay home with the baby. She herself was surprised by the decision since she had always been very driven in her career. But when she became a mother, her fundamental sense of meaning in life changed. She found she was willing to undergo great sacrifices for Alice's sake. Now she wanted the savings they had earmarked for a motorboat to go into a college fund. What happened to Maggie happens to many new mothers—the experience of parenthood is so profound that your whole notion of who you are and what you value gets reshuffled.

At first, Ken was confused by the changes in his wife. The woman he thought he knew was transforming before his eyes. But because they were in the habit of staying deeply connected, Ken was able to keep up to date on what Maggie was thinking and feeling. Too often when a new baby comes, the husband gets left behind. (More on this and ways of dealing with it in Chapter 9.) He can't keep up with his wife's metamorphosis, which he may not understand or be happy about. Knowing Maggie had always been a priority to Ken, so he didn't do what too many new fathers do—he didn't back away from this new charmed circle of mother and child. As a result they went through the transformation to parenthood together, without losing sight of each other or their marriage.

Having a baby is just one life event that can cause couples to lose their way without a detailed love map. Any major change—from a job shift to a move to illness or retirement—can have the same effect. Just the passage of time can do it as well. The more you know and understand about each other, the easier it is to keep connected as life swirls around you.

Love Maps Questionnaire

By giving honest answers to the following questions, you will get a sense of the quality of your current love maps. For the most accurate reading of how your marriage is doing on this first principle, both of you should complete the following.

Read each statement and circle **T** *for "true" or* **F** *for "false."*

1. I can name my partner's best friends. **T F**
2. I can tell you what stresses my partner is currently facing. **T F**
3. I know the names of some of the people who have been irritating my partner lately. **T F**
4. I can tell you some of my partner's life dreams. **T F**
5. I am very familiar with my partner's religious beliefs and ideas. **T F**
6. I can tell you about my partner's basic philosophy of life. **T F**

7. I can list the relatives my partner likes the least. **T F**

8. I know my partner's favorite music. **T F**

9. I can list my partner's three favorite movies. **T F**

10. My spouse is familiar with my current stresses. **T F**

11. I know the three most special times in my partner's life. **T F**

12. I can tell you the most stressful thing that happened to my partner as a child. **T F**

13. I can list my partner's major aspirations and hopes in life. **T F**

14. I know my partner's major current worries. **T F**

15. My spouse knows who my friends are. **T F**

16. I know what my partner would want to do if he or she suddenly won the lottery. **T F**

17. I can tell you in detail my first impressions of my partner. **T F**

18. Periodically I ask my partner about his or her world right now. **T F**

19. I feel that my partner knows me pretty well. **T F**

20. My spouse is familiar with my hopes and aspirations. **T F**

Scoring: Give yourself one point for each "true" answer.

10 or above: This is an area of strength for your marriage. You have a fairly detailed map of your spouse's everyday life, hopes, fears, and dreams. You know what makes your spouse "tick." Based on your score you'll probably find the love map exercises that follow easy and gratifying. They will serve as a reminder of how connected you and your partner are. Try not to take for granted this knowledge and understanding of each other. Keeping in touch in this way ensures you'll be well equipped to handle any problem areas that crop up in your relationship.

Below 10: Your marriage could stand some improvement in this area. Perhaps you never had the time or the tools to really get to know each other. Or perhaps your love maps have become outdated as your lives have changed over the years. In either case, by taking the time to learn more about your spouse now, you'll find your relationship becomes stronger.

There are few gifts a couple can give each other greater than the joy that comes from feeling known and understood. Getting to know each other shouldn't be a chore. That's why the first love map exercise below is actually a game! While you're having fun playing, you'll also be expanding and deepening your knowledge of each other. By the time you complete all of the exercises in this chapter, you'll know there's truth in that old song "To Know You Is to Love You."

Exercise 1: The Love Map
20 Questions Game

Play this game together in the spirit of laughter and gentle fun. The more you play, the more you'll learn about the love maps concept and how to apply it to your own relationship.

STEP 1. Each of you should take a piece of paper and pen or pencil. Together, randomly decide on twenty numbers between 1 and 60. Write the numbers down in a column on the left-hand side of your paper.

STEP 2. Below is a list of numbered questions. Beginning with the top of your column, match the numbers you chose with the corresponding question. Each of you should ask your partner this question. If your spouse answers correctly (you be the judge), he or she receives the number of points indicated for that question, and you receive one point. If your spouse answers incorrectly, neither of you receives any points. The same rules apply when you answer. The winner is the person with the higher score after you've both answered all twenty questions.

1. Name my two closest friends. (2)
2. What is my favorite musical group, composer, or instrument? (2)
3. What was I wearing when we first met? (2)
4. Name one of my hobbies. (3)
5. Where was I born? (1)
6. What stresses am I facing right now? (4)
7. Describe in detail what I did today, or yesterday. (4)
8. When is my birthday? (1)
9. What is the date of our anniversary? (1)
10. Who is my favorite relative? (2)

11. What is my fondest unrealized dream? (5)

12. What is my favorite flower? (2)

13. What is one of my greatest fears or disaster scenarios? (3)

14. What is my favorite time of day for lovemaking? (3)

15. What makes me feel most competent? (4)

16. What turns me on sexually? (3)

17. What is my favorite meal? (2)

18. What is my favorite way to spend an evening? (2)

19. What is my favorite color? (1)

20. What personal improvements do I want to make in my life? (4)

21. What kind of present would I like best? (2)

22. What was one of my best childhood experiences? (2)

23. What was my favorite vacation? (2)

24. What is one of my favorite ways to be soothed? (4)

25. Who is my greatest source of support (other than you)? (3)

26. What is my favorite sport? (2)

27. What do I most like to do with time off? (2)

28. What is one of my favorite weekend activities? (2)

29. What is my favorite getaway place? (3)

30. What is my favorite movie? (2)

31. What are some of the important events coming up in my life? How do I feel about them? (4)

32. What are some of my favorite ways to work out? (2)

33. Who was my best friend in childhood? (3)

34. What is one of my favorite magazines? (2)

35. Name one of my major rivals or "enemies." (3)

36. What would I consider my ideal job? (4)

37. What do I fear the most? (4)

38. Who is my least favorite relative? (3)

39. What is my favorite holiday? (2)

40. What kinds of books do I most like to read? (3)

41. What is my favorite TV show? (2)

42. Which side of the bed do I prefer? (2)

43. What am I most sad about? (4)

44. Name one of my concerns or worries. (4)

45. What medical problems do I worry about? (2)

46. What was my most embarrassing moment? (3)

47. What was my worst childhood experience? (3)

48. Name two of the people I most admire. (4)

49. Name my major rival or enemy. (3)

50. Of all the people we both know, who do I like the least? (3)

51. What is one of my favorite desserts? (2)

52. What is my social security number? (2)

53. Name one of my favorite novels. (2)

54. What is my favorite restaurant? (2)

55. What are two of my aspirations, hopes, wishes? (4)

56. Do I have a secret ambition? What is it? (4)

57. What foods do I hate? (2)

58. What is my favorite animal? (2)

59. What is my favorite song? (2)

60. Which sports team is my favorite? (2)

Play this game as frequently as you'd like. The more you play, the more you'll come to understand the concept of a love map and the kind of information yours should include about your spouse.

Exercise 2: Make Your Own Love Maps

Now that you have a clearer understanding of the love maps concept, it's time to focus more seriously on your love maps for each other's everyday lives. Even though these maps are "all in your head," it helps to write down some of the basics. Spend extra time on this exercise if you (or your spouse) believes that your current love map is inadequate or, as is often the case, has fallen out of date. Use the following form to interview each other as if you were reporters. (If your spouse is unavailable, you can fill out this form without his or her input, but obviously the major benefits of this exercise come from sharing information.) Take turns as listener and speaker, and write out the answers to these forms. (It's best to use a separate piece of paper, or better yet a notebook or journal that you can use for all of the exercises in this book.) Don't pass judgment on what your spouse tells you or try to give each other advice. Remember that you are simply on a fact-finding mission. Your goal is to listen and learn about your mate.

The cast of characters in my partner's life

Friends:

Potential friends:

Rivals, competitors, "enemies":

Recent important events in my partner's life

Upcoming events
(What is my partner looking forward to? Dreading?)

My partner's current stresses

My partner's current worries

My partner's hopes and aspirations (For self? For others?)

Although this exercise offers you just a snapshot of your partner's life, it can be quite illuminating. Couples who have completed our workshop say this exercise offered them plenty of surprises that helped them better understand their spouse. Joe, for example, never realized just how deeply Donna longed to be an author and how frustrated she was in her banking job until he asked her point-blank about her hopes and aspirations. And she never realized that his recent irritability was rooted in his concern about his new boss and his job performance, not her mother's visit.

This love maps form is useful for creating a broad outline of your current lives. But love maps shouldn't just be broad—they should also be deep. The next exercise will ensure that yours are.

Exercise 3: Who Am I?

The more you know about each other's inner world, the more profound and rewarding your relationship will be. This questionnaire is designed both to guide you through some self-exploration and to help you share this exploration with your partner. Work on this exercise even if you and your spouse consider yourselves open books. There's always more to know about each other. Life changes us, so neither of you may be the same person who spoke those wedding vows five, ten, or fifty years ago.

Many of the questions in this exercise are powerful. Please make sure you have enough time and privacy to do them justice. In fact, it may be best to reserve this exercise for an uninterrupted stretch when you do not have work to do, deadlines to meet, phone calls to answer, or children (or anybody else) to look after. Most likely you won't be able to complete this questionnaire in one sitting, nor should you try. Instead, break it up by section and do it slowly, over time together.

Answer the questions in each section as candidly as you can. You don't have to answer every aspect of each question—just respond to the parts that are relevant to your life. Write your answers in your private journal or notebook. If writing so much is hard, you can do it in outline form—but the process of writing this down is important to the success of the exercise. When you're ready, exchange notebooks and share with each other what you have written. Discuss each other's entries and what this added knowl-edge implies for your marriage and the deepening of your friendship.

My Triumphs and Strivings

1. What has happened in your life that you are particularly proud of? Write about your psychological triumphs, times when things went even bet-ter than you expected, periods when you came through trials and tribulations even better off. Include periods of stress and duress that you survived and mastered, small events that may still be of great importance to you, events from your childhood or the recent past, self-created challenges you met, periods when you felt powerful, glories and victories, wonderful friendships you maintained, and so on.

2. How have these successes shaped your life? How have they affected the way you think of yourself and your capabilities? How have they affected your goals and the things you strive for?

3. What role has pride (that is, feeling proud, being praised, expressing praise for others) played in your life? Did your parents show you that they were proud of you when you were a child? How? How have other people responded to your accomplishments?

4. Did your parents show you that they loved you? How? Was affection readily expressed in your family? If not, what are the effects and implications of this for your marriage?

5. What role does pride in your accomplishments play in your marriage? What role do your own strivings have in your marriage? What do you want your partner to know and understand about these aspects of your self, your past, present, and plans for the future? How do you show pride in one another?

My Injuries and Healings

1. What difficult events or periods have you gone through? Write about any significant psychological insults and injuries you have sustained, your losses, disappointments, trials, and tribulations. Include periods of stress and duress, as well as any quieter periods of despair, hopelessness, and loneliness.

Also include any deep traumas you have undergone as a child or adult. For example, harmful relationships, humiliating events, even molestation, abuse, rape, or torture.

2. How have you survived these traumas? What are their lasting effects on you?

3. How did you strengthen and heal yourself? How did you redress your grievances? How did you revive and restore yourself?

4. How did you gird and protect yourself against this ever happening again?

5. How do these injuries and the ways you protect and heal yourself affect your marriage today? What do you want your partner to know and understand about these aspects of your self?

My Emotional World

1. How did your family express the following when you were a child:
- Anger
- Sadness
- Fear
- Affection
- Interest in one another

2. During your childhood, did your family have to cope with a particular emotional problem, such as aggression between parents, a depressed parent, or a parent who was somewhat emotionally wounded? What implications does this have for your marriage and your other close relationships (friendships, relationships with your parents, your siblings, your children)?

3. What is your own philosophy about expressing feelings, particularly sadness, anger, fear, pride, and love? Are any of these difficult for you to express or to see expressed by your spouse? What is the basis of your perspective on this?

4. What differences exist between you and your spouse in the area of expressing emotion? What is behind these differences? What are the implications of these differences for you?

My Mission and Legacy

1. Imagine that you are standing in a graveyard looking at your own tombstone. Now write the epitaph you would like to see there. Begin with the words: "Here lies . . ."

2. Write your own obituary. (It does not have to be brief.) How do you want people to think of your life, to remember you?

3. Now you're ready to write a mission statement for your own life. What is the purpose of your life? What is its meaning? What are you trying to accomplish? What is your larger struggle?

4. What legacy would you like to leave when you die?

5. What significant goals have you yet to realize? This can be creating something, or having a particular experience. Minor examples are learning to play the banjo, climbing a mountain, and so on.

Who I Want to Become

Take a moment now to reflect on what you have just written. We are all involved in becoming the person we most want to be. In that struggle we all have demons to fight and overcome.

1. Describe the person you want to become.

2. How can you best help yourself become that person?

3. What struggles have you already faced in trying to become that person?

4. What demons in yourself have you had to fight? Or still have to fight?

5. What would you most like to change about yourself?

6. What dreams have you denied yourself or failed to develop?

7. What do you want your life to be like in five years?

8. What is the story of the kind of person you would like to be?

THE NEXT STEP

All of the above exercises and questions will help you develop greater personal insight and a more detailed map of each other's life and world. Getting to know your spouse better and sharing your inner self with your partner is an ongoing process. In fact, it's a life-long process. So expect to return to these pages from time to time to update your knowledge about yourselves and each other. Think about questions to ask your partner, like "If you could add an addition to our home what would it be?" or "How are you feeling about your job these days?" One therapist I know has taken to wearing a Bugs Bunny pin and advising couples that the key to sustaining a happy marriage is to ask periodically, "What's up, doc?"

But love maps are only a first step. Happily married couples don't "just" know each other. They build on and enhance this knowledge in many important ways. For starters, they use their love maps to express not only their understanding of each other but their fondness and admiration as well, the basis of my second principle.

4
Principle 2:
Nurture Your Fondness
and Admiration

*R*emember Dr. Rory, the husband whose love map was the size of a postage stamp? Who didn't even know the name of the family dog? For years his wife Lisa put up with his workaholism. But a turning point in their relationship occurred one year on Christmas Day, when Rory was, of course, working. Lisa decided to pack a Christmas picnic and bring the kids and herself to the hospital.

As they ate together in the waiting room, Rory turned on Lisa, his face like an angry mask. He told her he resented being surprised with a picnic. "Why did you do this? It is really embarrassing. None of the other doctors' wives would do this." Suddenly a resident called him on the waiting room phone. As Rory picked up the receiver, his face softened and his voice became helpful, warm, and friendly. When he hung up, he turned back to Lisa, his face again full of anger. Something snapped inside Lisa. She had had it. Clearly her husband was capable of kindness—but not toward her. She packed up the picnic and took the kids home.

Soon afterward she began going out in the evenings without him. After a while Rory asked her for a divorce. But in a last-ditch effort to work out their differences, they decided to try marital counseling. At first they got nowhere. When Lisa tried to be conciliatory toward Rory during their first session with a marital therapist, he was unable to respond in kind to her repair attempts.

But their marriage's hidden hope was discovered when the couple agreed to be taped in my lab for a segment of *Face to Face with Connie Chung*. The interviewer asked Rory and Lisa about their early years together. As Rory began to recall their first date, his face lit up. He explained that Lisa, unlike him, came from a traditional Armenian home. She was very sheltered by her parents and very inexperienced when it came to dating. Rory knew that getting her and her family to accept him would take a long time, but he was willing to hang in there. Here's a little of what they recalled:

RORY: I think she was very nervous, and I had some background about why she was nervous, some cultural things that she was trying to live with. And because of this I knew this was going to take a long, long time. So I wasn't nervous at all. I figured this was stage one of a five-year marathon. . . .
LISA: You mean you had a five-year plan on our first date?
RORY: Maybe that's exaggerating, but I knew it would take more than one lunch.
LISA: Wow.

Rory and Lisa actually held hands while they discussed this. Lisa was beaming—he had never before recounted his campaign to win her heart. This little vignette may not sound very dramatic (in fact, the TV show edited Rory and Lisa down to a snippet of air time), but to a trained observer there was much in this couple's interaction that offered hope for their marriage. Rory and Lisa's fond memories of their early days were evidence that underneath their mutual antagonism there were still glimmerings of what I call a fondness and admiration system. This means that they each retained some fundamental sense that the other was worthy of being respected and even liked.

If a couple still has a functioning fondness and admiration system, their marriage is salvageable. I'm not suggesting that the road to reviving a marriage as troubled as Rory and Lisa's is easy. But it can be done. By using techniques like those you'll find in the pages ahead, Rory and Lisa's therapist, Lois Abrams, showed them that they could unearth those positive feelings even more and put them to work to save their marriage.

Two years later everything has changed for this couple. Rory has revised his work schedule. He trained a resident to do much of the hospital work that he had been doing single-handedly. He now eats dinner every night with Lisa and the children. He and Lisa also go out together in the evenings, especially to folk dance. Despite the agony they put each other through, Rory and Lisa saved their marriage.

Fondness and admiration are two of the most crucial elements in a rewarding and long-lasting romance. Although happily married couples may feel driven to distraction at times by their partner's personality flaws, they still feel that the person they married is worthy of honor and respect. When this sense is completely missing from a marriage, the relationship cannot be revived.

LEARNING FROM HISTORY

As it was with Rory and Lisa, the best test of whether a couple still has a functioning fondness and admiration system is usually how they view their past. If your marriage is now in deep trouble, you're not likely to elicit much praise on each other's behalf by asking about the current state of affairs. But by focusing on your past, you can often detect embers of positive feelings.

Of course, some marriages do come up empty. In these relationships the antagonism has metastasized like a virulent cancer, even going backward in time and destroying the couple's positive memories. We saw that sad result in the marriage of Peter and Cynthia, who argued over washing her car. Their relationship was ruined by his contempt and her defensiveness. When they were asked the same questions about their early years, it became clear that their love was gone. They could remember very little about the beginning of their relationship. When asked what they used to do when they were dating, they gave each other a brief "help me out here" glance and then sat silently, racking their brains for an answer. Peter couldn't remember a single thing he admired about Cynthia back then. Their marriage was not salvageable.

> **I've found 94 percent of the time that couples who put a positive spin on their marriage's history are likely to have a happy future as well. When happy memories are distorted, it's a sign that the marriage needs help.**

In contrast, when another couple in my newlywed study, Michael and Justine, were asked about their history, they glowed. Their wedding was "perfect," the honeymoon was "fabulous." What's telling isn't just that they feel positive about their early years, but how vivid their memories are. Justine recalls that they had gone to the same high school, he a few years ahead of her. He was a big sports hero. She had such a crush on him that she had clipped his picture from the newspaper and kept it in a scrapbook. (She confessed and showed him the scrapbook on their fourth date.) They met formally a few years later, when she tagged along with his foster sister (a friend of hers) who was going to visit him at college for the weekend.

Michael sensed right away that Justine was the one, but he worried that she wouldn't like him. She recounts with a giggle discovering the letter he slipped under her leather purse at the end of that weekend to let her know how he felt about her. "I was never very aggressive about chasing women," he says. "She was the first girl I ever actually pursued. That's how I knew something was different about this one."

They recall the long walks and talks they had, the letters they wrote every day while he was at school. The only bad part of those days, says Michael, was "being away from Justine. Just missing her a lot." You can hear Justine's fondness, pride, and admiration for

Michael when she says, "I thought, 'God, if I don't marry this guy, someone else will. I'd better get him while I can.'" Michael says, "I would look at other girls, and I didn't want to be with them. I just wanted to be with her. I wanted to become a legal couple and let everybody know how special she is to me." Justine recalls the unity they felt in dealing with one of his buddies who resented that Justine was taking so much of Michael's time. "He didn't get it that I was *giving* her my time," Michael says.

It won't come as much of a surprise to hear that Michael and Justine continue to be happily married. That's because having a fundamentally positive view of your spouse and your marriage is a powerful buffer when bad times hit. Because they have this reserve of good feeling, Justine and Michael will not have cataclysmic thoughts about separation and divorce each time they have an argument.

THE ANTIDOTE TO CONTEMPT

At first, this may all seem obvious to the point of being ridiculous: People who are happily married like each other. If they didn't, they wouldn't be happily married. But fondness and admiration can be fragile unless you remain aware of how crucial they are to the friendship that is at the core of any good marriage. By simply reminding yourself of your spouse's positive qualities—even as you grapple with each other's flaws—you can prevent a happy marriage from deteriorating. The simple reason is that fondness and admiration are antidotes for contempt. If you maintain a sense of respect for your spouse, you are less likely to act disgusted with him or her when you disagree. So fondness and admiration prevent the couple from being trounced by the four horsemen.

If your mutual fondness and admiration have been completely extinguished, your marriage is in dire trouble. Without the fundamental belief that your spouse is worthy of honor and respect, where is the basis for any kind of rewarding relationship? But there are many couples like Rory and Lisa, whose fondness and admiration have receded to barely detectable levels. Although it seems that the fire is out, some embers still burn. Fanning them is the crucial first step in salvaging such a marriage.

Fondness and Admiration Questionnaire

To assess the current state of your fondness and admiration system, answer the following:

Read each statement and circle **T** *for "true" or* **F** *for "false."*

 1. I can easily list the three things I most admire about my partner. **T F**
 2. When we are apart, I often think fondly of my partner. **T F**
 3. I will often find some way to tell my partner "I love you." **T F**
 4. I often touch or kiss my partner affectionately. **T F**
 5. My partner really respects me. **T F**
 6. I feel loved and cared for in this relationship. **T F**
 7. I feel accepted and liked by my partner. **T F**
 8. My partner finds me sexy and attractive. **T F**
 9. My partner turns me on sexually. **T F**
 10. There is fire and passion in this relationship. **T F**
 11. Romance is definitely still a part of our relationship. **T F**
 12. I am really proud of my partner. **T F**
 13. My partner really enjoys my achievements and accomplishments. **T F**
 14. I can easily tell you why I married my partner. **T F**
 15. If I had it all to do over again, I would marry the same person. **T F**
 16. We rarely go to sleep without some show of love or affection. **T F**
 17. When I come into a room, my partner is glad to see me. **T F**
 18. My partner appreciates the things I do in this marriage. **T F**
 19. My spouse generally likes my personality. **T F**
 20. Our sex life is generally satisfying. **T F**

Scoring: Give yourself one point for each "true" answer.

10 or above: This is an area of strength for your marriage. Because you value each other highly, you have a shield that can protect your relationship from being overwhelmed by any negativity that also exists between you. Although it might seem obvious to you that people who are in love have a high regard for each other, it's common for spouses to lose sight of some of their fondness and admiration over time. Remember that this fondness and admiration is a gift worth cherishing. Completing the exercises in this chapter from time to time will help you to reaffirm your positive feelings for each other.

Below 10: Your marriage could stand some improvement in this area. Don't be discouraged by a low score. There are many couples in whom the fondness and admiration system has not died but is buried under layers of negativity, hurt feelings, and betrayal. By reviving the positive feelings that still lie deep below, you can vastly improve your marriage.

If your fondness and admiration are being chipped away, the route to bringing them back always begins with realizing how valuable they are. They are crucial to the long-term happiness of a relationship because they prevent contempt—one of the marriage-killing four horsemen—from becoming an overwhelming presence in your life. Contempt is a corrosive that, over time, breaks down the bond between husband and wife. The better in touch you are with your deep-seated positive feelings for each other, the less likely you are to act contemptuous of your spouse when you have a difference of opinion.

FANNING THE FLAMES

There's nothing complicated about reviving or enhancing your fondness and admiration. Even positive feelings that have long been buried can be exhumed simply by thinking and talking about them. You can do this by meditating a bit on your partner and what makes you cherish him or her. If you're feeling out of practice or have too much stress or anger to do this "free form," the following exercises will guide you. As simple as these exercises may seem to be, they have enormous power. When you acknowledge and openly discuss positive aspects of your partner and your marriage, your bond is strengthened. This makes it much easier to address the problem areas in your marriage and make some positive changes. Feel free to do these exercises as often as you wish. They are not intended only for troubled relationships. If your marriage is stable and happy, working through these exercises is an excellent way to heighten the romance.

Exercise 1: "I Appreciate . . ."

From the list below, circle three items that you think are characteristic of your partner. If there are more than three, still circle just three. (You can circle another three if you choose to do this exercise again.) If you're having difficulty coming up with three, feel free to define the word *characteristic* very loosely. Even if you can recall only one instance when your partner displayed this characteristic, you can circle it.

1. Loving	23. Resourceful
2. Sensitive	24. Athletic
3. Brave	25. Cheerful
4. Intelligent	26. Coordinated
5. Thoughtful	27. Graceful
6. Generous	28. Elegant
7. Loyal	29. Gracious
8. Truthful	30. Playful
9. Strong	31. Caring
10. Energetic	32. A great friend
11. Sexy	33. Exciting
12. Decisive	34. Thrifty
13. Creative	35. Full of plans
14. Imaginative	36. Shy
15. Fun	37. Vulnerable
16. Attractive	38. Committed
17. Interesting	39. Involved
18. Supportive	40. Expressive
19. Funny	41. Active
20. Considerate	42. Careful
21. Affectionate	43. Reserved
22. Organized	44. Adventurous

45. Receptive
46. Reliable
47. Responsible
48. Dependable
49. Nurturing
50. Warm
51. Virile
52. Kind
53. Gentle
54. Practical
55. Lusty
56. Witty
57. Relaxed
58. Beautiful
59. Handsome
60. Rich
61. Calm
62. Lively
63. A great partner
64. A great parent
65. Assertive
66. Protective
67. Sweet
68. Tender
69. Powerful
70. Flexible
71. Understanding
72. Totally silly

For each item you checked, briefly think of an actual incident that illustrates this characteristic of your partner. Write the characteristic and the incident in your notebook or journal as follows:

1. Characteristic _____

  Incident _____

2. Characteristic _____

  Incident _____

3. Characteristic _____

  Incident _____

Now, share your list with your partner. Let him or her know what it is about these traits that you value so highly.

  In my workshops, I can see the positive benefits of this exercise immediately. The room is filled with warm smiles and laughter. Couples who began the session sitting stiffly and awkwardly suddenly seem relaxed. Just looking at them, you can tell that something they had lost is being regained. The sense of hope that their marriage can be saved is almost palpable.

Exercise 2: The History and Philosophy of Your Marriage

Most couples are helped all the more by talking about the happy events of their past. Below is a version of the questionnaire that led Rory and Lisa to reconnect with their fondness and admiration for each other. Completing this questionnaire together will bring you face to face, once again, with the early years of your relationship, and help you remember how and why you became a couple.

You will need a few hours of uninterrupted time to complete this exercise. You can ask a close friend or relative to serve as interviewer, or you can just read the questions and talk about them together. There are no right or wrong answers to these questions—they are merely meant to guide you in recalling the love and perspective on marriage that led you to join your lives in the first place.

Part One: The History of Your Relationship

1. Discuss how the two of you met and got together. Was there anything about your spouse that made him or her stand out? What were your first impressions of each other?

2. What do you remember most about the time you were first dating? What stands out? How long did you know each other before you got married? What do you remember of this period? What were some of the highlights? Some of the tensions? What types of things did you do together?

3. Talk about how you decided to get married. Of all the people in the world, what led you to decide that this was the person you wanted to marry? Was it an easy decision? Was it a difficult decision? Were you in love? Talk about this time.

4. Do you remember your wedding? Talk to each other about your memories. Did you have a honeymoon? What do you remember about it?

5. What do you remember about the first year you were married? Were there any adjustments you needed to make?

6. What about the transition to becoming parents? Talk to each other about this period of your marriage. What was it like for the two of you?

7. Looking back over the years, what moments stand out as the really happy times in your marriage? What is a good time for you as a couple? Has this changed over the years?

8. Many relationships go through periods of ups and downs. Would you say that this is true of your marriage? Can you describe some of these periods?

9. Looking back over the years, what moments stand out as the really hard times in your marriage? Why do you think you stayed together? How did you get through these difficult times?

10. Have you stopped doing things together that once gave you pleasure? Explore these with one another.

Part Two: Your Philosophy of Marriage

11. Talk to each other about why you think some marriages work while others don't. Decide together who among the couples you know have particularly good marriages and who have particularly bad marriages. What is different about these two marriages? How would you compare your own marriage to each of these couples'?

12. Talk to each other about your parents' marriages. Would you say they were very similar to or different from your own marriage?

13. Make a chart of the history of your marriage, its major turning points, ups and downs. What were the happiest times for you? For your partner? How has your marriage changed over the years?

Most couples find that recalling their past together recharges their relationship in the here and now. Answering these questions often reminds couples of the love and great expectations that inspired their decision to marry in the first place. This can give couples who thought their marriage was already over the glimmerings of hope that lead them to struggle on to save their relationship. Just repeating the two exercises above from time to time may be enough to salvage and strengthen your fondness and admiration for each other. But if the negativity is deeply entrenched, a marriage may require a longer-term, more structured approach, which you'll find in the next exercise.

Exercise 3: A Seven-Week Course in Fondness and Admiration

This exercise is designed to get you into the habit of thinking positively about your partner when you're apart. If you are angry, stressed, or feeling distant from your spouse, you may tend to focus on his or her negative characteristics. This leads to distress-maintaining thoughts, which in turn leave you feeling ever more distant and isolated in your marriage. This exercise counteracts that tendency by training you to focus your thoughts on your partner's *positive* characteristics, even if you aren't having such a great day together.

For each day below there is a positive statement, or thought, followed by a task. Think about each statement and say it to yourself many times throughout the day while you and your spouse are apart. In some cases the thought may not seem to apply to your spouse or your marriage, especially if your fondness and admiration have dimmed. Keep in mind that the statement does not have to describe the typical state of affairs between you at the present time. If you can think of a single instant or episode where the statement applied, focus on that memory. For example, if you're not feeling overly attracted to your spouse these days, focus on one area of his or her anatomy that does appeal to you. Also be sure to complete the simple task that follows each positive statement. Do the exercise each day, no matter how you happen to be feeling about your relationship or your spouse. Don't stop even if you just had a major blow-up or are feeling very distant from each other.

Although this exercise might sound silly or hokey, it is based on a wide body of research into the power of rehearsing positive thoughts. This approach is one of the tenets of cognitive therapy, which has proven highly successful in helping people overcome depression. When people fall into a depression, their thinking may become disordered—they see everything in an extremely negative light, which just adds to their sense of hopelessness. But if, over time, they deliberately accustom their mind to a different, positive way of thinking, the sense of hopelessness can be lifted.

This exercise is an experiment in offering the same hope to marriage.

What you're really doing is rehearsing a more positive way to think about your partner and your relationship. Like any rehearsal, if you do it often enough, the words (and more importantly, the thoughts) will become second nature.

Note: Since most couples spend time apart on Monday through Friday, those are the days that are specified in the schedule below. You can switch the actual days around to better fit your schedule (if, for example, you work on the weekends), as long as you do the exercise five days a week.

Week 1

Monday

> Thought: I am genuinely fond of my partner.
> Task: *List one characteristic you find endearing or lovable.*

Tuesday

> Thought: I can easily speak of the good times in our marriage.
> Task: *Pick one good time and write a sentence about it.*

Wednesday

> Thought: I can easily remember romantic, special times in our marriage.
> Task: *Pick one such time and think about it.*

Thursday

> Thought: I am physically attracted to my partner.
> Task: *Think of one physical attribute you like.*

Friday

> Thought: My partner has specific qualities that make me proud.
> Task: *Write down one characteristic that makes you proud.*

Week 2

Monday

> Thought: I feel a genuine sense of "we" as opposed to "I" in this marriage.
> Task: *Think of one thing that you both have in common.*

Tuesday

> Thought: We have the same general beliefs and values.
> Task: *Describe one belief you share.*

Wednesday

> Thought: We have common goals.
>
> Task: *List one such goal.*

Thursday

> Thought: My spouse is my best friend.
>
> Task: *What secret about you does your spouse know?*

Friday

> Thought: I get lots of support in this marriage.
>
> Task: *Think of a time when your spouse was very supportive of you.*

Week 3

Monday

> Thought: My home is a place to come to get support and reduce stress.
>
> Task: *List a time when your spouse helped you reduce stress.*

Tuesday

> Thought: I can easily recall the time we first met.
>
> Task: *Describe that first meeting on paper.*

Wednesday

> Thought: I remember many details about deciding to get married.
>
> Task: *Write a sentence describing what you remember.*

Thursday

> Thought: I can recall our wedding and honeymoon.
>
> Task: *Describe one thing about them you enjoyed.*

Friday

> Thought: We divide up household chores in a fair way.
>
> Task: *Describe one way you do this on a regular basis. If you do not do your share, decide on a chore you will take on (such as doing the laundry).*

Week 4

Monday

> Thought: We are able to plan well and have a sense of control over our lives together.
>
> Task: *Describe one thing you both planned together.*

Tuesday

Thought: I am proud of this marriage.

Task: *List two things about this marriage that you are you proud of.*

Wednesday

Thought: I am proud of my family.

Task: *Recall a specific time when you especially felt this pride.*

Thursday

Thought: I don't like things about my partner, but I can live with them.

Task: *What is one of these minor faults you have adapted to?*

Friday

Thought: This marriage is a lot better than most I have seen.

Task: *Think of a marriage you know that's awful.*

Week 5

Monday

Thought: I was really lucky to meet my spouse.

Task: *List one benefit that being married to your spouse offers.*

Tuesday

Thought: Marriage is sometimes a struggle, but it's worth it.

Task: *Think of one difficult time you successfully weathered together.*

Wednesday

Thought: There is a lot of affection between us.

Task: *Plan a surprise gift for your mate for tonight.*

Thursday

Thought: We are genuinely interested in one another.

Task: *Think of something to do or talk about that would be interesting.*

Friday

Thought: We find one another to be good companions.

Task: *Plan an outing together.*

Week 6

Monday

Thought: There is lots of good loving in my marriage.

Task: *Think of a special trip you took together.*

Tuesday

Thought: My partner is an interesting person.

Task: *Plan something to ask your mate about that interests both of you.*

Wednesday

Thought: We respond well to each other.

Task: *Write a love letter to your spouse and mail it.*

Thursday

Thought: If I had it to do over again, I would marry the same person.

Task: *Plan an anniversary (or other) getaway.*

Friday

Thought: There is lots of mutual respect in my marriage.

Task: *Consider taking a class together (sailing, ballroom dancing, etc.). Or tell your spouse about a time recently when you admired something your spouse did.*

Week 7

Monday

Thought: Sex is usually (or can be) quite satisfying in this marriage.

Task: *Plan an erotic evening for the two of you.*

Tuesday

Thought: We have come a long way together.

Task: *Think of all you have accomplished as a team.*

Wednesday

Thought: I think we can weather any storm together.

Task: *Reminisce about having made it through a hard time.*

Thursday

Thought: We enjoy each other's sense of humor.

Task: *Rent a comedy video to watch together.*

Friday

Thought: My mate can be very cute.

Task: *Get very dressed up for an elegant evening together. Or if you don't like that kind of thing, plan another kind of evening out you would enjoy.*

By the end of the seven weeks, you're likely to find that your perspective on your partner and your marriage is far sunnier. Singing each other's praises can only benefit your marriage. But in order to ensure that the gains continue, you need to put your respect and affection to work. In the next chapter you'll do just that, by using them as the foundation for revamping—or reviving—your marriage's sense of romance.

5
Principle 3:
Turn toward Each Other
Instead of Away

one of the footage taped in our Love Lab would win anybody an Oscar. Our archives are filled with scenes in which the husband looks out the picture window and says, "Wow, look at that boat," and the wife peers over her magazine and says, "Yeah, it looks like that big schooner we saw last summer, remember?" and the husband grunts.

You might think I'd find viewing hour after hour of such scenes unbearably boring. On the contrary: When couples engage in lots of chitchat like this, I can be pretty sure that they will stay happily married. What's really happening in these brief exchanges is that the husband and wife are connecting—they are turning toward each other. In couples who go on to divorce or live together unhappily, such small moments of connection are rare. More often the wife doesn't even look up from her magazine—and if she does, her husband doesn't acknowledge what she says.

Hollywood has dramatically distorted our notions of romance and what makes passion burn. Watching Humphrey Bogart gather teary-eyed Ingrid Bergman into his arms may make your heart pound, but real-life romance is fueled by a far more humdrum approach to staying connected. It is kept alive each time you let your spouse know he or she is valued during the grind of everyday life. Comical as it may sound, romance actually grows when a couple are in the supermarket and the wife says, "Are we out of bleach?" and the husband says, "I don't know. Let me go get some just in case," instead of shrugging apathetically. It grows when you know your spouse is having a bad day at work and you take sixty seconds out of your own workday to leave words of encouragement on his voice mail. It grows when your wife tells you one morning, "I had the worst nightmare last night," and you say, "I'm in a big hurry, but tell me about it now so we can talk about it tonight," instead of "I don't have time." In all of these instances husband and wife are making a choice to turn toward each other rather than away. In marriage people periodically make what I call "bids" for their partner's attention, affection, humor, or support. People either turn toward one another after these bids or they turn away. Turning toward is the basis of emotional connection, romance, passion, and a good sex life.

So in the Love Lab my favorite scenes are the very ones that any Hollywood film editor would relegate to the cutting room floor. I know there's deep drama in the little moments: Will they read the Sunday paper together or silently alone? Will they chat while they eat lunch? Watching them is suspenseful because I know: Couples who turn toward each other remain emotionally engaged and stay married. Those that don't eventually lose their way.

The reason for the differing outcome of these marriages is what I've come to call the couple's emotional bank account. Partners who characteristically turn toward each other rather than away are putting money in the bank. They are building up emotional savings that can serve as a cushion when times get rough, when they're faced with a major life stress or conflict. Because they have stored up all of this goodwill, they are better able to make allowances for each other when a conflict arises. They can maintain a positive sense of each other and their marriage even during hard times.

The biggest payoff from this emotional bank account isn't the cushion it offers when the couple are stressed. As I said, turning toward your spouse in the little ways is also the key to long-lasting romance. Many people think that the secret to reconnecting with their partner is a candlelit dinner or a by-the-sea vacation. But the real secret is to turn toward each other in little ways every day. A romantic night out really turns up the heat only when a couple has kept the pilot light burning by staying in touch in the little ways. It's easy to imagine Justine and Michael, the couple who recalled their wedding and courtship with such delight, at a candlelit restaurant. But sit Peter and Cynthia, the couple who couldn't agree on car washing or much of anything else, in the same chairs, and the evening would most likely be a fiasco, filled with accusations, recriminations, or awkward silences.

Is Your Marriage Primed for Romance?

To get a good sense of how your relationship is faring (or is likely to fare in the future) in the romance department, answer the following questions.

Read each statement and circle **T** *for "true" or* **F** *for "false."*

1. We enjoy doing small things together, like folding laundry or watching TV. **T F**
2. I look forward to spending my free time with my partner. **T F**
3. At the end of the day my partner is glad to see me. **T F**
4. My partner is usually interested in hearing my views. **T F**
5. I really enjoy discussing things with my partner. **T F**
6. My partner is one of my best friends. **T F**
7. I think my partner would consider me a very close friend. **T F**
8. We just love talking to each other. **T F**
9. When we go out together, the time goes very quickly. **T F**
10. We always have a lot to say to each other. **T F**
11. We have a lot of fun together. **T F**
12. We are spiritually very compatible. **T F**

13. We tend to share the same basic values. **T F**

14. We like to spend time together in similar ways. **T F**

15. We really have a lot of common interests. **T F**

16. We have many of the same dreams and goals. **T F**

17. We like to do a lot of the same things. **T F**

18. Even though our interests are somewhat different, I enjoy my partner's interests. **T F**

19. Whatever we do together, we usually tend to have a good time. **T F**

20. My partner tells me when he or she has had a bad day. **T F**

Scoring: Give yourself one point for each "true" answer.

10 or above: Congratulations! This is an area of strength in your marriage. Because you are so often "there" for each other during the minor events in your lives, you have built up a hefty emotional bank account that will support you over any rough patches in your marriage (and keep many at bay). It's those little moments that you rarely think about—when you're shopping at the supermarket, folding laundry, or having a quickie catch-up call while you're both still at work—that make up the heart and soul of a marriage. Having a surplus in your emotional bank account is what makes romance last and gets you through hard times, bad moods, and major life changes.

Below 10: Your marriage could stand some improvement in this area. By learning to turn toward each other more during the minor moments in your day, you will make your marriage not only more stable but more romantic. Every time you make the effort to listen and respond to what your spouse says, to help him or her, you make your marriage a little better.

Couples often ignore each other's emotional needs out of mindlessness, not malice.

The first step in turning toward each other more is simply to be aware of how crucial these mundane moments are, not only to your marriage's stability, but to its ongoing sense of romance. For many couples, just realizing that they shouldn't take their everyday interactions for granted makes an enormous difference in their relationship. Remind yourself that being helpful to each other will do far more for the strength and passion of your marriage than a two-week Bahamas getaway. The following exercises will also help you make turning toward each other an easy, natural part of your lives together.

Exercise 1: The Emotional Bank Account

Keeping an account in your head of how much you're connecting with your spouse emotionally in little ways can greatly benefit your marriage. But for some couples the concept works best if they make their emotional bank account "real." You can do this by drawing a simple ledger and giving yourself one point each time you've turned toward your spouse during the course of the day. You probably wouldn't want to document every encouraging nod you gave while your spouse was talking. But you would include entries for such events as "Called J at work to see how meeting went" and "Took L's van to car wash."

Be careful not to turn this into a competition or a quid pro quo where you track each other's account "balance" and keep tabs on who has done what for whom. That approach defeats the purpose of this exercise. The goal is to focus on what *you* can do to improve your marriage—not on what your spouse should be doing but isn't. That means, for example, trying to turn toward your spouse even when you feel he or she is being difficult or hostile.

You can tally your daily or weekly balance by adding up your deposits and subtracting any withdrawals ("Forgot to get film for M's camera," "Was late getting home"). For this exercise to work it's important to be ruthlessly honest with yourself when you are negligent and turn away from your spouse. The more in the black your account is, the more likely you are to see your marriage improve. Don't be surprised if positive changes don't occur overnight, however. If you've gotten out of the habit of turning toward each other, it may take some time to see the benefits of this exercise. One of the challenges is to notice when your partner does turn toward you and vice versa. In one research study in which couples were closely observed in their own homes, happily married couples noticed almost all of the positive things the researchers observed their partners do

for them. However, unhappily married couples underestimated their partners' loving intentions by 50 percent!

Although you don't want your ledgers to become the focus of a competition, it makes sense to get each other's input about which areas of your
lives could benefit most from more emotional connection. That way you
can focus your efforts on where they'll have the greatest impact. Below is a
long list of activities that some couples do together—everything from washing dishes to going bowling. Choose the three that you most wish your
partner would do with you. You can also circle an item if you and your
spouse already do it jointly but you wish you did so more frequently or that
your spouse was more "there" emotionally during the activity. For example,
if you currently read the newspaper together every morning but wish your
spouse would discuss the news with you more instead of just reading
silently, you can circle that item.

1. Reunite at the end of the day and talk about how it went.
2. Shop for groceries. Make up the shopping list.
3. Cook dinner, bake.
4. Clean house, do laundry.
5. Shop together for gifts or clothes (for self, kids, or friends).
6. Go out (no kids) for brunch or dinner, or to your favorite haunt or bar.
7. Read the morning paper together.
8. Help each other with a self-improvement plan (e.g., a new class, weight loss, exercise, a new career).
9. Plan and host a dinner party.
10. Call and/or think about each other during the workday.
11. Stay overnight at a romantic hideaway.
12. Eat breakfast together during the work week.
13. Go to a church, mosque, or synagogue together.
14. Do yard work, shovel the walk, do home repairs, car maintenance, and washing.
15. Perform committee work in the community (e.g., volunteering).
16. Exercise together.
17. Go on weekend outings (e.g., picnic, drives).
18. Spend "everyday" time with kids —bedtimes, baths, homework.
19. Take the kids on outings (e.g., zoo, museum, dinner).

20. Attend school functions (e.g., teacher conferences).

21. Stay in touch with/spend time with kin (parents, in-laws, siblings).

22. Entertain out-of-town guests.

23. Travel together (plane, bus, train, car).

24. Watch TV or videos.

25. Order take out.

26. Double-date with friends.

27. Attend sporting events.

28. Engage in a favorite activity (e.g., bowl, go to amusement park, bicycle, hike, jog, horseback ride, camp, canoe, sail, water-ski, swim).

29. Talk or read together by an open fire.

30. Listen to music.

31. Go dancing or attend a concert, nightclub, jazz club, or theater.

32. Host your child's birthday party.

33. Take your child to lessons.

34. Attend your child's sporting events or performance (recital, play, etc.).

35. Pay bills.

36. Write letters or cards.

37. Deal with family medical events (take kids to the doctor, dentist, or emergency room).

38. Work at home, but still be together in some way.

39. Go to a community event (e.g., church auction).

40. Go to a party.

41. Drive to or from work together.

42. Celebrate milestones in your children's lives (confirmation, graduation).

43. Celebrate other milestones in your lives (e.g., promotion, retirement).

44. Play computer games, surf the Internet.

45. Supervise your children's play dates.

46. Plan vacations.

47. Plan your future together. Dream.

48. Walk the dog.

49. Read out loud together.

50. Play a board game or a card game.

51. Put on plays or skits together.

52. Do errands together on a weekend.
53. Engage in hobbies; e.g., painting, sculpting, making music.
54. Talk over drinks (alcohol, coffee, or tea).
55. Find time to just talk without interruptions—find time for spouse to really listen to you.
56. Philosophize.
57. Gossip (talk about other people).
58. Attend a funeral.
59. Help out other people.
60. Hunt for a new house or apartment.
61. Test-drive new cars.
62. Other _____ .

Now, share your top three choices with each other so you both know how best to turn toward each other and accrue points. Warning: Sometimes this exercise generates conflict when we do it as part of our workshop. For example, Dick may say he wants Renee to be there more when it comes to making weekend plans, but Renee claims she already does most of the weekend planning. To avoid this, remember that this exercise is really a way to flatter each other. What you're really telling your spouse is "I love you so much that I want more of you." So be sure to talk about your requests in that spirit. Rather than being critical of what your partner has not done in the past, focus on what you would like to have happen now. That means saying "I'd like it if you stayed with me most of the time at parties" instead of "You always abandon me."

The real benefit of this exercise comes when you both look at the three items your partner chose and follow through by committing to do one of them. This should be a firm agreement—in the workshops we actually call it a contract. Some couples find it helpful to put these contracts in writing, such as "I, Wendy, agree to join Bill in walking the dog every Monday and Thursday." This may sound stiff and formal, but an official agreement usually has the opposite effect: because it conveys respect for your request, you feel relieved and excited that your spouse is willing to give this to you. No wonder this exercise intensifies the sense of romance!

Exercise 2: The Stress-Reducing Conversation

Although you can earn points in your emotional bank account during just about any everyday activity listed above, we have found the first one, "Reunite at the end of the day and talk about how it went," to be the most effective. What this "How was your day, dear?" conversation does (or ought to do) is to help each of you manage the stress in your life that is *not* caused by your marriage. Learning to do this is crucial to a marriage's long-term health, according to research by my colleague Neil Jacobson, Ph.D., of the University of Washington. He has found that one of the key variables in relapse after his own approach to marital therapy is whether stress from other areas of your lives spills over into your relationship. Couples who are overrun by this stress see their marriages relapse, while those who can help each other cope with it keep their marriages strong.

Many couples automatically have this sort of calming-down conversation, perhaps at the dinner table or after the kids fall asleep. But too often this discussion does not have the desired effect—it *increases* your stress levels because you end up feeling frustrated with your spouse for not listening to you, whether you're the one venting or the one who's offering advice. If that's the case, you need to change your approach to these catch-up conversations to make sure they help you calm down.

For starters, think about the timing of the chat. Some people want to unburden themselves when they're barely through the door. But others need to decompress on their own for a while before they're ready to interact. So wait until you *both* want to talk.

On a typical day, spend twenty to thirty minutes on this conversation. The cardinal rule is that you talk about whatever is on your mind *outside of your marriage*. This is not the time to discuss any conflicts between you. It's an opportunity to support each other emotionally concerning other areas in your lives.

This exercise takes active listening, that classic technique of standard marital therapy, and stands it on its head. The goal of active listening is to hear your spouse's perspective with empathy and without judging him or her. That's all well and good. But this approach usually fails because couples are asked to use it when they are airing their gripes with each other. This is difficult to do and often about as painless as an IRS audit. It's virtually impossible not to feel frightened, hurt, or mad as hell when your spouse is blasting you.

But I have found that this same listening technique can be extremely beneficial if you use it during discussions where you are *not* your spouse's target. In this context, you'll feel far freer to be readily supportive and understanding of your spouse and vice versa. This can only heighten the love and trust you feel. Here are detailed instructions for having this discussion:

1. Take turns. Each partner gets to be the complainer for fifteen minutes.

2. Don't give unsolicited advice. If you quickly suggest a solution to your partner's dilemma, he or she is likely to feel that you are trivializing or dismissing the problem, which backfires. In effect you're saying, "That's not such a big issue. Why don't you just . . . ?" So the cardinal rule when helping your partner de-stress is that *understanding must precede advice*. You have to let your partner know that you fully understand and empathize with the dilemma before you suggest a solution. Oftentimes your spouse isn't asking you to come up with a solution at all—just to be a good listener, or offer a ready shoulder to cry on.

I have found a significant gender difference when it comes to this rule. Women are more sensitive to advice-giving than are men. In other words, when a wife tells her husband her troubles, she usually reacts very negatively if he tries to give her advice right away. Instead she wants to hear that he understands and feels compassion. Men are far more tolerant of immediate attempts to problem-solve, so a wife can probably "get away" with some gentle words of wisdom. Still, a man who emotes to his wife about his work troubles would probably prefer that she offer him sympathy rather than a solution.

In the workshops, when I tell couples that their role is not to solve each other's problems but to offer support, their relief is almost palpable. Men especially get caught up in thinking that when their wives are upset, their role is to take care of the problem. A huge burden is lifted once they realize that this is not their responsibility and is usually the opposite of what their wives want. It seems almost too good to be true that you earn points by *not* trying to solve your partner's problems, but that is the case.

3. Show genuine interest. Don't let your mind or eyes wander. Stay focused on your spouse. Ask questions. Make eye contact. Nod, say "uh-huh," and so on.

4. Communicate your understanding. Let your spouse know that you empathize: "What a bummer! I'd be stressed out, too. I can see why you feel that way."

5. Take your spouse's side. This means being supportive, even if you think his or her perspective is unreasonable. Don't side with the opposition—this will make your spouse resentful or dejected. If your wife's boss chewed her out for being five minutes late, don't say, "Oh, well, maybe Bob was just having a bad day." And certainly don't say, "Well, you shouldn't have been late." Instead, say, "That's so unfair!" The point isn't to be dishonest. It's just that timing is everything. When your partner comes to you for emotional support (rather than for advice), your job is not to cast moral judgment or to tell him or her what to do. Your job is to say "poor baby."

6. Express a "we against others" attitude. If your mate is feeling all alone in facing some difficulty, express solidarity. Let him or her know that the two of you are in this together.

7. Express affection. Hold your mate, put an arm on his or her shoulder, say, "I love you."

8. Validate emotions. Let your partner know that his or her feelings make sense to you. Phrases that do this include "Yeah, that is really so sad. That would have me worried, too. I can see why you'd be annoyed about that."

Here are two brief examples of a stress-reducing conversation to give you an idea of what to do—and what not to.

Don't:

HANK: I had another terrible meeting with Ethel today. She keeps challenging my knowledge, and she has been going to the boss telling him that she doubts my competence. I hate her.

WANDA: I think this is another example of you flying off the handle and overreacting. *(Criticizing)* I have seen her be very con-structive and reasonable. Maybe you are just not being sensitive to her concerns. *(Siding with the enemy)*

HANK: The woman is out to get me.

WANDA: That's your paranoid streak coming out. You've got to try to control that. *(Criticizing)*

HANK: Oh, forget it.

Do:

HANK: I had another terrible meeting with Ethel today. She keeps challenging my knowledge, and she has been going to the boss telling him that she doubts my competence. I hate her.

WANDA: I can't believe that woman! She is the meanest fighter and a terrible gossip. *(We against others)* What did you say? *(Showing genuine interest)*

HANK: I told her she is just out to get me. And that she's not going to succeed.

WANDA: She can make anyone become paranoid. I'm sorry she's putting you through this. *(Expressing affection)* I'd like to get even with her. *(We against others)*

HANK: So would I, but I think it'd be better to just forget it. Just ignore her.

WANDA: Your boss knows what she's like. Everyone does.

HANK: That's true. He doesn't share her opinions of me, and she goes around saying everyone is incompetent but her.

WANDA: That's bound to backfire.

HANK: I hope so, or she'll give me an ulcer.

WANDA: This is really stressing you out! I can understand why. *(Validating emotions)* You know, she's given her husband one.

HANK: He has an ulcer?

WANDA: I just heard about it.

HANK: Good Lord!

Below are some sample scenarios to help you practice being supportive during your spouse's whining session.

1. Your wife's sister yelled at her for not yet repaying money she loaned her two months ago. Your wife is feeling outraged and hurt by her sister's attitude. (She does owe her sister the money.)
   You say:

2. Your husband got a speeding ticket on his way home. "It was a speed trap!" he yells. "*Everyone* was going 80 mph. Why do I have to be the one who gets pulled over?"
   You say:

3. Your wife was late getting to a big job interview. Now she's worried she won't get the job. "I can't believe how stupid I was," she moans.
   You say:

4. Your husband asked his boss for a raise and was turned down. He got angry and stormed out of his boss's office. Now he's worried that his boss will hold this against him.
   You say:

Sample Answers

1. "I'm sorry she made you feel really hurt and angry." (Or "Poor baby.")
2. "How outrageous! That's so unfair!" (Or "Poor baby.")
3. "You weren't stupid. That could happen to anybody." (Or "Poor baby.")
4. "I understand how you feel." (Or "Poor baby.")

One last note: No one knows you better than your spouse. Sometimes advice may be just what you're looking for. The best strategy is to talk about what you'd each like from the other when you're feeling stressed. If your spouse is ranting about the promotion he didn't get, you can say something like "You're obviously really upset about this. How can I help you? Do you need me just to listen, or do you want me to help you brainstorm what to do next?"

If you have this sort of conversation every day, it can't help but benefit your marriage. You'll come away with the conviction that your partner is on your side, and that's one of the foundations of a long-lasting friendship.

**Once your marriage gets set at a more positive level,
it will be harder to knock it off course.**

As beneficial as turning toward each other can be, it can feel hurtful and rejecting when your spouse does the opposite. Often couples turn away from each other not out of malice but out of mindlessness. They get distracted and start taking each other for granted. Realizing the importance of the little moments and paying more attention to them is enough to solve the problem in many cases. But sometimes there are deeper reasons why couples keep missing each other. For example, when one partner rebuffs the other, it could be a sign of hostility over some festering conflict. But I have found that when one spouse regularly feels the other just doesn't connect enough, often the cause is a disparity between their respective needs for intimacy and independence.

Marriage is something of a dance. There are times when you feel drawn to your loved one and times when you feel the need to pull back and replenish your sense of autonomy. There's a wide spectrum of "normal" needs in this area—some people have a greater and more frequent need for connection, others for independence. A marriage can work even if people fall on opposite ends of this spectrum—as long as they are able to understand the reason for their feelings and respect their differences. If they don't, however, hurt feelings are likely to develop.

If you feel like your spouse gives you the cold shoulder in little ways throughout the day, or if your spouse's concept of closeness feels more like suffocation to you, the best thing you can do for your marriage is to talk it out. Looking at these moments together will give you greater insight into each other and help you both learn how to give each other what you need.

Exercise 3: What to Do When Your Spouse Doesn't Turn toward You

If one of you is feeling rebuffed by the other lately, or overwhelmed by your spouse's need for closeness, you should both fill out the form below and then share your answers. There is no answer key for these questions, they are merely a point of departure for discussions with your spouse. The bottom line of this approach is that there isn't one reality when a couple misses each other in little ways. There are two equally legitimate perspectives. Once you understand and acknowledge this, you'll find that reconnecting just comes naturally.

During this week I felt:

1.	Defensive.	A Great Deal	Definitely	A Little	Not at All
2.	Hurt.	A Great Deal	Definitely	A Little	Not at All
3.	Angry.	A Great Deal	Definitely	A Little	Not at All
4.	Sad.	A Great Deal	Definitely	A Little	Not at All
5.	Misunderstood.	A Great Deal	Definitely	A Little	Not at All
6.	Criticized.	A Great Deal	Definitely	A Little	Not at All
7.	Worried.	A Great Deal	Definitely	A Little	Not at All
8.	Righteously indignant.	A Great Deal	Definitely	A Little	Not at All
9.	Unappreciated.	A Great Deal	Definitely	A Little	Not at All
10.	Unattractive.	A Great Deal	Definitely	A Little	Not at All
11.	Disgusted.	A Great Deal	Definitely	A Little	Not at All
12.	Disapproving.	A Great Deal	Definitely	A Little	Not at All
13.	Like leaving.	A Great Deal	Definitely	A Little	Not at All
14.	Like my opinions didn't matter.	A Great Deal	Definitely	A Little	Not at All
15.	I had no idea what I was feeling.	A Great Deal	Definitely	A Little	Not at All
16.	Lonely.	A Great Deal	Definitely	A Little	Not at All

What triggered these feelings?

1.	I felt excluded.	A Great Deal	Definitely	A Little	Not at All
2.	I was not important to my spouse.	A Great Deal	Definitely	A Little	Not at All
3.	I felt cold toward my spouse.	A Great Deal	Definitely	A Little	Not at All
4.	I definitely felt rejected.	A Great Deal	Definitely	A Little	Not at All
5.	I was criticized.	A Great Deal	Definitely	A Little	Not at All
6.	I felt no affection toward my partner.	A Great Deal	Definitely	A Little	Not at All
7.	I felt that my partner was not attracted to me.	A Great Deal	Definitely	A Little	Not at All
8.	My sense of dignity was being compromised.	A Great Deal	Definitely	A Little	Not at All
9.	My partner was being domineering.	A Great Deal	Definitely	A Little	Not at All
10.	I could not persuade my partner at all.	A Great Deal	Definitely	A Little	Not at All

Now that you know what triggered this episode, it's time to see whether your emotional reaction is rooted in your past. Look over your answers to the "Who Am I?" exercise on p. 56. See if you can find connections there between earlier traumas or behavior and the current situation. Use the following checklist to facilitate this search for links between the past and present.

These recent feelings about my marriage come from:
(check all that apply)

___ The way I was treated in my family growing up
___ A previous relationship
___ Past injuries, hard times, or traumas I've suffered
___ My basic fears and insecurities
___ Things and events I have not yet resolved or put aside
___ Unrealized hopes I have
___ Ways other people treated me in the past
___ Things I have always thought about myself
___ Old "nightmares" or "catastrophes" I have worried about

After you've read each other's answers above, you will, I hope, come to see that many of your differences are really not matters of "fact." We are all complicated creatures whose actions and reactions are governed by a wide array of perceptions, thoughts, feelings, and memories. In other words, reality is subjective, which is why your partner's perspective on the past week may be different from yours without either of you being right or wrong about what really happened. In your notebook, write out a short description of your point of view, and then do the same for your partner's perspective.

It's natural to make the fundamental error of assuming that distance and loneliness are all your partner's fault. In truth they're nobody's fault. In order to break the pattern, you both need to admit playing some role (however slight at first) in creating the problem. To do that, read the following list and circle all that apply to you and that may have contributed to the turning away or the feelings of being swamped and smothered recently. (Do not try to do this until you have calmed down physiologically. Follow the steps for self-soothing on page 176 and then let go of thoughts that maintain the distress, thoughts of feeling misunderstood, righteous indignation, or innocent victimhood.)

1. I have been very stressed and irritable.	Yes, Definitely	Maybe a Little
2. I have not expressed much appreciation toward my spouse.	Yes, Definitely	Maybe a Little
3. I have been overly sensitive.	Yes, Definitely	Maybe a Little
4. I have been overly critical.	Yes, Definitely	Maybe a Little
5. I have not shared very much of my inner world.	Yes, Definitely	Maybe a Little
6. I have been depressed.	Yes, Definitely	Maybe a Little
7. I would say that I have a chip on my shoulder.	Yes, Definitely	Maybe a Little
8. I have not been very affectionate.	Yes, Definitely	Maybe a Little
9. I have not been a very good listener.	Yes, Definitely	Maybe a Little
10. I have been feeling a bit like a martyr.	Yes, Definitely	Maybe a Little

Overall, my contribution to this mess was:

How can I make this better in the future?

What one thing could my partner do next time to avoid this problem?

As you work through the exercises above, you'll become more adept at turning toward each other regularly, and the bond of camaraderie with your spouse will deepen. This more profound friendship will be a powerful shield against conflict. It may not forestall every argument, but it can prevent your differences of opinion from overwhelming your relationship. One of the ways friendship does this is by helping to balance the power between husband and wife.

When you honor and respect each other, you're usually able to appreciate each other's point of view, even if you don't agree with it. When there's an imbalance of power, there's almost inevitably a great deal of marital distress.

My next principle focuses on what can happen if one spouse is unwilling to share power with the other—and how to overcome this difficulty. Although power-mongering is more common in husbands, there are wives who have just as hard a time acceding to their spouse's wishes, so my fourth principle really applies to everybody.

6
Principle 4:
Let Your Partner
Influence You

*J*ack was considering buying a used blue Honda. The car seemed like a great deal since the seller, Phil, had only owned it for a month. The car was for sale because Phil's company was suddenly transferring him to London. Jack liked the car's handling and power, not to mention the state-of-the-art sound system. He was ready to do a deal, but first, he told Phil, he wanted a mechanic to check the car. "Why?" said Phil. "It's really a new car. It only has three hundred miles, and you get the manufacturer's warranty."

"True," said Jack, "but I promised my wife I wouldn't buy a car without having it inspected first."

Phil gave Jack a withering look. "You let your *wife* tell you what to do about cars?" he asked.

"Sure," said Jack. "Don't you?"

"Well, no. I don't—didn't. I'm divorced," said Phil.

"Well," Jack chuckled. "Maybe that's why."

Jack had the car checked by his mechanic, and it turned out that the rear bumper needed to be replaced, so he never bought Phil's car. But more importantly, he never bought Phil's attitude toward women. Jack has made his wife a partner in his decision making. He respects and honors his wife and her opinions and feelings. He understands that for his marriage to thrive, he has to share the driver's seat.

There was a time when Phil's macho attitude wasn't necessarily a liability for a husband. But our data suggest that this is no longer the case. In our long-term study of 130 newlywed couples, now in its eighth year, we have found that, even in the first few months of marriage, men who allow their wives to influence them have happier marriages and are less likely to divorce than men who resist their wives' influence. Statistically speaking, when a man is not willing to share power with his partner, there is an 81 percent chance that his marriage will self-destruct.

Obviously, it takes two to make or break a marriage, so we're not singling out men here. The point of this chapter is not to scold, bash, or insult men. It's certainly just as important for wives to treat their husbands with honor and respect. But my data indicate that the vast majority of wives—even in unstable marriages—already do that. This doesn't mean that they don't get angry and even contemptuous of their husbands. It just means that they let their husbands influence their decision making by taking their opinions and feelings into account. But too often men do not return the favor.

"ANYTHING YOU SAY, DEAR"?

That was the sound bite that some members of the media used, erroneously, to sum up my study on accepting influence. It was parodied on *Saturday Night Live,* pilloried by Rush Limbaugh, and picked on by Bill Maher, the host of *Politically Incorrect.* I got the biggest chuckle from one newspaper cartoon that depicted Saddam Hussein's wife asking him to take out the garbage and him refusing until she held a machine gun to his head and he finally said, "Yes, dear."

Our study didn't really find that men should give up all of their personal power and let their wives rule their lives. But we did find that the happiest, most stable marriages in the long run were those where the husband treated his wife with respect and did not resist power sharing and decision making with her. When the couple disagreed, these husbands actively searched for common ground rather than insisting on getting their way.

To arrive at these findings, we looked intently at what happened when these newlyweds discussed an area of conflict and also when they talked about the history of their romance. When we analyzed the data, we were struck by a significant gender difference. Although the wives would sometimes express anger or other negative emotions toward their husbands, they rarely responded to their husbands by *increasing* the negativity. Most of them either tried to tone it down or matched it. So if a husband said, "You're not listening to me!" the wife would usually say something like "Sorry, I'm listening now" (a repair that tones down the negativity) or "I'm finding it hard to listen to you!" which matched her husband's anger but didn't go beyond it.

But 65 percent of the men did not take either of these approaches. Instead, their response *escalated* their wives' negativity. They did this in a very specific way: by trotting out one of the four horsemen (criticism, contempt, defensiveness, or stonewalling). If the wife of one of these men said, "You're not listening to me!" the husband would either ignore her (stonewall), be defensive ("Yes, I am!"), be critical ("I don't listen because what you say never makes any sense"), or be contemptuous ("Why waste my time?"). Using one of the four horsemen to escalate a conflict is a telltale sign that a man is resisting his wife's influence.

Rather than acknowledging his wife's feelings, this husband is using the four horsemen to drown her out, to obliterate her point of view. This is the opposite of accepting her influence. One way or another, this approach leads to instability in the marriage. Even if the husband doesn't react this way very often, there's an 81 percent chance that his marriage will be damaged.

Although it is always important for both husband and wife to try to keep the four horsemen from taking over in times of conflict, it is especially important that men be aware of the danger to their marriage when they use one of them to escalate the negativity. For some reason, when a wife uses the four horsemen in the same manner, the marriage does not become more unstable. At this point, the data do not offer an explanation for this disparity. But we know that as a general rule women *do* accept influence from their husbands, which may help to explain the gender differences in our findings. So although it certainly makes sense for both partners to avoid escalating conflicts in this way, the bottom line is that husbands put their marriage at added risk when they do.

SIGNS OF RESISTANCE

I've met enough angry husbands and sparred with enough angry radio talk show hosts to know that some men are quite up front in their refusal to share power with their wives. Even in these days of gender equity there are still husbands who simply refuse to consider any opinions their wives air, and never take their feelings or ideas into account when making decisions.

Some men claim that religious conviction requires them to be in control of their marriages and, by extension, their wives. But there's no religion I know of that says a man should be a bully. I am not advocating a particular spiritual belief system about the roles of men and women. Our research has included couples who believe the man should be the head of the family as well as couples who hold egalitarian viewpoints. In both kinds of marriages, emotionally intelligent husbands have figured out the one big thing: *how to convey honor and respect*. All spiritual views of life are consistent with loving and honoring your spouse. And that's what accepting influence is all about. After all, do you really want to make decisions that leave your wife feeling disrespected? Is *that* really consistent with religious beliefs? It is not.

This was brought home to me by a colleague, Dana Kehr, who is a Mormon bishop. Traditional Mormon doctrine exalts patriarchy. It holds that the husband should make all decisions for the family. But Kehr and his wife have an emotionally intelligent marriage. Kehr says he sees no conflict between his beliefs and accepting influence from his wife. He told me, "I wouldn't think about making a decision she disagreed with. That would be very disrespectful. We talk and talk about it till we both agree, and *then* I make the decision." Kehr intuitively realizes that a marriage can't work unless both partners honor and respect each other. That's true whatever your belief system.

In many cases, I suspect, men who resist letting their wives influence them are not even aware of this tendency. There are men who consider themselves feminists who interact with their wives in ways that belie this label. Case in point: a hardworking software engineer named Chad. If you asked him in the abstract his view on gender roles, he'd come out squarely on the side of a fifty-fifty marriage. But that's not what was playing out in the new home into which he and his wife Martha just moved. One night he announced that he would have to work late that Thursday. Martha reminded him that her mother was coming to visit on Friday and that she was counting on him to help her clean the house and get the guest room ready. "I'm really upset with you," Martha said bluntly. "Don't you remember that my mother is coming? Why can't you shift your schedule around?"

"Why didn't *you* remember I have this big project due? There's no way I can change my schedule. I have to work—maybe even the entire weekend," said Chad. His response upped the ante. First he was defensive—instead of responding to Martha's complaint, he volleyed back a complaint of his own: Why didn't she remember *his* schedule? Then he threatened her by suggesting that he would have to work even more than he had initially said. This was really a kind of belligerence. He goaded her in "here's mud in your eye" style.

Martha became furious. She called him a lot of unfortunate names and stormed out of the room. Chad felt like he had just been victimized. After all, he *had* to work. As usual, her fury seemed to have come out of nowhere. His heart started racing, and his head was pounding. He had become flooded, which made it difficult to think about the problem clearly or come up with a solution. All he wanted was to escape from his wife's unfair, irrational attitude. He certainly wasn't in the mood to find a compromise. So, feeling victimized, he poured himself a beer and turned on the TV. When Martha came back into the room, wanting to talk, he simply ignored her. When she started to cry, he left the room and announced he was going to bed early.

There's certainly plenty of blame to go around in this scene. Martha's harsh startup didn't exactly put Chad in the mood for compromise. But there is a history to Martha's reaction. Her mother lived in Canada and she rarely got to see her. Martha had been planning this visit for a month and had talked to Chad on many occasions about how excited she was to show her mother their new house and to have her finally get to spend time with her two grandchildren.

When Chad announced matter-of-factly that he would be working late, without even acknowledging the impact it would have on his mother-in-law's visit, it became clear to Martha that Chad didn't even remember that her mother was coming. Or if he did remember, it was such a low priority for him that he didn't consider his working to be in any way a crisis. He had arrived at his decision without discussing the problem with her first. Because Chad had a history of being "in his own world," as Martha described it, she went ballistic as soon as he made his announcement.

When a couple have an argument like this, there are so many accusations and counteraccusations that sometimes it can be hard to determine the underlying cause. In the case of Martha and Chad, though, there's a glaring clue that the fundamental problem is his unwillingness to be influenced by her: When she becomes negative ("I'm really upset with you"—a straightforward complaint), he responds by *escalating* the conflict. In come belligerence and the third horseman, defensiveness. Martha becomes furious and Chad becomes flooded, which leads him to stonewall—the fourth horseman. Their marriage has just taken a nasty tumble down the cascade toward divorce.

Think of how differently Martha and Chad would be feeling if, instead of getting defensive, Chad had apologized to Martha and acknowledged that he had been feeling so overwhelmed at work that he really had forgotten about her mother's imminent visit. Or if, after this row, Chad had attempted some repair. Martha might still have been upset, but she wouldn't have felt devalued by Chad. If he had listened to her vent her anger without being defensive or belligerent, she might have calmed down. Then together they could have come up with a solution to the problem.

Accepting influence doesn't mean never expressing negative emotions toward your partner. Marriages can survive plenty of flashes of anger, complaints, even criticisms. Trying to suppress negative feelings in your spouse's presence wouldn't be good for your marriage or your blood pressure. The problem comes when even mild dissatisfaction on the wife's part is met by a barrage from her husband that, instead of toning down or at the most matching her degree of negativity (yelling back, complaining, etc.), goes beyond it.

> **The wives of men who accept their influence are far less likely to be harsh with their husbands when broaching a difficult marital topic. This increases the odds their marriage will thrive.**

Any man who isn't sold on the need to accept his wife's influence more should consider the many pluses. Studies have shown that marriages where the husband resists sharing power are four times more likely to end or drone on unhappily than marriages where the husband does not resist. We see again and again that when the man shares power, the four horsemen aren't so prevalent. In large part this is because his wife is far less likely to use a harsh startup when she's upset. Because she's not angered, frustrated, or humiliated by her husband, she is apt to begin difficult discussions without being critical or contemptuous.

Another reason these marriages fare so well is that they have a firm foundation for compromising. After all, the better able you are to listen to what your spouse has to say and to consider her perspective respectfully, the more likely it is that you'll be able to come up with a solution or approach to a problem that satisfies you both. If your ears are closed to your spouse's needs, opinions, and values, compromise just doesn't have a chance.

WHAT HUSBANDS CAN LEARN FROM WIVES

Perhaps most importantly, when a husband accepts his wife's influence, his open attitude also heightens the *positive* in his relationship by strengthening his friendship with his wife. This will make it far easier for him to follow the first three principles: deepening his love map, bolstering fondness and admiration, and turning toward his wife as a matter of course.

This occurs not just because the absence of frequent power struggles makes the marriage more pleasurable, but because such a husband is open to learning from his wife. And there's no doubt that women have plenty to teach men about friendship. In his book *The Complete Book of Guys,* Dave Barry writes about the huge gap between men and women in this regard. He recounts that every year he and his wife get together with some old friends. The wives immediately begin an intense catching-up conversation about their inner feelings. He and the other husband watch the playoffs. The men do get emotional at times—usually when deciding which kind of pizza to order. Later, when the couples have parted company, Barry's wife will say something like "Isn't it amazing how well George has adjusted to having his leg amputated?" And Barry will pretend that of course he had noticed George was missing a leg. Barry is exaggerating, but the story is funny because it reveals a basic truth: Women are more oriented toward discussing and understanding feelings than are men.

I'm not suggesting that all women are savvier about emotions and have better "people skills" than all men. There are plenty of women who are tone deaf to social nuances and insensitive to others. But usually women are more emotionally intelligent than their husbands for one simple reason: They've had an enormous head start in acquiring these skills. Observe children at any playground, and you'll see that head start in action. When young boys play (usually run-and-chase games) their priority is the game itself—not their relationship with each other and their feelings. But for little girls, feelings are paramount. A cry of "I'm not your friend anymore" will stop a game cold. Whether it starts up again will depend on whether the girls make up.

Even when a boy and girl play with the same toy, the gender difference is apparent. When four-year-old best friends Naomi and Eric shared her baby doll *she* wanted to play that the doll was their baby and they were going to show it off to their friends (relationship-based play). *He* went along with this for about ten minutes, and then the game roller-coasted into boy territory: "Hey Naomi, this baby is dead!" he announced. "We have to get it to the hospital right away!" He climbed into a pretend ambulance and away he went, "Brrrrrrrrr." Naomi urged him not to drive too fast. Suddenly they both became surgeons and saved the baby's life. (Eric wanted Naomi to be the nurse, but she objected that girls can be surgeons too, so some things have changed!) After the baby's life was saved, they went back to playing Naomi's way—showing off the baby to friends.

The play styles of Naomi and Eric are equally charming and delightful. But the plain truth is that "girlish" games offer far better preparation for marriage and family life because they focus on relationships. As a general rule, boys don't even include games with relationship and domestic themes in their repertoire. Think about it: While no preschool dress-up corner would be complete without bridal costumes, you never see tuxedos for little pretend grooms!

Where does this difference in play styles between boys and girls originate? Because it occurs in virtually every culture, I suspect that it is caused mostly by biology rather than by socialization. But whether nature or nurture is the cause of these differences, their effect is undeniable. Because their play emphasizes social interactions and feelings, girls undergo an extensive education into emotions by childhood's end. Boys learn how to pitch overhand. A boy's experience at playing cooperatively and quickly resolving conflicts will be an asset later in the boardroom or on the construction site, but it will be a liability in marriage if it comes at the expense of understanding the emotions behind his wife's perspectives.

This difference in training is heightened by the fact that as they get older, boys rarely play with girls, so they miss the chance to learn from them. Although about 35 percent of preschool best friendships are between boys and girls (like Naomi and Eric), by age seven that percentage plummets to virtually 0 percent. From then till puberty the sexes will have little or nothing to do with each other. This is a worldwide phenomenon. Many explanations have been given for this voluntary segregation. One intriguing theory, by psychologist Eleanor Maccoby, Ph.D., at Stanford University, dovetails with my findings on accepting influence. She found that even at very young ages (1½ years), boys will accept influence only from other boys when they play, whereas girls accept influence equally from girls or boys. At around ages five to seven, girls become fed up with this state of affairs and stop wanting to play with boys. From that age until puberty, our culture (and virtually all others) offers no formal structure for ensuring that boys and girls continue to interact.

By the time Naomi and Eric are grown, the difference in their knowledge of homemaking will be apparent. Once a couple move in together or get engaged, the groom-to-be is suddenly immersed in what is probably an alien world. In the Broadway play *In Defense of the Cave Man,* a man says that when he was first married, he saw his wife cleaning the bathroom and asked her, "Are we moving?" In his bachelor days that was the only time he and his roommates bothered to clean the bathroom. Many young husbands discover they have a lot to learn from their wives about maintaining a home.

You can see the shell-shocked look on the face of the typical young fiancé in any home furnishings store. He neither knows nor cares about the difference between taffeta and chintz. All of the china and silver patterns look remarkably alike to him. Most of all he's thinking that this is taking an awfully long time, and if he turns around suddenly he will do about $10,000 worth of damage since all of the shelves are made of glass and placed about two feet apart, probably just to intimidate guys like him. How will he react? If pretty soon he hears himself saying, "Hey, that's a great pattern," another emotionally intelligent husband has been born.

EMOTIONALLY INTELLIGENT HUSBANDS

My data on newlywed couples indicate that more husbands are being transformed in this way. About 35 percent of the men we've studied fall into this category. Research from previous decades suggests the number used to be much lower. Because this type of husband honors and respects his wife, he will be open to learning more about emotions from her. He will come to understand her world and those of his children and friends. He may not emote in the same way that his wife does, but he will learn how to better connect with her emotionally. As he does so, he'll make choices that show he honors her. When he's watching the football game and she needs to talk, he'll turn off the TV and listen. He is choosing "us" over "me."

I believe the emotionally intelligent husband is the next step in social evolution. This doesn't mean that he is superior to other men in personality, upbringing, or moral fiber. He has simply figured out something very important about being married that the others haven't—yet. And that is how to honor his wife and convey his respect to her. It is really that elementary.

The new husband is likely to make his career less of a priority than his family life because his definition of success has been revised. Unlike husbands before him, he naturally incorporates the first three principles into his daily life. He makes a detailed map of his wife's world. He keeps in touch with his admiration and fondness for her, and he communicates it by turning toward her in his daily actions.

This benefits not only his marriage but his children as well. Research shows that a husband who can accept influence from his wife also tends to be an outstanding father. He is familiar with his children's world and knows all about their friends and their fears. Because he is not afraid of emotions, he teaches his children to respect their own feelings—and themselves. He turns off the football game for them, too, because he wants them to remember him as having had time for them.

This new type of husband and father leads a meaningful and rich life. Having a happy family base makes it possible for him to create and work effectively. Because he is so connected to his wife, she will come to him not only when she is troubled but when she is delighted. When the city awakens to a beautiful fresh snowstorm, his children will come running for him to see it. The people who matter most to him will care about him when he lives and mourn him when he dies.

The other kind of husband and father is a very sad story. He responds to the loss of male entitlement with righteous indignation, or he feels like an innocent victim. He may become more authoritarian or withdraw into a lonely shell, protecting what little he has left. He does not give others very much honor and respect because he is engaged in a search for the honor and respect he thinks is his due. He will not accept his wife's influence because he fears any further loss of power. And because he will not accept influence he will not have very much influence. The consequence is that no one will much care about him when he lives nor mourn him when he dies.

THE CHANGE IS HERE

Although there are men in traditional marriages who are masters at accepting influence from their wives, the reality is that sharing marital power is a relatively new concept and has come about in the wake of vast social changes over the past few decades. "Wearing the pants" was once the norm for a husband, but times have changed.

Maybe all of this sounds like a feminist line, but it's also the reality. With more than 60 percent of married women working, the male's role as the sole breadwinner is on the wane. Increasingly women's jobs provide them with a source not only of income and economic power but of self-esteem as well. A significant number of the core issues we see between couples today have to do with this change in gender roles. Often wives complain that men still aren't doing their fair share of domestic chores and child care. This is not just an issue for young couples. We have seen the same pattern among couples in their forties and sixties. Men who are willing to accept influence are happily married. Those who are not see their marriages become unstable. As one unhappy husband put it, "I married June Cleaver and she turned into Murphy Brown. It's not fair. I didn't bargain for this."

It's understandable that some men have problems with the shift in the husband's role. For centuries men were expected to be in charge of their families. That sense of responsibility and entitlement gets passed down from father to son in so many subtle ways that revising the husband's role can be a challenge for many men.

Some men may resist being influenced by their wives because they still believe that the upheaval in gender roles is a passing fad— or that the pendulum has swung to an extreme and soon things will revert. But there is scientific evidence that we are living through a cultural transformation that will not come undone. Anthropologist Peggy Sanday, Ph.D., a professor at the University of Pennsylvania, has devoted her career to studying and comparing hunter-gatherer cultures all over the world. On the surface our lives may seem very different from those of the peoples she studies. But human nature is fundamentally the same. Sanday has identified certain factors that determine whether a culture will be male dominant or egalitarian. (Interestingly, no cultures were female dominant.) She has also studied the signs that a culture is moving in one direction or the other.

According to her research, male-dominated societies are characterized by the following:

1. Food is quite scarce and daily life is hard. Danger lurks in the environment.
2. Meat from large game animals is almost always more valued

than other foods. Hunting large game is almost always an entirely male activity.

3. Men do not participate in the care and raising of infants. They may care for children but not for babies.

4. There is limited female representation in the culture's sacred symbols, especially in its creation myths.

Sanday found that the cultures in which these factors were the most extreme were also the most male dominant. And when these factors moved in the opposite direction, the culture also shifted to an egalitarian mode where men and women shared power. I believe you can see such a change happening in our culture today. Consider:

1. Food is plentiful, and environmental conditions are not very harsh. Enforced laws keep the bulk of people feeling relatively safe.

2. Men are no longer the sole breadwinners or "hunters" for food.

3. Many men now want to participate in the care and raising of infants. There has been an explosion in the number of men who attend childbirth classes with their wives, are present at the birth of their children, and share in the diapering, feeding, and bathing of their babies. Go to the park on Sunday, and you're likely to see young fathers carrying Snuglis and pushing strollers. Many women feel that men still don't do enough caretaking of the very young, but it's clear there's been a shift in attitude.

4. There is an increasingly strong female representation in our culture's sacred symbols. Catholicism has seen an important growth in worship involving Mary, the mother of Christ. Not only has worship increasingly involved Mary, but her role has shifted dramatically from being the passive recipient of the Holy Spirit to being a woman who bravely and actively *chooses* to accept the role of mother in her encounter with

the angel Gabriel (Luke 1:26–38). She intercedes on behalf of supplicants with love, compassion, and understanding.

In Judaism, the Conservative and Reform movements have rewritten prayer books to emphasize the female in the sacred. The importance of the matriarchs is recognized, as well as the *Shechinah,* the female qualities of God: forgiveness, compassion, understanding, and love.

True, not all marriages have become more egalitarian. Many men are still disengaged from family life. Yet a growing number are seeking guidance in coping with the cultural change. Witness the growing popularity of organized men's movements such as the Promise Keepers, the Robert Bly mythopoetic movement, the Million Man March, and the men's rights movement. People are now marching on Washington not to demand political change but to make new vows about their role in families. Whatever your opinion of each of these groups, their very existence is a symptom of the seismic shift in social relations that has left many men lost and befuddled.

The challenge for each man is to decide how to deal with this great transformation. Our research clearly indicates that the only effective approach is to embrace the change rather than to react with anger and hostility. Time and again we can separate the happy from the unstable couples based on whether the husband is willing to accept influence from his wife.

LEARNING TO YIELD

Perhaps the fundamental difference between these two kinds of husbands is that the "new" husband has learned that often in life he needs to yield in order to win. When you drive through any modern city, you encounter frustrating bottlenecks and unexpected barricades that block your normal and rightful passage. You can take one of two approaches to these impossible situations. One is to stop, become righteously indignant, and insist that the offending obstacle move. The other is to drive around it. The first approach will eventually earn you a heart attack. The second approach—which I call yielding to win—will get you home.

The classic example of a husband yielding to win concerns the ubiquitous toilet seat issue. The typical woman gets irritated when her husband leaves the toilet seat up, even though it only takes her a millisecond to put it down herself. For many women a raised toilet seat is symbolic of the male's sense of entitlement. So a man can score major points with his wife just by putting the seat down. The wise husband smiles at how smart he is as he drops the lid.

Accepting influence is an attitude, but it's also a skill that you can hone if you pay attention to how you relate with your spouse. In your day-to-day life, this means working on the first three principles by following the advice and exercises in Chapters 3, 4, and 5. And when you have a conflict, the key is to be willing to compromise. You do this by searching through your partner's request for something you can relinquish. For example, Chad, who infuriated Martha by working late when her mother was due to visit, might not be able to compromise on working more than usual, but perhaps he could switch the timing of his work. He could, for example, postpone the late night until Friday so that at least he could help Martha get the house ready for her mother's visit. Perhaps she, Grandma, and little sister could take their son to soccer practice on Saturday (traditionally his task) so that he could get some work done then.

If despite plenty of effort a man is still unable to accept influence from his wife on a particular issue, it's a sign that an unacknowledged, unsolvable problem is stymieing his attempts. In such a case, the key is to learn how to cope with the unsolvable problem, using the advice in Chapter 10. One couple we studied, Tim and Kara, faced this dilemma. They constantly argued about his friend Buddy, who Kara thought was anything but a pal. Unemployed, he often fought with his live-in girlfriend and ended up boozing and then crashing on their living room sofa. Kara feared that Buddy would be a bad influence on Tim and saw his frequent presence in their home as an invasion and a threat. But whenever she tried to talk to Tim about it, he insisted that this was his home and that he could invite over anyone he wanted. When she disagreed with him, he would stonewall, which made her so angry she would start yelling. Then he would accuse her of being the one with the problem, not Buddy. Kara was infuriated by Tim's attitude. As she saw it, he refused to respect that this was her home, too, and that he had to share decisions about houseguests with her.

> **More than 80 percent of the time it's the wife who brings up sticky marital issues, while the husband tries to avoid discussing them. This isn't a symptom of a troubled marriage—it's true in most happy marriages as well.**

When I interviewed Tim and Kara, Tim's unwillingness to accept influence from Kara seemed to be the core of their problem—especially since he admitted that he saw no grounds for compromise on the issue. Then I asked him what his friendship with Buddy meant to him. It turned out there was more to the story. Tim explained that he and Buddy had been pals since childhood. During high school, when Tim's parents were going through a bitter divorce and his home life was coming apart, Tim spent countless nights on Buddy's couch. He believed it was now his responsibility to help out the friend who had helped him. He felt that Kara was trying to get him to abandon Buddy. Doing so would go against his sense of honor. He wasn't concerned that Buddy would be a bad influence. He saw himself as a stable, married man and took pride in his ability to help his friend.

The more Tim talked about Buddy, the clearer it became that he and Kara were grappling with a perpetual problem in their relationship about their views of friendship and loyalty. By recognizing that and working on the problem together, the issue was transformed. Tim stopped thinking about it in the context of his "right" to do what he wanted in his own home. Kara acknowledged that it had been Tim's "piggish" attitude—not just Buddy's presence—that was making her so angry. She told him that she really admired his loyalty—it was one of the things she loved about him. She just worried that Buddy was taking advantage of him. He acknowledged that Buddy could be a "user." By identifying the issue for what it was—a perpetual problem—and agreeing to work on it with Kara, Tim had effectively accepted her influence. They each became better able to see the other's perspective. In the end they agreed that Buddy could continue to use their living room as a crash pad, but less frequently than before.

It took getting to the heart of a perpetual problem before Tim was able to accept influence from his wife. But in most cases the key is just for the husband to be open to sharing power with his wife, then to get plenty of practice doing so. A husband can start by taking the quiz below, which will give you a sense of how skilled you currently are at accepting your wife's influence. There's no reason why wives shouldn't take the quiz as well, since the more open to influence you both are, the smoother your marriage will be. Then work through the fun exercises that follow. They will help you hone your ability to share power.

Accepting Influence Questionnaire

*Read each statement and circle **T** for "true" or **F** for "false."*

1. I am really interested in my spouse's opinions on our basic issues. **T F**
2. I usually learn a lot from my spouse even when we disagree. **T F**
3. I want my partner to feel that what he or she says really counts with me. **T F**
4. I generally want my spouse to feel influential in this marriage. **T F**
5. I can listen to my partner, but only up to a point. **T F**
6. My partner has a lot of basic common sense. **T F**
7. I try to communicate respect even during our disagreements. **T F**
8. If I keep trying to convince my partner, I will eventually win out. **T F**
9. I don't reject my spouse's opinions out of hand. **T F**

10. My partner is not rational enough to take seriously when we discuss our issues. **T F**

11. I believe in lots of give and take in our discussions. **T F**

12. I am very persuasive and usually can win arguments with my spouse. **T F**

13. I feel I have an important say when we make decisions. **T F**

14. My partner usually has good ideas. **T F**

15. My partner is basically a great help as a problem solver. **T F**

16. I try to listen respectfully, even when I disagree. **T F**

17. My ideas for solutions are usually much better than my spouse's. **T F**

18. I can usually find something to agree with in my partner's position. **T F**

19. My partner is usually too emotional. **T F**

20. I am the one who needs to make the major decisions in this marriage. **T F**

Scoring: 1. Give yourself one point for each "true" answer, *except* for questions 5, 8, 10, 12, 17, 19, 20.

2. *Subtract* one point for each "true" answer to questions 5, 8, 10, 12, 17, 19, 20.

6 or above: This is an area of strength in your marriage. You willingly cede power to your spouse, a hallmark of an emotionally intelligent marriage.

Below 6: Your marriage could stand some improvement in this area. You are having some difficulty accepting influence from your spouse, which can cause a marriage to become dangerously unstable. The first step in righting the situation is to understand just what it means to accept influence. Reread this chapter if you're still unclear about why it is so essential to share power with your partner. Then the following exercises will show you how to do so.

Exercise 1: Yield to Win

Below is a series of common situations faced by couples I've studied. Try to visualize these scenes as if you and your wife were the ones having this conflict. (Wives who are doing this exercise should flip the genders accordingly.) The more vividly you put yourself into each situation, the more effective the exercise will be. No matter how negative you envision your partner as sounding in these scenarios, try to think of the negativity as her way of emphasizing how important this issue is—not as an attack on you. In other words, try to respond to the message, not to your partner's tone of voice. Assume that within that message is a reasonable request with which you could easily agree. In your notebook describe that reasonable request in a sentence. (In some of these scenarios the demand is implied rather than directly spoken.) Then write down what you could say to express your cooperation. There are no right answers to these exercises, but you'll find examples of effective responses to each of these scenarios on pages 121–122.

EXAMPLE: When you come home tired from work, you like to eat dinner and then watch TV. But your wife, who works at home all day, wants to go out. One night she gets very angry and claims that you are inconsiderate of her need to escape from the house. You say that you are just too tired to do anything at night. She yells, "Well, what about me? I will go crazy if I can't get out and have contact with other people!"

Reasonable part of wife's request: To get out of the house.

You say: "I'm sorry you're going so stir crazy. What if we have a relaxing dinner at home so I can rest, and then go out for dessert?"

1. You and your wife have not been getting along lately. Part of the problem is that you think she spends way too much money. Now she's insisting that you undergo expensive marital counseling. You point out that there is simply no money to pay for that until expenses are cut somewhere else. Your wife says, "I disagree. We can't afford *not* to get counseling. It's like borrowing for a needed vacation. We've got to do it!"

Reasonable part of wife's request:

You say:

2. Since your wife is not working, you've asked that she clean the house and have dinner on the table by the time you come home. Tonight you walk in to find that the laundry isn't folded and dinner isn't made. You complain, and she says, "You never notice how much I *have* done during the day. You just don't appreciate how much work it takes to keep the house going."

Reasonable part of wife's request:

You say:

3. You've gone down to the local bar with a few friends to have a couple of beers. You and your wife have argued frequently about your going out drinking too often. Tonight she keeps calling you at the bar to say that if you don't come home right now, she's going to come get you. When you finally walk in the door, she is crying. "Instead of spending all your free time with your buddies at the bar, why don't you ever take me dancing?"

Reasonable part of wife's request:

You say:

4. It's a Saturday afternoon, and your wife has been cleaning and telling you about some repairs the house needs. You feel that she is not willing to make the financial sacrifices in other areas so that you can afford these repairs. She says, "You just don't think that what I want is important. You'll find money for things if *you* want them."

Reasonable part of wife's request:

You say:

5. For the past few days your wife has been complaining about your not being very affectionate and considerate when you have sex with her. Tonight after having sex your wife tells you she feels dissatisfied and wants you to touch her more. You tell her that you're not used to doing things that way. She says, "I understand how you feel, but we've got to learn how to turn each other on more. I'll try to help you."

Reasonable part of wife's request:

You say:

6. When you come home from work, the first thing you like to do is to get comfortable, have a drink, read the paper, and take off your shoes and socks. Sometimes you make a bit of a mess in the living room, but you usually clean it up after dinner when you have more energy. One night, when you haven't cleaned up, your wife says, "It really makes me mad the way you leave your stuff around. I'm tired, too, and I wish I didn't have to pick up after you. Why can't you clean up before dinner?"

Reasonable part of wife's request:

You say:

7. Money has been tight lately, so you've come up with a system in which you and your wife discuss every purchase beforehand. Tonight you come home, and she announces she's bought new bulbs to replace the outside lights, which just blew. She says she bought them without consulting you because she feels the bulbs are absolutely necessary—she doesn't feel safe at night unless the lights are on. You tell her they may be necessary, but you can't afford them. She says, "We need to have them whether we can afford them or not."

Reasonable part of wife's request:

You say:

8. You decide to surprise your wife by buying a new car. As soon as she sees it, she gets very upset. She says, "That's terrible! I'll never ride in it. Take it back!"

Reasonable part of wife's request:

You say:

9. You've just come home from work feeling tired, and you still have to run to the hardware store. Your wife, who stays home to raise the kids, says that she has just had a terrible day with them. She asks you to take them with you to the store so she can have some alone time.

Reasonable part of wife's request:

You say:

10. You like to stay up late and work or watch TV. Your wife likes to go to sleep by eleven. One night around ten-thirty she comes into the den where you're watching TV and asks you to come to bed. She says that it bothers her that you don't come to bed until after she's asleep, because she'd like to have sex more often.

Reasonable part of wife's request:

You say:

Sample Answers

1. Reasonable part of wife's request: Your marriage does need help.
You say: "I agree that improving our marriage is very important. Maybe counseling *is* the answer. Let's think about how we can cut down

somewhere else so we can afford it. Then I won't be so worried about the money."

2. Reasonable part of wife's request: To feel appreciated for the work she does around the house.

You say: "I'm sorry. You're right, I haven't noticed. Let's start over again. Help me to appreciate what has been done. Then maybe I can also pitch in and fold some of this laundry. You have been doing a lot lately. Maybe tonight we should go out to dinner."

3. Reasonable part of wife's request: To spend more of your free time with her.

You say: "Great idea. Let's go down to McSorley's and dance until we see dawn together like in the old days."

4. Reasonable part of wife's request: Your house does need some repairs.

You say: "Okay, maybe you're right. What repairs do you think we need to do?"

5. Reasonable part of wife's request: For you to focus on what turns her on.

You say: "This is hard for me to talk about, but I'll try to listen to you. Tell me how you want to be touched."

6. Reasonable part of wife's request: For you to clean up before dinner.
You say: "Sorry, okay, I'll clean up." Then do it.

7. Reasonable part of wife's request: Buying the outside lights was necessary.

You say: "You're absolutely right that we need them. It's fine that you bought the lights. Thank you for doing it. But next time can we talk it over first, like we usually do?"

8. Reasonable part of wife's request: Not to surprise her with a new car.

You say: "We need to talk about this car. Tell me why you're upset."

9. Reasonable part of wife's request: To get a break from the kids.

You say: "Okay. Let's go for a ride, kids. Ice cream on the way for everybody!"

10. Reasonable part of wife's request: To have sex more often.

You say: "Great idea. Can you wear the satin nightie? I love making love to you."

Now that you've worked through these examples, you should have a better sense of what it means to "give" in a relationship. The next step is to get used to giving to your spouse and sharing power more in your own marriage. The following fun exercise lets you work on making decisions together. As you do it, remember that the goal is for both of you to be influential and to accept each other's influence.

Exercise 2: The Gottman Island Survival Game

Imagine that your cruise ship just sank in the Caribbean, and you awaken to find yourselves on a tropical desert island. Gilligan and Ginger are nowhere in sight—the two of you are the only survivors. One of you is injured. You have no idea where you are. You think there's some chance that people know of the ship's distress, but you're not sure. A storm appears to be on the way. You decide that you need to prepare to survive on this island for some time and also to make sure you'll be spotted by a rescue party. There is a bunch of stuff from the ship on the beach that could help you, but you can only carry ten items.

Your Mission

STEP 1: Each of you writes down on a separate piece of paper what you consider the ten most important items to keep from the inventory list below, based on your survival plan. Then rank-order these items based on their importance to you. Give the most crucial item a 1, the next most crucial a 2, and so on. There are no right or wrong answers.

Ship's Inventory

1. Two changes of clothing
2. AM-FM and short-wave radio receiver
3. Ten gallons of water
4. Pots and pans

5. Matches
6. Shovel
7. Backpack
8. Toilet paper
9. Two tents
10. Two sleeping bags
11. Knife
12. Small life raft, with sail
13. Sunblock lotion
14. Cookstove and lantern
15. Long rope
16. Two walkie-talkie sender-receiver units
17. Freeze-dried food for seven days
18. One change of clothing
19. One fifth of whiskey
20. Flares
21. Compass
22. Regional aerial maps
23. Gun with six bullets
24. Fifty packages of condoms
25. First-aid kit with penicillin
26. Oxygen tanks

STEP 2: Share your list with your partner. Together come up with a consensus list of ten items. That means talking it over and working as a team to solve the problem together. Both of you need to be influential in discussing the problem and in making the final decisions.

When you've finished, it's time to evaluate how the game went. You should both answer the questions below.

1. How effective do you think you were at influencing your spouse?
   a) Not at all effective
   b) Neither effective nor ineffective
   c) Somewhat effective
   d) Very effective

2. How effective was your spouse at influencing you?
   a) Not at all effective
   b) Neither effective nor ineffective
   c) Somewhat effective
   d) Very effective

3. Did either of you try to dominate the other, or were you competitive with each other?
   a) A lot
   b) Somewhat
   c) A little
   d) Not at all

4. Did you sulk or withdraw?
   a) A lot
   b) Somewhat
   c) A little
   d) Not at all

5. Did your partner sulk or withdraw?
   a) A lot
   b) Somewhat
   c) A little
   d) Not at all

6. Did you have fun?
   a) Not at all
   b) A little
   c) Somewhat
   d) A lot

7. Did you work well as a team?
   a) Not at all
   b) A little
   c) Somewhat
   d) A great deal

8. How much irritability or anger did you feel?
   a) A lot
   b) Some
   c) A little
   d) None

9. How much irritability or anger did your partner feel?
   a) A lot
   b) Some
   c) A little
   d) None

10. Did you both feel included?
   a) Not at all
   b) A little
   c) A reasonable amount
   d) A great deal

Scoring: Give yourself one point for each "a" answer, two points for each "b" answer, three points for each "c" answer, and 4 points for each "d" answer. Tally your score.

If your final number is over 24, you're doing a good job of accepting each other's influence and working together as a team. If you scored 24 or below, your marriage needs further work in this area.

If you're having difficulty accepting influence, one of the best things you can do for your marriage is to acknowledge the problem and talk with your spouse about it. Nobody can change old habits overnight. But if you're able to take responsibility for the parts of your marital troubles that are caused by your difficulty with sharing power, that in itself will be a major leap forward for your marriage. Your spouse is likely to feel a great sense of relief and renewed optimism about improving your marriage. The next step is to make your partner an ally in your crusade to overcome this problem. Ask her (or him) to gently point out to you instances where you are being unwittingly domineering, defensive, or disrespectful.

Because all of the Seven Principles are interrelated, the more you work on the others, the easier it will become for you to share power. And of course, the more skilled you become at accepting influence, the easier it will be for you to adhere to the other principles. A willingness to share power and to respect the other person's view is a prerequisite of compromising. For that reason, becoming more adept at accepting influence will help you cope far better with marital conflict—the focus of Principles 5 and 6. As you'll see, there are two major categories of disagreements that virtually all couples experience. When coping with either kind, accepting influence will be a cornerstone of success.

7

The Two Kinds of
Marital Conflict

*E*very marriage is a union between two individuals who bring to it their own opinions, personality quirks, and values. So it's no wonder that even in very happy marriages the husband and wife must cope with a profusion of marital issues. Some conflicts are just minor irritants, but others can seem overwhelmingly complex and intense. Too often couples feel mired in conflict or have distanced themselves from each other as a protective device.

Although you may feel your situation is unique, we have found that *all* marital conflicts, ranging from mundane annoyances to all-out wars, really fall into one of two categories: Either they can be resolved, or they are perpetual, which means they will be a part of your lives forever, in some form or another. Once you are able to identify and define your various disagreements, you'll be able to customize your coping strategies, depending on which of these two types of conflict you're having.

PERPETUAL PROBLEMS

Unfortunately, the majority of marital conflicts fall into this category—69 percent, to be exact. Time and again when we do four-year follow-ups of couples, we find that they are still arguing about precisely the same issue. It's as if four minutes have passed rather than four years. They've donned new clothes, altered their hairstyles, and gained (or lost) a few pounds and wrinkles, but they're still having the same argument. Here are some typical perpetual problems that the happy couples in our studies are living with:

1. Meg wants to have a baby, but Donald says he's not ready yet—and doesn't know if he ever will be.
2. Walter wants sex far more frequently than Dana.
3. Chris is lax about housework and rarely does his share of the chores until Susan nags him, which makes him angry.
4. Tony wants to raise their children as Catholics. Jessica is Jewish and wants their children to follow her faith.
5. Angie thinks Ron is too critical of their son. But Ron thinks he has the right approach: Their son has to be taught the proper way to do things.

Despite their differences these couples remain very satisfied with their marriages because they have hit upon a way to deal with their unbudgeable problem so it doesn't overwhelm them. They've learned to keep it in its place and to have a sense of humor about it. For example, one couple we studied, Melinda and Andy, have an ongoing conflict over his reluctance to go on outings with her family. But when they talk to me about this problem, they don't get angry, they simply relate good-naturedly what happens. Andy starts to tell me what he always ends up saying. Melinda, who knows it all so well, jumps in and offers up his quote for him, mimicking his put-upon voice: "All right, I'll go." Then Andy adds that he also says, "Okay, sure, anything you say, dear."

"We still continue to do that," Melinda explains to me. Then Andy chuckles and adds, "We don't even disagree good, do we?"

Melinda and Andy haven't solved their problem, but they've learned to live with it and approach it with good humor.

Despite what many therapists will tell you, you don't have to resolve your major marital conflicts for your marriage to thrive.

Another happy couple, Carmen and Bill, have a perpetual problem over their disparate degrees of orderliness. Carmen has the discipline of a drill sergeant, while he is a classic absentminded professor. For Carmen's sake, Bill tries to think about where he's putting things. For his sake, she tries not to nag him when things get lost. When she finds, say, last month's phone bill under a two-foot pile of newspapers in their recycling bin, she'll make her point by gently teasing him—unless she's feeling excess stress that day, in which case she'll probably throw a fit, after which he'll make her a mug of hot chocolate as contrition, and they'll go on happily with their day. In other words, they are constantly working it out, for the most part good-naturedly. At times it gets better, other times it gets worse. But because they keep acknowledging the problem and talking about it, their love for each other isn't overwhelmed by their difference.

These couples intuitively understand that problems are inevitably part of a relationship, much the way chronic physical ailments are inevitable as you get older. They are like a trick knee, a bad back, an irritable bowel, or tennis elbow. We may not love these problems, but we are able to cope with them, to avoid situations that worsen them, and to develop strategies and routines that help us deal with them. Psychologist Dan Wile said it best in his book *After the Honeymoon*: "When choosing a long-term partner . . . you will inevitably be choosing a particular set of unsolvable problems that you'll be grappling with for the next ten, twenty or fifty years."

Marriages are successful to the degree that the problems you choose are ones you can cope with. Wile writes: "Paul married Alice and Alice gets loud at parties and Paul, who is shy, hates that. But if Paul had married Susan, he and Susan would have gotten into a fight before they even got to the party. That's because Paul is always late and Susan hates to be kept waiting. She would feel taken for granted, which she is very sensitive about. Paul would see her complaining about this as her attempt to dominate him, which *he* is very sensitive about. If Paul had married Gail, they wouldn't have even gone to the party because they would still be upset about an argument they had the day before about Paul's not helping with the housework. To Gail, when Paul does not help, she feels abandoned, which she is sensitive about, and to Paul, Gail's complaining is an attempt at domination, which he is sensitive about." And so it goes.

In *unstable* marriages, perpetual problems like these eventually kill the relationship. Instead of coping with the problem effectively, the couple gets gridlocked over it. They have the same conversation about it over and over again. They just spin their wheels, resolving nothing. Because they make no headway, they feel increasingly hurt, frustrated, and rejected by each other. The four horsemen become ever more present when they argue, while humor and affection become less so. They become all the more entrenched in their positions. Gradually they feel physiologically overwhelmed. They start a slow process of trying to isolate or enclose this problem area. But actually they have started becoming emotionally disengaged from each other. They are on the course toward parallel lives and inevitable loneliness—the death knell of any marriage.

THE SIGNS OF GRIDLOCK

If you're not sure whether you've gridlocked over a perpetual problem or are coping well with it, this checklist will help. The characteristics of a gridlocked problem are:

- The conflict makes you feel rejected by your partner.
- You keep talking about it but make no headway.
- You become entrenched in your positions and are unwilling to budge.
- When you discuss the subject, you end up feeling more frustrated and hurt.

- Your conversations about the problem are devoid of humor, amusement, or affection.
- You become even more unbudgeable over time, which leads you to vilify each other during these conversations.
- This vilification makes you all the more rooted in your position and polarized, more extreme in your view, and all the less willing to compromise.
- Eventually you disengage from each other emotionally.

If this sounds painfully familiar, take comfort in knowing that there is a way out of gridlock, no matter how entrenched in it you are. As you'll see when we get to Principle 6, all you need is motivation and a willingness to explore the hidden issues that are really causing the gridlock. The key will be to uncover and share with each other the significant personal dreams you have for your life. I have found that unrequited dreams are at the core of every gridlocked conflict. In other words, the endless argument symbolizes some profound difference between you that needs to be addressed before you can put the problem in its place.

SOLVABLE PROBLEMS

These problems may sound relatively simple compared with unsolvable ones, but they can cause a great deal of pain between husband and wife. Just because a problem is solvable doesn't mean it gets resolved. When a solvable problem causes excessive tension, it's because the couple haven't learned effective techniques for conquering it. They aren't to blame—far too many of the conflict resolution ideas recommended by marriage manuals and therapists are not easy to master or apply. Most of these strategies focus on validating your partner's perspective and learning to be a good listener. There's nothing wrong with this—except that it's very hard for most people to do at any time, much less when they're distressed.

My fifth principle for making marriage work tackles solvable problems head on. It offers an alternative approach to conflict resolution based on my research into what goes right when emotionally intelligent couples handle a disagreement. I will show you how to (1) make sure your startup is soft rather than harsh, (2) learn the effective use of repair attempts, (3) monitor your physiology during tense discussions for warning signs of flooding, (4) learn how to compromise, and (5) become more tolerant of each other's imperfections. Follow this advice, and you're likely to find that solvable problems no longer interfere with your marital happiness.

TELLING THE DIFFERENCE

If you and your spouse are entrenched in conflict, it may not be obvious which of the two types of disagreement you're having— gridlocked or solvable. One way to identify solvable problems is that they seem less painful, gut-wrenching, or intense than perpetual, gridlocked ones. That's because when you argue over a solvable problem, your focus is only on a particular dilemma or situation. There is no underlying conflict that's fueling your dispute.

For example, both Rachel and Eleanor complain that their husbands drive too fast. Eleanor has been arguing with her husband Dan about this for years. He always tells her the same thing—she's overreacting. He's never had an accident, he reminds her. He says he is not an aggressive driver, he's an assertive one. She tells him she doesn't understand why he can't change his driving habits so she'll feel less nervous in the car. She ends up yelling that he's selfish, that he doesn't care if he kills both of them, and so on. He tells her the real problem is that she doesn't trust him. Each time they have this squabble, they feel all the more frustrated and hurt and ever more entrenched in their positions. There's a lot of vilifying on both sides: Dan accuses her of being distrustful. She accuses him of being uncaring.

For Eleanor and Dan, speeding constitutes a perpetual problem they will probably never fully resolve. That's because their disagreement symbolizes deeper conflicts between them. They are really arguing about Big Issues like trust, security, selfishness. To keep their ongoing battles over driving from ruining their marriage, they'll need to understand the deeper meaning that this battle has for each of them. Only then will they be able to manage it effectively.

But for Rachel and Jason, disagreements over driving speeds constitute a solvable problem. Every morning they commute together from their suburban home to downtown Pittsburgh. She thinks he drives too fast. He says he has to speed because she takes so long to get ready. If he doesn't make up for her dawdling by speeding, they'll both be late to work. Rachel says it takes her so long in the morning because he showers first and takes forever. Plus, he always leaves the breakfast dishes on the table. While she's busy washing them, he's honking the horn for her to hurry. Every workday starts with accusations and counteraccusations about showering time and household chores. By the time Jason drops Rachel off at her office, he's stonewalling and she's fighting back tears.

This couple's difficulty over driving is a solvable problem because, for starters, it is situational—it occurs only when they are going to work, and it doesn't reverberate into other areas of their lives. Unlike Eleanor and Dan, they don't vilify each other. Their arguments aren't about his selfishness or her being distrustful—they're simply about driving and their morning routine. By learning a more effective way to talk with each other about the issue, they could readily find a compromise. They could put blame aside and work out a schedule that got them to work on time, without passing the speed limit. Maybe they could set their alarm fifteen minutes earlier, or she could shower first, or he could just remember to deal with the dishes.

However, if they don't work to find a compromise on this issue, it's likely that they will become increasingly resentful and entrenched in their positions. The conflict could deepen and take on more symbolic meaning. In other words, it could evolve into a gridlocked, perpetual problem.

Below I've described various scenarios of marital conflict. For each one, mark whether you think it's solvable or perpetual.

I. Cliff and Lynn agree that it's Cliff's job to take out the kitchen trash every evening after dinner. But lately he's been so distracted by a big deadline looming at work that he forgets. Either Lynn ends up throwing out the garbage herself or the trash just sits there. By morning the apartment smells like a city dump, and Lynn is in a rage.

Solvable ___ **Perpetual** ___

2. Elise wants to spend less time with Joel and more time with her friends. Joel says this makes him feel abandoned. Elise says that she needs time away from him. He seems very needy to her, and she's feeling suffocated by him.

Solvable ___ **Perpetual** ___

3. Ingrid wishes that Gary would bring up things that are bothering him rather than sulking. But when he does try to tell her when he's upset by some things that she's done, she gets critical about how he has brought them up. She asks him not to mention so many at the same time. He says that since it's so hard for him to discuss such things, he wants a reward when he does: Namely, he wants Amy to say she's sorry instead of criticizing his style of communication.

Solvable ___ **Perpetual** ___

4. Helena gets together with her friends every Monday night. Jonathan wants her to take a ballroom dancing class together with him, but the only night the class is held is Monday. Helena doesn't want to give up her girls' night out.

Solvable ___ **Perpetual** ___

5. Penny complains that Roger expects her to do all the work taking care of their newborn son. Roger says he'd like to do more, but because he works during the day, he isn't as experienced as his wife at diapering, bathing, and the like. Whenever he does try to do something, like pick up the baby when he cries, Penny tells him he's doing it wrong. This makes him angry and he ends up telling her to do it herself.

Solvable ___ **Perpetual** ___

6. Jim works full time while Thea is a stay-at-home mom. He wants her to be more organized about running the house—to clean it more, and to do a better job of planning the mornings so the kids get to school on time. He acts smug and superior to her and gives her the sense that the disorganization in their house is due to a character flaw she has. She feels attacked and gets defensive whenever he raises the subject. She says their house is supposed to be a home, not an army barracks, and that he needs to relax about these issues because his demands are unreasonable. They have been arguing about this for four years.

Solvable ____   **Perpetual** ____

7. Whenever Brian and Allyssa have a disagreement, he quickly raises his voice. Allyssa feels intense stress when he yells and tells him to stop. Brian says he doesn't see anything wrong with yelling when he's upset. Allyssa starts to cry and tells him she can't take it. So they find themselves fighting over his yelling rather than whatever issue they disagreed about.

Solvable ____   **Perpetual** ____

8. Ever since their baby was born, Kurt has felt that Irene is squeezing him out of her life. She insists on doing all of the child care herself and doesn't seem to have time for him anymore. She has been thinking a lot about her own childhood. (Her parents divorced when she was two and she was shuffled between relatives' homes for years.) She tells Kurt she doesn't want their son Brendan to feel abandoned by her, as she did by her own mother. But Kurt feels betrayed because one of the things he's always loved about Irene is how nurturing and motherly she is toward him. Now that's all being directed at the baby, and he feels cheated.

Solvable ____   **Perpetual** ____

9. Oscar just inherited $5,000 from his great-aunt. He wants to use it to buy home exercise equipment. But Mary thinks they should save it for a down payment on a house. Oscar says the inheritance is really not enough to make a dent in a down payment, so why not use it for something they could enjoy right away? But Mary believes that every little bit adds up and that they have to save as much as they can all the time.

Solvable ____ **Perpetual** ____

10. Anita thinks Bert is stingy about tipping waiters, cab drivers, and so on. This upsets her because part of her image of a strong, sexy man is someone who's generous. When she's disappointed with Bert, she gets very contemptuous of him. Meanwhile, Bert believes that Anita is too loose with their money, which makes him nervous. To him, money represents security and a sense of control over his life, so it's hard to give any of it up.

Solvable ____ **Perpetual** ____

Answers

1. Solvable. Cliff has stopped taking out the garbage only recently and for a specific reason that's not related in any deep way to his relationship with Lynn—namely, he's under a lot of stress at work. This problem could be solved in any number of ways—from putting a sign on the refrigerator door to remind him, to reshuffling their domestic chores so that Lynn gets garbage detail for a while until Cliff's work deadline passes.

2. Perpetual. This problem suggests a core difference between Elise and Joel in their personalities and what they need from each other to feel close and connected. This difference is unlikely to change—they'll need to adjust to it.

3. Perpetual. Ingrid and Gary are engaged in a metacommunication war. This means that they aren't having difficulty communicating about a certain issue, they're having difficulty communicating about how to communicate. This is not related to a specific situation but is present whenever they have a disagreement.

4. Solvable. Helena and Jonathan can resolve this issue in a number of ways. Perhaps they could switch off weekly between dancing class and Helena's girls' night out. Or maybe her friends would be willing to switch the night. Or Jonathan could find another dancing class on another night or on the weekend. Or one of them could simply agree not to push it.

5. Solvable. Roger just needs to spend more time with his son so he can get up to speed on his care. And Penny needs to back off and let Roger approach baby care his way. Because this issue isn't related to deep-seated needs either of them has, it can be readily solved through compromise.

6. Perpetual. This problem probably started out as a situational one about housecleaning and organization. Perhaps Jim and Thea have different tolerance levels for clutter, dirt, and how planned out one's life should be. But because they haven't found a compromise position about running their house, they have continued to argue about these differences. Thea has come to feel her husband doesn't value or respect her role, while he feels that she's not holding up her end of the marriage by keeping the household well organized. The argument has become about their mutual resentment rather than about housekeeping.

7. Perpetual. Brian and Allyssa have different emotional styles. He tends to be volatile, meaning that he's very passionate and "out there" with his emotions. Allyssa prefers to discuss issues quietly and rationally. When Brian starts yelling at her, she feels overwhelmed and quickly becomes flooded. Since emotional style is part of one's personality, neither of them is likely to change. But by becoming aware of and respecting each other's emotional style, they can find an approach to conflict resolution they are both comfortable with.

8. Perpetual. At the core Irene and Kurt have different emotional needs. The huge change in their marriage that was created by their child's birth has thrown what they need from each other out of sync.

9. Solvable. Oscar and Mary may have different philosophies about savings. But their conflict over money doesn't appear to be symbolic. Instead, it's a straightforward difference of opinion about what to do with Oscar's inheritance. For that reason, they could probably find a straightforward compromise. Perhaps, for example, they could spend half of the amount on equipment and save the rest.

10. Perpetual. Money has very different meanings to Bert and Anita. Since the symbolic significance of money is usually rooted in childhood experiences, it's unlikely that Bert will naturally transform into a big tipper or that Anita will suddenly learn to love clipping coupons. But if they work together on this perpetual problem (and especially Anita's contempt for her husband about this issue), it will cease to be a major sore spot in their relationship.

Assessing Your Marital Conflicts Questionnaire

Now that you have a greater understanding of the differences between solvable and perpetual problems, it's time to categorize your own marital issues in this way. By doing so you'll know which strategies to use to cope with them. Below is a list of seventeen common causes of conflict in a marriage. For each, mark whether it is a perpetual problem in your marriage, a solvable problem for you, or not a problem right now. If it is either a solvable or a perpetual problem, check all of the specific subareas that you think are currently troublesome.

1. We are becoming emotionally distant.

Perpetual ____   Solvable ____   Not a problem right now ____

Check any of the specific items below that are problems within this general area:
__ We have difficulty just simply talking to each other.
__ We are staying emotionally in touch with each other less.

___ I feel taken for granted.

___ I feel my spouse doesn't know me right now.

___ My spouse is (or I am) emotionally disengaged.

___ We spend less time together.

Comments:

_____

_____

_____

2. There is spillover of nonmarital stresses (such as job tension) into our marriage.

Perpetual ____ **Solvable** ____ **Not a problem right now** ____

Check any of the specific items below that are problems within this general area:

___ We don't always help each other reduce daily stresses.

___ We don't talk about these stresses together.

___ We don't talk together about stress in a helpful manner.

___ My spouse doesn't listen with understanding about my stresses and worries.

___ My spouse takes job or other stresses out on me.

___ My spouse takes job or other stresses out on the children or others.

Comments:

_____

_____

_____

3. Our marriage is becoming nonromantic and passionless; the fire is dying.

Perpetual ____ **Solvable** ____ **Not a problem right now** ____

Check any of the specific items below that are problems within this general area:

___ My spouse has stopped being verbally affectionate.

___ My spouse expresses love or admiration less frequently.

___ We rarely touch each other.

__ My spouse (or I) have stopped feeling very romantic.
__ We rarely cuddle.
__ We have few tender or passionate moments.
Comments:

_____

_____

_____

4. We are having problems in our sex life.

Perpetual ____ **Solvable** ____ **Not a problem right now** ____

Check any of the specific items below that are problems within this general
area:
__ Sex is less frequent.
__ I (or my spouse) get less satisfaction from sex.
__ We have problems talking about sexual problems.
__ Each of us wants different things sexually.
__ Desire is less than it once was.
__ Our lovemaking feels less loving.
Comments:

_____

_____

_____

5. Our marriage is not dealing well with an important change (such as the
birth of a child, a job loss, move, illness, or death of a loved one).

Perpetual ____ **Solvable** ____ **Not a problem right now** ____

Check any of the specific items below that are problems within this general
area:
__ We have very different views on how to handle things.
__ This event has led my partner to be very distant.
__ This event has made us both irritable.
__ This event has led to a lot of fighting.
__ I'm worried about how this will all turn out.

__ We are now taking very different positions.
Comments:

_____

_____

_____

6. Our marriage is not handling well a major issue about children. (This category includes whether to have a child.)

Perpetual ____   Solvable ____   Not a problem right now ____

Check any of the specific items below that are problems within this general area:
__ We have very different goals for our children.
__ We differ on *what* to discipline children for.
__ We differ on *how* to discipline our children.
__ We have issues on how to be close to our kids.
__ We are not talking about these problems well.
__ There is much tension and anger about these differences.
Comments:

_____

_____

_____

7. Our marriage is not handling well a major issue or event concerning in-laws or another relative(s).

Perpetual ____   Solvable ____   Not a problem right now ____

Check any of the specific items below that are problems within this general area:
__ I feel unaccepted by my partner's family.
__ I sometimes wonder which family my spouse is in.
__ I feel unaccepted by my own family.
__ There is tension between us about what might happen.
__ This issue has generated a lot of irritability.
__ I worry about how this will turn out.

Comments:

_____

_____

_____

8. One of us is flirtatious outside the marriage, or may have had a recent affair, and/or there is jealousy.

Perpetual ____ **Solvable** ____ **Not a problem right now** ____

Check any of the specific items below that are problems within this general area:

___ This area is the source of a lot of hurt.

___ This is an area that creates insecurity.

___ I can't deal with the lies.

___ It is hard to reestablish trust.

___ There is a feeling of betrayal.

___ It's hard to know how to heal over this.

Comments:

_____

_____

_____

9. Unpleasant fights have occurred between us.

Perpetual ____ **Solvable** ____ **Not a problem right now** ____

Check any of the specific items below that are problems within this general area:

___ There are more fights now.

___ Fights seem to come out of nowhere.

___ Anger and irritability have crept into our marriage.

___ We get into muddles where we are hurting each other.

___ I don't feel very respected lately.

___ I feel criticized.

Comments:

_____

_____

_____

10. We have differences in our basic goals and values or desired lifestyle.

Perpetual ____ **Solvable** ____ **Not a problem right now** ____

Check any of the specific items below that are problems within this general area:

__ Differences have arisen in life goals.
__ Differences have arisen about important beliefs.
__ Differences have arisen on leisure time interests.
__ We seem to want different things out of life.
__ We are growing in different directions.
__ I don't much like who I am with my partner.
Comments:

_____

_____

_____

11. Very disturbing events (for example, violence, drugs, an affair) have occurred within our marriage.

Perpetual ____ **Solvable** ____ **Not a problem right now** ____

Check any of the specific items below that are problems within this general area:

__ There has been physical violence between us.
__ There is a problem with alcohol or drugs.
__ This is turning into a marriage I hadn't bargained for.
__ Our marriage "contract" is changing.
__ I find some of what my partner wants upsetting or repulsive.
__ I am now feeling somewhat disappointed by this marriage.
Comments:

_____

_____

_____

12. We are not working well as a team.

Perpetual ____ **Solvable** ____ **Not a problem right now** ____

Check any of the specific items below that are problems within this general area:

___ We used to share more of the family's workload.

___ We seem to be pulling in opposite directions.

___ My spouse does not fairly share in housework or child care.

___ My spouse is not carrying his or her weight financially.

___ I feel alone managing this family.

___ My spouse is not being very considerate.

Comments:

_____

_____

_____

13. We are having trouble sharing power and influence.

Perpetual ____ **Solvable** ____ **Not a problem right now** ____

Check any of the specific items below that are problems within this general area:

___ I don't feel influential in decisions we make.

___ My spouse has become more domineering.

___ I have become more demanding.

___ My spouse has become passive.

___ My spouse is "spacey," not a strong force in our marriage.

___ I am starting to care a lot more about who is running things.

Comments:

_____

_____

_____

14. We are having trouble handling financial issues well.

Perpetual ____ **Solvable** ____ **Not a problem right now** ____

Check any of the specific items below that are problems within this general area:

___ One of us doesn't bring in enough money.

___ We have differences about how to spend money.

__ We are stressed about finances.

__ My spouse is financially more interested in self than in us.

__ We are not united in managing our finances.

__ There is not enough financial planning.

Comments:

_____

_____

_____

15. We are not having much fun together these days.

Perpetual ____   Solvable ____   Not a problem right now ____

Check any of the specific items below that are problems within this general area:

__ We don't seem to have much time for fun.

__ We try but don't seem to enjoy our times together very much.

__ We are too stressed for fun.

__ Work takes up all our time these days.

__ Our interests are so different, there are no fun things we like to do together.

__ We plan fun things to do, but they never happen.

Comments:

_____

_____

_____

16. We are not feeling close about spiritual issues these days.

Perpetual ____   Solvable ____   Not a problem right now ____

Check any of the specific items below that are problems within this general area:

__ We do not share the same beliefs.

__ We do not agree about religious ideas and values.

__ We differ about the specific church, mosque, or synagogue.

__ We do not communicate well about spiritual issues.

__ We have issues about spiritual growth and change.

__ We have spiritual issues involving family or children.

Comments:

_____

_____

_____

17. We are having conflict(s) about being a part of and building community together.

Perpetual ____ Solvable ____ Not a problem right now ____

Check any of the specific items below that are problems within this general area:

___ We feel differently about being involved with friends and other people or groups.

___ We don't care to the same degree about the institutions that build community.

___ We have different opinions about putting time into the institutions of community (political party, school, hospital, church, mosque, synagogue, agencies, and the like).

___ We disagree about doing projects or working for charity.

___ We disagree about doing other good deeds for others.

___ We have different views about whether to take a leadership role in the service of our community.

Scoring: For each of the seventeen general areas that cause you problems, count up the number of specific bones of contention that you've checked. If you've checked more than two, then this is an area of significant conflict in your marriage. For solvable problems, you'll find advice in Chapter 8. But if some of your problems are perpetual, follow the advice in Chapter 10 as well. No doubt you'll find that your marriage, like most, is coping with both types of problems.

THE KEY TO *ALL* CONFLICT RESOLUTION

In the chapters ahead you will find specific techniques that will help you to manage your marital troubles, whether perpetual or solvable.

But first, some overall advice. The basis for coping effectively with either kind of problem is the same: communicating basic acceptance of your partner's personality. Human nature dictates that it is virtually impossible to accept advice from someone unless you feel that that person understands you. So the bottom-line rule is that, before you ask your partner to change the way he or she drives, eats, or makes love, you must make your partner feel that you are understanding. If either (or both) of you feels judged, misunderstood, or rejected by the other, you will not be able to manage the problems in your marriage. This holds for big problems and small ones.

You may discover that your partner is more conciliatory during arguments than you realized— once you know what to listen for.

It's probably easiest to acknowledge this truth if you think about it from your own perspective. Say you want your spouse's advice on handling a disagreement you're having with your boss. If your spouse immediately begins criticizing you and insisting that your boss is right, you're wrong, and what's the matter with you for picking a fight with your boss anyway, you'd probably regret having brought it up. Most likely you'd get defensive, angry, offended, hurt, or any combination of these. And yet your spouse might honestly say, "But I was only trying to help." There's a big difference between "You are such a lousy driver. Would you please slow down before you kill us?" and "I know how much you enjoy driving fast. But it makes me really nervous when you go over the speed limit. Could you please slow down?"

Maybe that second approach takes a bit longer. But that extra time is worth it since *it is the only approach that works.* It's just a fact that people can change only if they feel that they are basically liked and accepted as they are. When people feel criticized, disliked, and unappreciated they are unable to change. Instead, they feel under siege and dig in to protect themselves.

Adults could learn something in this regard from research into child development. We now know that the key to instilling in children a positive self-image and effective social skills is to communicate to them that we understand their feelings. Children grow and change optimally when we acknowledge their emotions ("That doggie scared you," "You're crying because you're sad right now," "You sound very angry. Let's talk about it") rather than belittle or punish them for their feelings ("It's silly to be afraid of such a little dog," "Big boys don't cry," "No angry bears allowed in this house—go to your room till you calm down"). When you let a child know that his or her feelings are okay to have, you are also communicating that the child himself or herself is acceptable even when sad or crabby or scared. This helps the child to feel good about himself or herself, which makes positive growth and change possible. The same is true for adults. In order to improve a marriage, we need to feel accepted by our spouse.

Another important lesson I have learned is that in all arguments, both solvable and perpetual, no one is ever right. There is no absolute reality in marital conflict, only two subjective realities. The following exercise will, I hope, help you come to see that by walking you through an analysis of the last argument you had—of either type.

Exercise: Your Last Argument

Answer the questions below in regard to the last argument you two had. You'll see that this exercise is very similar to the one on p. 93 ("What to Do When Your Spouse Doesn't Turn toward You"). That's because both of these situations are founded in what I call "subjective reality." In other words, when you and your spouse are not in sync, either in little ways (not turning toward each other) or in bigger ways (actually fighting), your perspectives on what happened and why are likely to be very different. Whether your conflict is perpetual or solvable, you'll find coping with it far easier the more you are able to respect each other's point of view, even if it is very different from your own.

There is no answer key for the following questions. Use them to spark some mutual soul-searching with your spouse.

During this argument I felt:

1.	Defensive.	A Great Deal	Definitely	A Little	Not at All
2.	Hurt.	A Great Deal	Definitely	A Little	Not at All
3.	Angry.	A Great Deal	Definitely	A Little	Not at All
4.	Sad.	A Great Deal	Definitely	A Little	Not at All
5.	Misunderstood.	A Great Deal	Definitely	A Little	Not at All
6.	Criticized.	A Great Deal	Definitely	A Little	Not at All
7.	Worried.	A Great Deal	Definitely	A Little	Not at All
8.	Righteously indignant.	A Great Deal	Definitely	A Little	Not at All
9.	Unappreciated.	A Great Deal	Definitely	A Little	Not at All
10.	Unattractive.	A Great Deal	Definitely	A Little	Not at All
11.	Disgusted.	A Great Deal	Definitely	A Little	Not at All
12.	Disapproving.	A Great Deal	Definitely	A Little	Not at All
13.	Like leaving.	A Great Deal	Definitely	A Little	Not at All
14.	Like my opinions didn't matter.	A Great Deal	Definitely	A Little	Not at All
15.	I had no idea what I was feeling.	A Great Deal	Definitely	A Little	Not at All
16.	Lonely.	A Great Deal	Definitely	A Little	Not at All

What triggered these feelings?

1.	I felt excluded.	A Great Deal	Definitely	A Little	Not at All
2.	I was not important to my spouse.	A Great Deal	Definitely	A Little	Not at All
3.	I felt cold toward my spouse.	A Great Deal	Definitely	A Little	Not at All
4.	I definitely felt rejected.	A Great Deal	Definitely	A Little	Not at All
5.	I was criticized.	A Great Deal	Definitely	A Little	Not at All
6.	I felt no affection toward my partner.	A Great Deal	Definitely	A Little	Not at All

7. I felt that my partner was not attracted to me.	A Great Deal	Definitely	A Little	Not at All
8. My sense of dignity was being compromised.	A Great Deal	Definitely	A Little	Not at All
9. My partner was being domineering.	A Great Deal	Definitely	A Little	Not at All
10. I could not persuade my partner at all.	A Great Deal	Definitely	A Little	Not at All

Now that you know what triggered this episode, it's time to see whether your emotional reaction is rooted in your past. Look over your answers to the "Who Am I?" exercise on p. 56. See if you can find connections there between earlier traumas or behavior and the current situation. Use the checklist below to facilitate this search for links between the past and present.

This recent argument was rooted in:

(check all that apply)

__ The way I was treated in my family growing up
__ A previous relationship
__ Past injuries, hard times, or traumas I've suffered
__ My basic fears and insecurities
__ Things and events I have not yet resolved or put aside
__ Unrealized hopes I have
__ Ways other people treated me in the past
__ Things I have always thought about myself
__ Old "nightmares" or "catastrophes" I have worried about

After you've read each other's answers above, you will, I hope, come to see that we are all complicated creatures whose actions and reactions are governed by a wide array of perceptions, thoughts, feelings, and memories. In other words, reality is subjective, which is why your partner's perspective on the argument may be different from yours without either of you being right or wrong about what really happened.

It's natural to make the fundamental error of believing that the fight is all your partner's fault. To break the pattern, you both need to admit some role (however slight at first) in creating the conflict. In order to do that, read the following list and circle all that apply to you and that may have contributed to the argument. (Do not try to do this until you have calmed down physiologically. Follow the steps for self-soothing on p. 176 and then let go of thoughts that maintain the distress: thoughts of feeling misunderstood, righteous indignation, or innocent victimhood.)

1.	I have been very stressed and irritable lately.	Yes, Definitely	Maybe a Little
2.	I have not expressed much appreciation toward my spouse lately.	Yes, Definitely	Maybe a Little
3.	I have been overly sensitive lately.	Yes, Definitely	Maybe a Little
4.	I have been overly critical lately.	Yes, Definitely	Maybe a Little
5.	I have not shared very much of my inner world.	Yes, Definitely	Maybe a Little
6.	I have been depressed lately.	Yes, Definitely	Maybe a Little
7.	I would say that I have a chip on my shoulder lately.	Yes, Definitely	Maybe a Little
8.	I have not been very affectionate.	Yes, Definitely	Maybe a Little
9.	I have not been a very good listener lately.	Yes, Definitely	Maybe a Little
10.	I have been feeling a bit like a martyr.	Yes, Definitely	Maybe a Little

Overall, my contribution to this mess was:

How can I make this better in the future?

What one thing could my partner do next time to avoid this argument?

If, after working through this exercise, you or your spouse still find it hard to accept each other's perspective, it may help you to work together more on the exercises in Chapter 4 (strengthening your fondness and admiration system). I have found that couples who have remained happily married for many years are able to enjoy each other—foibles and all—because of the strength of their fondness and admiration. Many of the older couples I studied with colleagues Bob Levenson and Laura Carstensen in the San Francisco Bay Area were masters at this. They had been married for a very long time—some for more than forty years. Through the course of their marriages, they had learned to view their partners' shortcomings and oddities as amusing parts of the whole package of their spouse's character and personality.

One wife, for example, accepted with a chuckle that her husband would never stop being a Dagwood—always running late and frantic. She found ways around it. Whenever they had to get to the airport, she'd tell him their plane left thirty minutes sooner than the actual takeoff time. He knew she was deceiving him, and they laughed about it. Then there was the husband who looked upon his wife's weekly shopping sprees with as much amusement as dread, even though her shopping style made bill-paying very confusing— she almost always returned about half of her purchases.

Somehow couples such as these have learned to mellow about their partner's faults. So although they communicate to each other every emotion in the spectrum, including anger, irritability, disappointment, and hurt, they also communicate their fundamental fondness and respect. Whatever issue they are discussing, they give each other the message that they love and accept each other, "warts and all."

When couples are not able to do this, sometimes the problem is that they are unable to forgive each other for past differences. It's all too easy to hold a grudge. For a marriage to go forward happily, you need to pardon each other and give up on past resentments. This can be hard to do, but it is well worth it. When you forgive your spouse, you both benefit. Bitterness is a heavy burden. As Shakespeare wrote in *The Merchant of Venice,* mercy is "twice blessed. It blesses him that gives and him that takes."

8

Principle 5:
Solve Your Solvable Problems

*I*t stands to reason that when a husband and wife respect each other and are open to each other's point of view, they have a good basis for resolving any differences that arise. And yet too often couples lose their way when trying to persuade each other or settle disagreements. A conversation that could have been productive instead ends in a screaming match or angry silence. If this sounds like you, and you're certain the problem you want to tackle is indeed solvable (see Chapter 7), then the key to resolving this difficulty is to learn a new approach to settling conflict. (The advice offered here will also be somewhat helpful in coping with gridlocked problems, but it won't be enough. To break the stranglehold a perpetual problem has on your marriage, be sure to read about Principle 6, "Overcome Gridlock," in Chapter 10.)

The popular approach to conflict resolution, advocated by many marital therapists, is to attempt to put yourself in your partner's shoes while listening intently to what he or she says, and then to communicate empathetically that you see the dilemma from his or her perspective. It's not a bad method—if you can do it. But, as I've said, many couples can't—including many very happily married couples. Plenty of the people we studied who had enviable, loving relationships did not follow the experts' rules of communication when they argued. But they were still able to resolve their conflicts.

By studying intently what these couples *did* do, I have come up with a new model for resolving conflict in a loving relationship. My fifth principle entails the following steps:

1. Soften your startup
2. Learn to make and receive repair attempts
3. Soothe yourself and each other
4. Compromise
5. Be tolerant of each other's faults

These steps take very little "training" because we all pretty much have these skills already; we just get out of the habit of using them in our most intimate relationship. To a certain degree, my fifth principle comes down to having good manners. It means treating your spouse with the same respect you offer to company. If a guest leaves an umbrella, we say, "Here. You forgot your umbrella." We would never think of saying, "What's wrong with you? You are constantly forgetting things. Be a little more thoughtful, for God's sake! What am I, your slave to go picking up after you?" We are sensitive to the guest's feelings, even if things don't go so well. When a guest spills wine, we say, "No problem. Would you like another glass?" not, "You just ruined my best tablecloth. I can't depend on you to do anything right, can I? I will never invite you to my home again."

Remember Dr. Rory, who was so nasty to his wife during their Christmas Day picnic at the hospital? When a resident phoned, he was very pleasant to *him.* This is not an infrequent phenomenon. In the midst of a bitter dispute, the husband or wife picks up a ringing telephone and is suddenly all smiles: "Oh, hi. Yes, it would be great to have lunch. No problem, Tuesday would be fine. Oh, I am so sorry to hear that you didn't get the job. You must feel so disappointed," and so on. Suddenly the angry, rigid spouse has been transformed into a flexible, rational, understanding, and compassionate being—until the phone call is over. Then he or she just as suddenly morphs back into someone scowling and immovable all for the partner's benefit. It just doesn't have to be that way. Keep in mind, as you work your way through these steps, that what's really being asked of you is no more than would be asked if you were dealing with an acquaintance, much less the person who has vowed to share his or her life with you.

STEP 1: SOFTEN YOUR STARTUP

If there's one similarity between happy and unhappy marriages, it's that in both circumstances the wife is far more likely than the husband to bring up a touchy issue and to push to resolve it. But there's a dramatic difference in *how* the wife brings it up. Remember Dara, who lit into her husband, Oliver, as soon as they began discussing housework? Within a minute she was being sarcastic and batting down every suggestion he made: "Do you think you really work well with lists?" and "I think you do a pretty good job of coming home and lying around and disappearing into the bathroom."

Compare Dara's harsh approach with that of Justine, who is happily married to Michael but has the same problem: He doesn't do his share around the house. What bugs her the most is that she always ends up folding the laundry, which she hates. Here's what she says in the Love Lab, when she broaches the topic with Michael.

JUSTINE: Okay *(deep breath)*. Housework.

MICHAEL: Yeah. Well, I mean I definitely clean off the counters in the kitchen and the table whenever we do stuff. *(Defensive)*

JUSTINE: Hm-hmm. You do. *(Repair attempt)*

MICHAEL: Hm-hmm. *(He's relaxed; Justine's repair attempt was successful.)*

JUSTINE: I think it's just, like, sometimes when things are just kind of left, or the laundry just piles up . . . *(Softened startup)*

MICHAEL: Yeah. I haven't even been thinking about laundry *(laughs)*. I mean, I just haven't been thinking about it at all. *(Not defensive)*

JUSTINE *(laughs)*: That's kind of cute. Who do you think's doing it? You keep having clothes to wear.

MICHAEL: Yeah, I guess.

JUSTINE: And maybe that's okay. But it just gets to me after a while.

MICHAEL: Well, it hasn't even crossed my mind that, like, we have to do the laundry. *(Chuckles.)*

JUSTINE: Actually, Tim's been folding them. *(A neighbor in their apartment complex—the washer and dryer are in a communal laundry room.)* I left a load in, and then when I passed by, the sheets were folded.

MICHAEL: Maybe we should put our hamper in his room?

JUSTINE *(laughs)*. *(Shared humor deescalates tension and lowers heart rates.)*

MICHAEL: So, okay, like maybe every other day or something when I first get back home from work . . .

JUSTINE: Yeah, you could fold what makes sense, especially towels and underwear and the sheets. . . .

MICHAEL: Yeah, I'll just look in the basket. *(He is accepting her influence.)*

JUSTINE: Okay.

Perhaps the most important quality of this exchange is the virtual absence of the Four Horsemen of the Apocalypse—criticism, contempt, defensiveness, and stonewalling—those hallmarks of marriage-harming conflict. The reason for their absence is that Justine's startup is soft. In contrast, a *harsh* startup usually begins the cycle of the four horsemen, which leads to flooding and, in turn, increased emotional distance and loneliness that lets the marriage wither. Only 40 percent of the time do couples divorce because they are having frequent, devastating fights. More often marriages end because, to avoid constant skirmishes, husband and wife distance themselves so much that their friendship and sense of connection are lost.

That's why it's so important that when Michael admits that he doesn't even think about the laundry, Justine doesn't get critical or contemptuous. She laughs and says she thinks that's "cute."

Because Justine is gentle with Michael, their conversation actually produces a result: They come up with a plan to resolve the conflict. Since they are able to do this, their discussion leaves them feeling positive about themselves and their marriage. That feeling is "money in the bank" for any couple—it inspires an optimistic attitude that will help them resolve the next conflict that comes along.

In another happy marriage, the big issue is that the wife, Andrea, wants her husband, Dave, to become more involved with the church. But she hardly bangs him over the head with a Bible. Instead she says, "Going to church is not something I need every day. But it's a comfort." Then she tells him, "I don't like you going just because of me." By the time she tells him directly, "I want a little bit more involvement from you than just Easter, Christmas, and Mother's Day," he is ready to compromise. "Okay, I'll go to church on big important days and . . . maybe some Sundays."

A soft startup doesn't necessarily have to be this diplomatic. It just has to be devoid of criticism or contempt. In a healthy, volatile marriage, which can be very confrontational, the wife is more likely to say something like "Hey, I know I can be a slob sometimes myself, but I'm really angry that you walked by the laundry basket last night without stopping to fold any sheets. I didn't like having to fold them all myself." Or: "I feel really strongly that we need to go to church together more often. This is very important to me." These are soft startups because they are direct complaints rather than criticisms or contemptuous accusations.

Softening the startup is crucial to resolving conflicts because, my research finds, *discussions invariably end on the same note they begin.* That's why 96 percent of the time I can predict the fate of a conflict discussion in the first three minutes! If you start an argument harshly—meaning you attack your spouse verbally—you'll end up with at least as much tension as you began. But if you use a softened startup—meaning you complain but don't criticize or otherwise attack your spouse—the discussion is likely to be productive. And if most of your arguments start softly, your marriage is likely to be stable and happy.

Although either spouse can be responsible for a harsh startup, we've found that the vast majority of the time the culprit is the wife. This is because in our culture the wife is far more likely than her husband to bring up difficult issues and push to get them resolved. Husbands are more likely to try to distance themselves from hard-to-face concerns. As I've noted, there are physiological reasons for this gender gap. Men tend to experience flooding much more easily because their bodies are more reactive to emotional stress than their wives'. So they are more inclined to avoid confrontation.

Harsh Startup Questionnaire

To get a sense of whether harsh startup is a problem in your marriage, answer the following questions.
*Read each statement and circle **T** for "true" or **F** for "false."*

When we begin to discuss our marital issues:

1. My partner is often very critical of me. **T F**
2. I hate the way my partner raises an issue. **T F**
3. Arguments often seem to come out of nowhere. **T F**
4. Before I know it, we are in a fight. **T F**
5. When my partner complains, I feel picked on. **T F**
6. I seem to always get blamed for issues. **T F**
7. My partner is negative all out of proportion. **T F**
8. I feel I have to ward off personal attacks. **T F**
9. I often have to deny charges leveled against me. **T F**
10. My partner's feelings are too easily hurt. **T F**
11. What goes wrong is often not my responsibility. **T F**
12. My spouse criticizes my personality. **T F**
13. Issues get raised in an insulting manner. **T F**
14. My partner will at times complain in a smug or superior way. **T F**
15. I have just about had it with all this negativity between us. **T F**
16. I feel basically disrespected when my partner complains. **T F**
17. I just want to leave the scene when complaints arise. **T F**

18. Our calm is suddenly shattered. **T F**

19. I find my partner's negativity unnerving and unsettling. **T F**

20. I think my partner can be totally irrational. **T F**

Scoring: Give yourself one point for each "true" answer.

Under 5: This is an area of strength in your marriage. You and your spouse initiate difficult discussions with each other gently—without being critical or contemptuous. Because you avoid being harsh, your chances of resolving your conflict or learning to manage it successfully together are dramatically increased.

5 or above: Your marriage could stand some improvement in this area. Your score suggests that when you address areas of disagreement with your spouse, one of you tends to be harsh. That means you immediately trot out at least one of the four horsemen, which automatically prevents the issue from being resolved.

Although the wife is usually responsible for a harsh startup, the secret to avoiding it is for *both of you* to work together on the first four principles. Do this, and the wife's startup softens as a matter of course. So if your spouse tends to raise issues harshly, the best advice I can give is to make sure she (or he) is feeling known, respected, and loved by you, and that you accept her influence. Harsh startup is often a reaction that sets in when a wife feels her husband doesn't respond to her low-level complaints or irritability. So if you comply with a minor request like "It's your turn to take out the garbage, please," you avoid having the situation escalate into "What the hell is wrong with you? Are you deaf? Take out the damn garbage!"

If you are the one most responsible for harsh startups in your relationship, I can't emphasize enough how important it is to the fate of your marriage to soften up. Remember: If you go straight for the jugular, you're going to draw plenty of blood. The result will be war or retreat on your partner's part, rather than any kind of meaningful, productive discussion. If you're angry with your spouse, it's worth taking a deep breath and thinking through how to broach the subject before leaping in. It will be easier to do this if you constantly remind yourself that by being gentle, you are more likely to resolve the conflict. If you feel too angry to discuss the matter gently, your best option is not to discuss it at all until you've calmed down. Follow the steps for self-soothing on page 176 before talking it out with your spouse.

Here are some suggestions to ensure that your startup is soft:

Complain but don't blame. Let's assume that you're angry because your spouse insisted on buying a dog despite your reservations. He swore up and down that he'd clean up after the dog. But now you're finding poop all over the yard whenever you take out the garbage. It's certainly okay to complain. You could say something like "Hey, there's poop all over the backyard. We agreed you'd clean up after Banjo. I'm really upset about this." While this is confrontational, it's not an attack. You're simply complaining about a particular situation, not your partner's personality or character.

What's not okay is to say something like "Hey, there's poop all over the backyard. This is all your fault. I just knew you'd be irresponsible about that dog. I should never have trusted you about it in the first place." However justified you may feel in blaming your spouse, the bottom line is that this approach is not productive. Even if it does lead your partner to clean up the yard, it also leads to increased tension, resentment, defensiveness, and so on.

Make statements that start with "I" instead of "You." "I" statements have been a staple of interpersonal psychology ever since the mid-1960s, when acclaimed psychologist Haim Ginott noted that phrases starting with *I* are usually less likely to be critical and to make the listener defensive than statements starting with *you*. You can see the difference:

"You are not listening to me," versus "I would like it if you'd listen to me."

"You are careless with money," versus "I want us to save more."

"You just don't care about me," versus "I'm feeling neglected."

Clearly, the "I" statements above are gentler than their "You" counterparts. Of course, you can also buck this general rule and come up with "I" statements like "I think you are selfish" that are hardly gentle. So the point is not to start talking to your spouse in some stilted psychobabble. Just keep in mind that if your words focus on how *you're* feeling rather than on accusing your spouse, your discussion will be far more successful.

Describe what is happening, don't evaluate or judge. Instead of accusing or blaming, just describe what you see. Instead of "You never watch the baby," say, "I seem to be the only one chasing after Charlie today." Again, this will help prevent your spouse from feeling attacked and waging a defense rather than really considering your point.

Be clear. Don't expect your partner to be a mind reader. Instead of "You left the dining room a total mess," say, "I'd appreciate it if you would clean your stuff off the dining room table." Instead of "Would you take care of the baby for once?" say, "Please change Emmy's diaper and give her a bottle."

Be polite. Add phrases such as "please" and "I would appreciate it if . . ."

Be appreciative. If your partner has, at some point, handled this situation better, then couch your request within an appreciation of what your partner did right in the past and how much you miss that now. Instead of "You never have time for me anymore," say, "Remember how we used to go out every Saturday night? I loved spending so much time alone with you. And it felt so good knowing that you wanted to be with me, too. Let's start doing that again."

Don't store things up. It's hard to be gentle when you're ready to burst with recriminations. So don't wait too long before bringing up an issue—otherwise it will just escalate in your mind. As the Bible says (Ephesians 4:26), "Let not the sun go down upon your wrath."

To see how all of these steps combine to create a softened startup, compare what Iris says in the following two dialogues:

Harsh Startup

IRIS: Another Saturday, and once again I'm spending my free time picking up after you. The trouble with you, Richard, is that . . . *(Criticism, blame)*

RICHARD: Yep, here we go again. "The trouble with you, Richard, the trouble with you, Richard." There's nothing wrong with me!

IRIS: Then why do I always have to tell you what to do? Never mind, I've finished cleaning up your stuff anyway, or were you too busy reading the Sunday paper to notice? *(Contempt)*

RICHARD: Look, I hate cleaning up. I know you do, too. I've been thinking about what we should do. *(Repair attempt)*

IRIS: This I've got to hear. *(More contempt)*

RICHARD: Well, actually I was thinking that we could use a vacation. Wouldn't it be nice for you to be waited on hand and foot? *(Second repair attempt)*

IRIS: Come on, we can't afford a cleaning lady, much less a vacation like that.

Softened Startup

IRIS: This house is an incredible mess, and we're having company tonight. *(Describing)* I am really upset that I am doing all this cleaning, alone, on a Saturday. *("I" statement)* Come on, please help me. Maybe you could do the vacuuming? *(Being clear)*

RICHARD: All right. I hate cleaning up, but I guess vacuuming is the best of the worst. I'll do the bathrooms, too.

IRIS: That'd be a big help. *(Appreciation)* Thank you. *(Politeness)*

RICHARD: When we're done, we deserve a reward—let's go out for lunch.

IRIS: Okay.

When you switch to a soft startup, your spouse may not automatically react so sweetly. He or she may still be anticipating criticism or contempt from you and therefore respond negatively. Don't give up or fall into the trap of then escalating the conflict. Continue to broach the topic gently, and eventually you will see a change in how your spouse responds, especially if you are working on all of the other aspects of Principle 5 together.

Here are some other examples that illustrate the difference between a harsh startup and a softened alternative:

Harsh startup: You never touch me.

Softened alternative: I loved it when you kissed me in the kitchen the other day. You are a natural-born kisser. Let's do that some more.

Harsh startup: I see you dented the car again. When are you going to stop being so reckless?

Softened alternative: I saw that new dent. What happened? I am really getting worried about your driving, and I want you to be safe. Can we talk about this?

Harsh startup: You always ignore me!

Softened alternative: I have been missing you lately, and I'm getting a little lonely.

Exercise 1: Softened Startup

Now test your own ability to soften a harsh startup. For each item below, supply a softened alternative. (Sample answers follow, but try not to peek.)

I. When your mother-in-law visits tonight, you plan to tell her how much it hurts you when she criticizes your parenting skills. You want your partner, who is very defensive when it comes to Mom, to back you up.

   Harsh startup. I can't stand it when your mother comes over.

   Your softened alternative:

2. You wish that your partner would cook dinner tomorrow night or take you out to dinner.

Harsh startup. You never take me anywhere. I'm sick of doing all the cooking.

Your softened alternative:

3. You think that your partner spends too much time with other people instead of you when you go to parties. Tonight, you want your partner to stick by you.

Harsh startup. I just know that tonight you're gonna be flirting shamelessly again at the party.

Your softened alternative:

4. You're upset that you have not made love in some time. You're feeling unsure that your partner finds you attractive. You wish that the two of you could make love tonight.

Harsh startup. You're always so cold to me!

Your softened alternative:

5. You want your partner to ask for a raise.

Harsh startup. You're too wimpy to get a raise for your own family.

Your softened alternative:

6. You want to do more fun things together on the weekends.
   Harsh startup. You have no idea how to have a good time. You're a workaholic.

Your softened alternative:

7. You wish that the two of you could save more money.
   Harsh startup. You don't have a clue about how to manage money.

Your softened alternative:

8. You wish your partner would spend more money buying you surprise presents.
   Harsh startup. When was the last time you bought me anything?

Your softened alternative:

Sample Answers

1. I'm worried that your mom is going to be critical of.me tonight and that you won't back me up.
2. I'm tired of cooking. It'd be real nice if you took me out.
3. I'm feeling very shy tonight again. Please spend time with me and make it easier for me to talk to other people. You're so good at that.
4. I'm really missing you lately, you know how much you turn me on. Let's make love!
5. It would be great if you could get a raise soon. What if we talked about a plan for getting one?

6. I really want to spend some fun time with you this weekend. How about not working and let's do something fun together? There's a great movie I'd really like to see.

7. I'm feeling anxious about our savings. Let's come up with a savings plan, okay?

8. I'm feeling very deprived lately, and I would love it if we surprised each other with a present out of the blue this week. What do you think?

STEP 2: LEARN TO MAKE AND RECEIVE REPAIR ATTEMPTS

When you take driving lessons, the first thing you're taught is how to stop the car. Putting on the brakes is an important skill in a marriage, too. When your discussion starts off on the wrong foot, or you find yourself in an endless cycle of recriminations, you can prevent a disaster if you know how to stop. I call these brakes *repair attempts.*

When Michael gets defensive and says, "I definitely clean off the counters in the kitchen and the table whenever we do stuff," Justine doesn't immediately discount his point. "Hm-hmm, you do," she says. This is a repair attempt. It deescalates the tension so that Michael is more receptive to finding a compromise. What separates stable, emotionally intelligent marriages from others is not that their repair attempts are necessarily more skillful or better thought out, but that their repair attempts get through to their spouse. This is because the air between them hasn't been clouded by a lot of negativity.

Repair Attempts Questionnaire

To assess the effectiveness of repair attempts in your own relationship, answer the following.
Read each statement and circle **T** *for "true" or* **F** *for "false."*

During our attempts to resolve conflict:

1. We are good at taking breaks when we need them. **T F**
2. My partner usually accepts my apologies. **T F**
3. I can say that I am wrong. **T F**
4. I am pretty good at calming myself down. **T F**
5. We can maintain a sense of humor. **T F**
6. When my partner says we should talk to each other in a different way, it usually makes a lot of sense. **T F**
7. My attempts to repair our discussions when they get negative are usually effective. **T F**
8. We are pretty good listeners even when we have different positions on things. **T F**
9. If things get heated, we can usually pull out of it and change things. **T F**
10. My spouse is good at soothing me when I get upset. **T F**
11. I feel confident that we can resolve most issues between us. **T F**
12. When I comment on how we could communicate better my spouse listens to me. **T F**
13. Even if things get hard at times I know we can get past our differences. **T F**
14. We can be affectionate even when we are disagreeing. **T F**
15. Teasing and humor usually work to get my spouse over negativity. **T F**
16. We can start all over again and improve our discussion when we need to. **T F**
17. When emotions run hot, expressing how upset I feel makes a real difference. **T F**
18. We can discuss even big differences between us. **T F**
19. My partner expresses appreciation for nice things I do. **T F**
20. If I keep trying to communicate it will eventually work. **T F**

Scoring: Give yourself one point for each "true" answer.

6 or above: This is an area of strength in your marriage. When marital discussions are at risk of getting out of hand, you are able to put on the brakes and effectively calm each other down.

Below 6: Your marriage could stand some improvement in this area. By learning how to repair your interactions when negativity engulfs you, you can dramatically improve the effectiveness of your problem solving and develop a more positive perspective of each other and your marriage.

GETTING THE MESSAGE THROUGH

As I said, the key factor in whether a repair attempt is effective is the state of the relationship. In happy marriages, couples send and receive repair attempts with ease. In unhappy ones, even the most eloquent repair attempt can fall on deaf ears. But now that you know this, you can "buck the system." You don't have to wait for your marriage to improve before you start hearing each other's repair attempts. Start now by focusing intently on these "brakes" and training each other to recognize when one is sent your way. Do this, and you can pull yourselves out of the downward cycle of negativity.

> **Your future together can be bright even if your disagreements tend to be very negative. The secret is learning the right kind of damage control.**

One reason couples miss each other's repair attempts is that they don't always come sugarcoated. If your spouse yells, "You're getting off the topic!" or grumbles, "Can we take a break?" that's a repair attempt despite the negative delivery. If you listen to your partner's tone rather than the words, you could miss his real message, which is "Stop! This is getting out of hand." Because repair attempts can be difficult to hear if your relationship is engulfed in negativity, the best strategy is to make your attempts obviously formal in order to emphasize them. Below you'll find a long list of scripted phrases. These are specific words you can say to your spouse to deescalate the tension. By using them when arguments get too negative, you'll be able to keep your discussions from spiraling out of control. Some couples even copy this list and stick it on their refrigerator for handy reference.

Many, if not all, of these phrases probably sound phony and unnatural to you right now. That's because they offer a very different way of speaking with your spouse when you're upset. But their phoniness is not a reason to reject them. If you learned a better and more effective way to hold your tennis racket, it would feel "wrong" and "unnatural" initially, simply because you weren't used to it yet. The same goes for these repair attempts. Over time they'll come easily to you, and you'll modify them to more closely suit your style of speech and personality.

I Feel

1. I'm getting scared.
2. Please say that more gently.
3. Did I do something wrong?
4. That hurt my feelings.
5. That felt like an insult.
6. I'm feeling sad.
7. I feel blamed. Can you rephrase that?
8. I'm feeling unappreciated.
9. I feel defensive. Can you rephrase that?
10. Please don't lecture me.
11. I don't feel like you understand me right now.
12. I am starting to feel flooded.
13. I feel criticized. Can you rephrase that?
14. I'm getting worried.

I Need to Calm Down

1. Can you make things safer for me?
2. I need things to be calmer right now.
3. I need your support right now.
4. Just listen to me right now and try to understand.
5. Tell me you love me.
6. Can I have a kiss?
7. Can I take that back?

8. Please be gentler with me.
9. Please help me calm down.
10. Please be quiet and listen to me.
11. This is important to me. Please listen.
12. I need to finish what I was saying.
13. I am starting to feel flooded.
14. I feel criticized. Can you rephrase that?
15. Can we take a break?

Sorry

1. My reactions were too extreme. Sorry.
2. I really blew that one.
3. Let me try again.
4. I want to be gentler to you right now, and I don't know how.
5. Tell me what you hear me saying.
6. I can see my part in all this.
7. How can I make things better?
8. Let's try that over again.
9. What you are saying is . . .
10. Let me start again in a softer way.
11. I'm sorry. Please forgive me.

Get to Yes

1. You're starting to convince me.
2. I agree with part of what you're saying.
3. Let's compromise here.
4. Let's find our common ground.
5. I never thought of things that way.
6. This problem is not very serious in the big picture.
7. I think your point of view makes sense.
8. Let's agree to include both our views in a solution.
9. I am thankful for . . .
10. One thing I admire about you is . . .
11. I see what you're talking about.

Stop Action!

1. I might be wrong here.
2. Please, let's stop for a while.
3. Let's take a break.
4. Give me a moment. I'll be back.
5. I'm feeling flooded.
6. Please stop.
7. Let's agree to disagree here.
8. Let's start all over again.
9. Hang in there. Don't withdraw.
10. I want to change the topic.
11. We are getting off track.

I Appreciate

1. I know this isn't your fault.
2. My part of this problem is . . .
3. I see your point.
4. Thank you for . . .
5. That's a good point.
6. We are both saying . . .
7. I understand.
8. I love you.
9. I am thankful for . . .
10. One thing I admire about you is . . .
11. This is not your problem, it's *our* problem.

Formalizing repair attempts by using these scripted phrases can help you defuse arguments in two ways. First, the formality of a script ensures that you will use the type of words that work well for putting on the brakes. Second, these phrases are like megaphones—they help ensure that you pay attention to a repair attempt when you're on the receiving end.

Now it's time to use the above checklist to help you resolve an issue in your marriage. Choose a low-intensity conflict to discuss.

Each of you gets to talk for fifteen minutes. Make sure you both use at least one phrase from the list of phrases during the discussion. Announce to your partner beforehand that you're about to make a repair attempt. You can even refer to the attempt by number, as in, "I'm making repair attempt number six under *I Feel:* 'I'm feeling sad.'"

When your partner announces a repair attempt, your job is simply to try to accept it. View the interruption as a bid to make things better. Accept the attempt in the spirit in which it was intended. This entails accepting your partner's influence. For example, if he or she says, "I need to finish what I'm saying," acknowledge that need and then encourage your partner to keep talking to you. As you continue to use the list in your conversations, eventually you might consider replacing it with some other ritual, like raising your hand and announcing point-blank, *"This is a repair attempt!"* Or you may come up with other effective repairs that better fit your personality and relationship. For example, a couple we know say "clip clop" to each other if one of them introduces one of the four horsemen into a discussion. The humor in this repair helps defuse the negativity all the more.

STEP 3: SOOTHE YOURSELF AND EACH OTHER

While Justine is in the middle of discussing laundry with Michael, he does something that seems incidental but really has great significance for their chances of a happy future: He yawns. Cleaning house is not the most fascinating subject, but Michael doesn't yawn because Justine is boring him. He yawns because he is relaxed. When you're feeling angry or anxious, yawning is just about the least likely physiological reaction you're going to have. Michael's yawn is like an announcement that he's feeling soothed by Justine, even though she's discussing an area of conflict. Because no alarms are going off in his body (or mind), he is able to discuss housework and reach a compromise with Justine easily.

It is harder for a man's body to calm down after an argument than a woman's.

In less stable marriages, however, conflict discussions can lead to the opposite reaction—they can trigger flooding. When this occurs, you feel overwhelmed both emotionally and physically. Most likely you think thoughts of righteous indignation ("I don't have to take this anymore") or innocent victimhood ("Why is she always picking on me?"). Meanwhile, your body is in distress. Usually your heart is pounding, you're sweating, you're holding your breath.

I have found that in the vast majority of cases, when one spouse does not "get" the other's repair attempt, it's because the listener is flooded and therefore can't really hear what the spouse is saying. When you're in this condition, the most thoughtful repair attempt in the world won't benefit your marriage.

Flooding Questionnaire

To discover whether flooding is a significant problem in your relationship, answer the following questions:
Read each statement and circle **T** *for "true" or* **F** *for "false."*

1. Our discussions get too heated. **T F**
2. I have a hard time calming down. **T F**
3. One of us is going to say something we will regret. **T F**
4. My partner gets too upset. **T F**
5. After a fight I want to keep my distance. **T F**
6. My partner yells unnecessarily. **T F**
7. I feel overwhelmed by our arguments. **T F**
8. I can't think straight when my partner gets hostile. **T F**
9. Why can't we talk more logically? **T F**
10. My partner's negativity often comes out of nowhere. **T F**
11. There's often no stopping my partner's temper. **T F**
12. I feel like running away during our fights. **T F**
13. Small issues suddenly become big ones. **T F**

14. I can't calm down very easily during an argument. **T F**

15. My partner has a long list of unreasonable demands. **T F**

Scoring: Give yourself one point for each "true" answer.

Below 6: This is an area of strength in your marriage. You are able to confront differences of opinion with your spouse without feeling over-whelmed. This means that you are not feeling victimized or hostile toward your spouse during disagreements. That's good news since it indicates that you are able to communicate with each other without negativity getting out of hand. As a result, you're better able to resolve conflicts (and avoid grid-lock over issues that are unresolvable).

6 or above: Your marriage could stand some improvement in this area. Your score suggests that you tend to get flooded during arguments with your spouse. When this occurs, any likelihood that the problem can be resolved ceases. You are feeling too agitated to really hear what your spouse is saying or to learn any helpful conflict-resolution skills. Read on to find out how to cope with this problem.

Exercise 2: Self-Soothing

The first step is to stop the discussion. If you keep going, you'll find yourself exploding at your spouse or imploding (stonewalling), neither of which will get you anywhere other than one step farther down the marital cascades that lead to divorce. The only reasonable strategy, therefore, is to let your spouse know that you're feeling flooded and need to take a break. That break should last at least twenty minutes, since it will be that long before your body calms down. It's crucial that during this time you avoid thoughts of righteous indignation and innocent victimhood. Spend your time doing something soothing and distracting, like listening to music or exercising.

Many people find that the best approach to self-soothing is to focus on calming the body through a meditative technique. Here's a simple one:

1. Sit in a comfortable chair, or lie on your back on the floor.

2. Focus on controlling your breathing. Usually when you get flooded, you either hold your breath a lot or breathe shallowly. So close your eyes and focus on taking deep, regular breaths.

3. Relax your muscles. One at a time, tightly squeeze the muscle groups that seem tense (usually, your forehead and jaw, neck, shoulders, arms, and back). Hold for two seconds, then release.

4. Let the tension flow out of each muscle group, and get that muscle group to feel *heavy* by imagining that it is.

5. Let the tension flow out of each (now-heavy) muscle group, and get that muscle group to feel *warm*. One way is to keep your eyes closed and focus on one calming vision or idea. Many people find it effective to think of a place they associate with calmness, like a forest, a lake, or a beach. Imagine this place as vividly as you can. Keep focused on this calming vision for about thirty seconds.

6. Find a personal image that brings all of this soothing to mind. For example, I think of a place I know on Orca Island in Washington State, where the loudest sound is the wind rustling the trees as young eagles residing in a nearby rookery soar by. Conjuring that image relaxes me and automatically triggers all of the other steps of self-soothing.

I think taking a break of this sort is so important that I schedule this exercise into the conflict-resolution section of every workshop I run. Invariably I get the same response from participants. At first, they moan and groan about being forced to relax. Some are quite cynical about relaxation exercises and can't see how closing their eyes and thinking about a lake can help cure their marital woes. And yet once they do the exercise, they realize how powerful and helpful it really is. Suddenly everybody in the room relaxes. You can see the difference in how couples relate to each other. Their voices get softer; there is more chuckling. Soothing themselves has made them better able to work on their conflicts as a team rather than as adversaries.

In one of our latest experiments, we interrupted couples after fifteen minutes and told them we needed to adjust the equipment. We asked them not to talk about their issue, but just to read magazines for half an hour. When they started talking about their issue again, their heart rates were significantly lower and their interaction more productive.

Exercise 3: Soothing Each Other

Once you've calmed yourself, you can benefit your marriage enormously if you then take some time to calm each other. Obviously this can be quite difficult to do if you're feeling very angry or hurt. But the results can be so impressive that it's worth trying. Remember: Only do this after you've already spent twenty minutes calming down on your own.

Soothing your partner is of enormous benefit to a marriage because it's really a form of reverse conditioning. In other words, if you frequently have the experience of being calmed by your spouse, you will stop seeing your partner as a *trigger* of stress in your life and instead associate him or her with feeling relaxed. This automatically increases the positivity in your relationship.

To comfort each other, you first need to talk earnestly about flooding. Ask yourself and each other these questions:

- What makes me (you) feel flooded?
- How do I (you) typically bring up issues or irritability or complaints?
- Do I (you) store things up?
- Is there anything I can do that soothes you?
- Is there anything you can do that soothes me?
- What signals can we develop for letting the other know when we feel flooded? Can we take breaks?

If your heart rate exceeds 100 beats per minute you won't be able to hear what your spouse is trying to tell you no matter how hard you try. Take a twenty-minute break before continuing.

There are many different ways to calm your spouse. What matters most is that your partner determines the method and enjoys it. Some couples find massage the perfect antidote to a stressful discussion. Another helpful technique is to take turns guiding each other through a meditation like the one described on pages 178–179. Think of it as a verbal massage. You can even write an elaborate script in which you have your spouse tighten and relax different muscle groups and then visualize a calm, beautiful scene that brings him or her pleasure. You can tape-record your rendition for future use—perhaps give it to your spouse as a special gift. You don't need to wait for a tense situation to use this exercise. Soothing each other regularly is a wonderful way to prevent future flooding and generally enrich your marriage.

STEP 4: COMPROMISE

Like it or not, the only solution to marital problems is to find a compromise. In an intimate, loving relationship it just doesn't work for either of you to get things all your way, even if you're convinced that you're right. This approach would create such inequity and unfairness that the marriage would suffer.

Usually, though both partners do make an earnest effort to compromise on issues, they fail because they go about trying to compromise in the wrong way. Negotiation is possible only after you've followed the steps above—softening startup, repairing your discussion, and keeping calm. These prime you for compromise by getting you into a positive mode.

Before you try to resolve a conflict, remember that *the cornerstone of any compromise is the fourth principle of marriage—accepting influence*. This means that for a compromise to work, you can't have a closed mind to your spouse's opinions and desires. You don't have to agree with everything your spouse says or believes, but you have to be honestly open to *considering* his or her position. That's what accepting influence is really all about. If you find yourself sitting with your arms folded and shaking your head no (or just thinking it) when your spouse is trying to talk out a problem with you, your discussion will never get anywhere.

As I've said, men have a harder time accepting influence from their wives than vice versa. But whatever your gender, an inability to be open-minded is a real liability when it comes to conflict resolution. So if you haven't already, work through the exercises in Chapter 6. Realize that it may take time and continued self-awareness to break out of this tendency. Your spouse can assist you in seeing things from his or her perspective. Ask your spouse questions to help you see his or her point of view. Remember to search for the part of your spouse's perspective that, by objective standards, is reasonable.

Once you're ready, there's nothing magical about finding a solution you both can live with. Often compromise is just a matter of talking out your differences and preferences in a systematic way. This is not difficult to do as long as you continue to follow the steps above to prevent your discussion from becoming overwhelmingly negative.

Exercise 4: Finding Common Ground

Decide together which solvable problem you want to tackle. Then sit separately and think about the problem. On a piece of paper, draw two circles—a smaller one inside a larger one. In the inner circle make a list of the aspects of the problem you can't give in on. In the outer circle list all of the aspects of the problem you *can* compromise about. Remember the aikido principle of yielding to win—the more able you are to compromise, the better able you'll be to persuade your spouse. So try hard to make your outer circle as large as possible and your inner circle as small as possible.

Here are the inner and outer circles of a couple named Raymond and Carol, who were both dissatisfied with their sex life.

Raymond

Inner Circle:
   1. I want sex to be more erotic.
   2. I want there to be fantasy play with you wearing very sexy lingerie.
Outer Circle:
   1. I can compromise on whether to have sex in the morning or at night even when I'm tired.
   2. I can compromise on our talking during sex.

Carol

Inner Circle:
  1. I want to feel like we're making love when we're having sex.
  2. I want Raymond to hold me and stroke me a lot. I want a lot of foreplay.

Outer Circle:
  1. I prefer to have sex at night because I love falling asleep in your arms afterward, but sex in the morning would be okay too.
  2. Talking to me a lot while we make love is nice, but I can compromise on this too.

Once you've filled in your circles (your lists may be much longer than Raymond's and Carol's), come back and share them with each other. Look for common bases of agreement. Remember as you discuss this to make use of all the other problem-solving strategies outlined in this chapter—namely, softened startup and soothing yourself or each other if flooding occurs.

In the case of Carol and Raymond, their inner circles are very different, but they are not incompatible. Once they accept and respect their sexual differences, they can create lovemaking sessions that incorporate his desire for erotic fantasy with her longing for intimacy and lots of touching. And although their outer circles are in opposition as well, they are willing to give in these areas, so compromise should be easy. Maybe they'll decide to switch off with morning and evening sex depending on how tired Raymond is. And they can vary how much they speak during sex as well.

The goal of this circle exercise is to try to develop a common way of thinking about the issue so that you work together to construct a real plan that you can both live with. As you share your circles, ask yourselves the following questions:

  1. What do we agree about?
  2. What are our common feelings or the most important feelings here?
  3. What common goals can we have here?
  4. How can we understand this situation, this issue?
  5. How do we think these goals should be accomplished?

Most likely if you're grappling with a solvable problem, following these steps will lead you to find a reasonable compromise. Once you do, try out the solution for an agreed-upon time before revisiting it and deciding if it's working. If it's not, begin the process again and work together to resolve it.

From time to time it's a good idea to recharge your compromising skills by focusing together on solving a problem that is not related to your marital issues. What follows is a fun exercise that will give you practice in coming to consensus decisions by working as a team and giving and accepting influence.

Exercise 5: Paper Tower

This exercise is especially fun to do with other couples. Consider having a paper tower party or contest where each couple is a separate team. You can take turns being builders and scorekeepers.

Your mission: Build a free-standing paper tower using the supplies listed below. The goal is to build the highest, most stable, and most beautiful tower you can. You may have very different ideas about how to go about this, so remember to work out your differences of opinion using the compromise approach described in this chapter. During this exercise try to be a team. Try both to give and to accept influence. Include your partner. Ask questions. Take about half an hour for this task. The finished product should not adhere exactly to either of your visions but should include both of them. When you're finished, have a third party (or another couple) score your tower. No doubt the scoring will be highly subjective since it values creativity more than engineering prowess. But your final score is beside the point, which is to have fun building your tower together. When you're finished you'll have created a monument to your marriage and your enhanced compromising skills.

Supplies

1 Sunday newspaper	Crayons
Ball of string	Colored cellophane

Scotch tape   Construction paper
Stapler   Cardboard pieces
Markers

Score: Have a third party (or another couple) score your tower. The top score is 90. You get:
Up to 20 points for height
Up to 20 points for strength (stability)
Up to 50 points for beauty and originality.

STEP 5: BE TOLERANT OF EACH OTHER'S FAULTS

Too often, a marriage gets bogged down in "if onlies." If only your spouse were taller, richer, smarter, neater, or sexier, all of your problems would vanish. As long as this attitude prevails, conflicts will be very difficult to resolve. Until you accept your partner's flaws and foibles, you will not be able to compromise successfully. Instead, you will be on a relentless campaign to alter your spouse. Conflict resolution is not about one person changing, it's about negotiating, finding common ground and ways that you can accommodate each other.

When you have mastered the general problem-solving skills outlined in this chapter, you'll find that many of your problems find their own solutions. Once you get past the barriers that have prevented clear communication, difficulties are easy to resolve. In fact, the next chapter offers some creative and simple solutions to some of the most common conflicts couples face—money, sex, housework, kids, work stress. But remember: These solutions work only for problems that can be solved. If compromise still seems like a distant goal to you, then the problem you are grappling with may not be solvable after all. That means it's time to turn to the advice on coping with perpetual problems in Chapter 10.

9

Coping with Typical Solvable Problems

Work stress, in-laws, money, sex, housework, a new baby: These are the most typical areas of marital conflict, so there's a good chance at least some of them are hot buttons in your relationship. Even in very happy and stable marriages, these issues are perennials. Although every relationship is different, there's a reason why these particular conflicts are so common: They touch upon some of the marriage's most important work.

Many people pay lip service to the notion that a good marriage takes "work." But what specifically does this mean? Every marriage is faced with certain emotional tasks that husband and wife need to accomplish together for the marriage to grow and deepen. These tasks come down to attaining a rich understanding between husband and wife. A marriage needs this understanding in order for both people to feel safe and secure in it. When these tasks are not accomplished, the marriage feels not like a port in the storm of life but just another storm.

When there's conflict in one of these six common areas, usually it's because husband and wife have different ideas about these tasks, their importance, or how they should be accomplished. If the conflict is perpetual, no amount of problem-solving savvy will fix it. The tension will deescalate only when you both feel comfortable living with your ongoing difference. But when the issue is solvable, the challenge is to find the right strategy for conquering it. (If you're not sure whether your conflict is solvable or perpetual, see page 134.) Here we've listed these six hot spots, the task they each represent for a marriage, and practical advice for addressing the solvable disagreements they often trigger.

STRESS AND MORE STRESS

The task: *Making your marriage a place of peace.*

Most days Stephanie and Todd get home from work within a few minutes of each other. Too often, instead of a loving reunion, they find themselves in a shouting match. Todd, who has been kowtowing to a difficult boss all day, gets annoyed when he can't find the mail because Stephanie moved it off the table for the nth time. Stephanie, who has a deadline at work and knows she'll be up late working, feels her anger surge when she opens the refrigerator and discovers nothing but Strawberry Snapple. "There's no food!" she yells. "I can't believe you didn't go to the supermarket like you promised. What's wrong with you?"

The real question is what's going wrong between Todd and Stephanie. The answer is that they are bringing their work stress home, and it is sabotaging their marriage.

> **Scheduling formal griping sessions can prevent the spillover of everyday stress into your marriage.**

There's no doubt that work stress has become an increasing factor in marital dissatisfaction. Today's couples work an average of one thousand hours more each year than people did thirty years ago. There is less time for talking, relaxing, eating, and even sleeping. No wonder the days of the cheerful "Honey, I'm home!" are history for so many families. Most likely "Honey" is working too and has come home with a stack of papers she needs to prepare for tomorrow's presentation to a client. Or maybe she's been waiting tables all day, and the last thing she wants to do is to wait on her man.

Solution Acknowledge that at the end of a long, stressful day you may need time to yourselves to decompress before interacting with each other. If you are feeling suddenly outraged by something your spouse did, realize that the incident may be overblown in your mind because you're feeling so tense. Likewise, if your spouse comes home with a cloud over his head and your "What's wrong?" gets answered with a snarl, try not to take it personally. He or she probably just had a bad day. Rather than making the situation worse by lashing out, let it go.

Build time to unwind into your daily schedule. Make it a ritual, whether it entails lying on your bed and reading your mail, going for a jog, or meditating. Of course, some couples find that the easiest way to relax is to enlist each other's help. If so, try the soothing techniques described in detail on pages 178–179.

Once you're both feeling relatively composed, it's time to come together and talk about each other's day. Consider this a sanctioned whining session during which each person gets to complain about any catastrophes that occurred while the other is understanding and supportive.

RELATIONS WITH IN-LAWS

The task: *Establishing a sense of "we-ness," or solidarity, between husband and wife.*

Although mother-in-law jokes told by men are a traditional staple of comedy routines, the real family tension is more frequently between the wife and her mother-in-law. Invariably the differences between the two women's opinions, personalities, and life views become evident the more time they spend together. A decision to go out to dinner can create dissension over such minutiae as where to eat, when to eat, what to eat, how much to spend, who gets the check, and so on. Then, of course, there are the deeper issues of values, jobs, where to live, how to live, how to pray, and whom to vote for.

Although such conflicts usually surface quite early in a marriage, in-law difficulties can be triggered or revived at many other times, such as when children are born or pass major milestones in their development, and again as the parents age and become increasingly dependent on the couple.

At the core of the tension is a turf battle between the two women for the husband's love. The wife is watching to see whether her husband backs her or his mother. She is wondering, "Which family are you really in?" Often the mother is asking the same question. The man, for his part, just wishes the two women could get along better. He loves them both and does not want to have to choose. The whole idea is ridiculous to him. After all, he has loyalties to each, and he must honor and respect both. Unfortunately, this attitude often throws him into the role of peacemaker or mediator, which invariably makes the situation worse.

Solution The only way out of this dilemma is for the husband to side with his wife against his mother. Although this may sound harsh, remember that one of the basic tasks of a marriage is to establish a sense of "we-ness" between husband and wife. So the husband must let his mother know that his wife does indeed come first. His house is his and his wife's house, not his mother's. He is a husband first, then a son. This is not a pleasant position to take. His mother's feelings may be hurt. But eventually she will probably adjust to the reality that her son's family unit, where he is the husband, takes precedence to him over all others. It is absolutely critical for the marriage that the husband be firm about this, even if he feels unfairly put upon and even if his mother cannot accept the new reality.

This is not to suggest that a man do anything that he feels demeans and dishonors his parents or goes against his basic values. He should not compromise who he is. But he has to stand with his wife and not in the middle. He and his wife need to establish their own family rituals, values, and lifestyle and insist that his mother (and father) respect them.

For this reason, creating or renewing your sense of solidarity with your spouse may involve some rending and tearing away from your primary families. That's the challenge David faced when his parents came for a weekend visit to his new home, a visit that led to what he now calls the Great Osso Buco Crisis. Here's what happened: His wife Janie had made Saturday dinner reservations for all of them at her favorite Italian restaurant. She was very excited about showing the restaurant off to her Italian in-laws, especially because she often felt upstaged by her mother-in-law, who was very knowledgeable about cuisine. But while she and David were out running errands, the older woman went to the butcher and the supermarket and prepared David's favorite dish for dinner—osso buco.

When David and Janie arrived home, the savory aroma of garlic and veal wafted through the air. Janie was furious—but not surprised—when David's mother said she "forgot" about the reservations. David was face to face with a dilemma. The veal looked delicious, and he knew how hurt his mother would be if he didn't eat it. He really wanted to tell Janie to cancel the reservations.

Although this hardly sounds like a major crisis, it led to a turning point in David and Janie's marriage. Janie had dreaded her in-laws' visit to begin with because she felt her mother-in-law always acted as if Janie was sweet but incompetent while she was the great savior who would set their household right. Janie was always polite but distant with David's mom. Privately she would give David an earful about what a control freak his mother was. David always insisted Janie was imagining or exaggerating slights. This just made her angrier.

Now Janie held her breath as she watched David survey the feast his mother had prepared. He cleared his throat, put his arm around his mother, and thanked her for cooking such a wonderful meal. Then he insisted it would keep for another day in the refrigerator. He explained that it was important to him and Janie to share with her and his dad how they liked to spend Saturday night together as a couple at their favorite restaurant.

His mother looked highly offended. She got teary-eyed and made a bit of a scene. (David let his father deal with that.) But it was worth it to David to see Janie look so happy and triumphant. In the end, David's message was loud and clear: She comes first, Mom. Get used to it. "That's when our *real* marriage began," Janie recalls. "When he let his mother know that I was now first in his heart."

An important part of putting your spouse first and building this sense of solidarity is not to tolerate any contempt toward your spouse from your parents. Noel and Evelyn's marriage was heading for disaster until Noel learned that lesson. After their son was born, it was very important to Noel that his parents view him as a good father. Although he was a very busy lawyer and didn't get to spend much time with the baby, every other weekend he would bring the baby with him for a visit with his parents, who lived in the next town. This gave Evelyn some desperately needed time to herself.

Often Evelyn would join them at the end of the day. From the moment she entered the house, she felt like an outsider, as if she had been cut out of the baby's life. Noel's parents pretty much ignored her. They'd make a big fuss over the baby and go on and on about what a great father Noel was. At times they were even sarcastic toward Evelyn—issuing snide comments, for example, about the fact that she was still nursing the baby at six months. Since Evelyn knew that Noel wanted her to wean the baby, she suspected that Noel was complaining to his parents about her behind her back. In our laboratory we helped the couple talk about this issue, and it turned out she was completely right. In an effort to impress his parents, Noel was sacrificing his "we-ness" with Evelyn by bad-mouthing her.

Once Noel realized that his need for his parents' approval was playing out against Evelyn and their marriage, he was able to change. He began to spend less time at his parents' house with the baby, so that his parents saw their grandson mostly when they were on Evelyn's home turf. When his mother expressed concern that the baby wasn't getting enough to eat, Noel piped up that Evelyn had just taken him to the pediatrician, who declared him perfectly plump and healthy. When his father suggested that the baby needed a heavier snowsuit, Noel told him that Evelyn was the mother and knew better than anyone else what was best for their son. At first Noel's parents were miffed by his new attitude. But as time went on, they came to accept the change. And Noel and Evelyn found that their marriage flourished. They finally developed a sense that they were a team. They had mastered the task of building "we-ness."

Exercise 1: On-law Problems

If you are having ongoing in-law problems in your marriage, filling out this brief questionnaire can help. It will let you focus on your relationships with each other's kin so that you can determine whether your sense of "we-ness" as a couple needs to be strengthened when it comes to a particular relative. You should both jot down your answers to this form on separate paper.

1. Think of your relationship with various members of your spouse's family. If you feel that your spouse isn't necessarily on your side in any of these relationships or that there are ongoing issues with a particular family member, check off the appropriate box.

❏ Spouse's mother
❏ Spouse's stepmother
❏ Spouse's father
❏ Spouse's stepfather
❏ Spouse's brother(s) _____
❏ Spouse's sister(s) _____
❏ Other family member _____

Describe the successes so far:

Describe the conflict(s) that remain:

2. Think about your spouse's relationship with your kin. If you feel that your spouse isn't necessarily on your side in any of these relationships or that there are ongoing issues with a particular family member, check off the appropriate box.

❏ Mother
❏ Stepmother
❏ Father
❏ Stepfather
❏ Brother(s) _____
❏ Sister(s) _____
❏ Other family member _____

Describe the successes so far:

Describe the conflict(s) that remain:

Now get together with your spouse and read over each other's responses. Discuss what can be done to increase the amount of support and solidarity you are getting from each other. Try not to be defensive if your spouse perceives a problem and you don't. Remember that much about relationships has to do with perception. So, for example, if your wife believes that you side with your own mother against her, that's something you need to work on in your marriage, even if you don't agree with her perception of the situation.

MONEY, MONEY, MONEY

The task: *Balancing the freedom and empowerment money represents with the security and trust it also symbolizes.*

Whether their bank account is teeming or they're just scrimping by, many couples confront significant money conflicts. Often such disputes are evidence of a perpetual issue, since money is symbolic of many emotional needs—such as for security and power—and goes to the core of our individual value system. But when a simpler, solvable financial problem arises, the key to resolving it is to first understand a marriage's task in this area. While money buys pleasure, it also buys security. Balancing these two economic realities can be work for any couple, since our feelings about money and value are so personal and often idiosyncratic.

I find that solvable financial differences are usually the province of newlyweds rather than longer-term couples. That's because as a marriage goes on, these issues either become resolved successfully or develop into perpetual problems about money's symbolic meanings. However, long-term couples may also find themselves facing a solvable money issue as their circumstances change. Differences of opinion over job changes, financing the children's education, planning for retirement, and caring for elderly parents are common sources of friction in midlife.

Solution Some clearheaded budgeting is called for. Below are some simple steps you can take to get a handle on how much you'd like to be spending—and on what. Keep in mind, though, that managing complex financial matters is beyond the scope of this book. If you need extra help with financial planning and investing, you'll find plenty of resources at your local library or bookstore. In particular I recommend *Get a Financial Life* by Beth Kobliner (Fireside Books, 1996) and *Your Money or Your Life* by Joe Dominguez and Vicki Robin (Penguin, 1992). What's most important in terms of your marriage is that you work as a team on financial issues and that you express your concerns, needs, and fantasies to each other before coming up with a plan. Make sure you don't end up with a budget that forces either of you to become a martyr. This will only build up resentment. You'll each need to be firm about items that you consider nonnegotiable.

Step 1: Itemize Your Current Expenditures

Use a form like the one that follows to record how you have spent your money over the last month, six months, or year, whichever is most appropriate to your situation. You may be able to do this just by reviewing your checkbook and credit card statements.

Expenditures

Food
Mortgage or rent
  Vacation rentals
  Remodeling
  Property taxes
  Condo maintenance fees
Home office supplies
Utilities
  Electricity
  Gas
  Heat
  Water
  Phone
  E-mail, Internet
Household maintenance
  Housecleaning
  Laundry
  Dry cleaning
  Supplies and equipment (vacuum, bathroom cleaner, etc.)
Clothes
Personal care (Haircuts, manicures, sundries)
Car
  Gas
  Maintenance and repairs
  License renewal
  Insurance
  Parking, tolls
  Payments
Other Transportation
  Bus, train, ferry fares
Trips
  Business
  Visiting family
  Other vacations

Recreation
  Eating out or takeout
  Baby-sitters
  Dates (movies, plays, concerts, sports)
  Home entertainment (video rentals, CDs)
Health
  Insurance premiums
  Doctor
  Pharmacy
  Health club membership
  Other (eyeglasses, massages, counseling, etc.)
Appliances and electronics (TV, computer, answering machine)
Gifts
Charitable contributions
Interest on loans, bank charges, credit cards
Life insurance
Investments and savings (stocks, etc.)

Step 2: Manage Everyday Finances

1. Write down every expense from the list above that you consider essential for your sense of happiness and well-being.

2. Look carefully at your income and assets. Now try to create a budget that allows you to manage everyday finances and other "essentials" based on your means.

3. Come up with a plan for paying bills on a regular basis. Determine who writes the checks and when, and who balances the checkbook.

4. Discuss your separate lists and plans with each other. Look for common ground between your two approaches. Decide on a workable strategy that allows both of you to meet your "essential" needs. Agree to sit down and revisit your plan in a few months to make sure it's working for both of you.

Step 3: Plan Your Financial Future

1. Imagine your life 5, 10, 20, or 30 years from now. What would be your ideal circumstance? Think of things you want (house, and so on) and the kind of life you would ideally like to lead. Also think through the kinds of financial disasters you would most want to avoid. For example, some people's greatest financial fear is not having enough money to retire. Others fear not being able to fund a child's college education.

2. Now list your long-term financial goals, taking into account what you most desire and what you most fear. For example, your goals might include buying your own home or weekend home, as well as having a well-funded retirement account.

3. Share your lists with each other. Look for similarities in your long-term goals. Discuss your perspectives.

4. Come up with a long-range financial plan that will help you both meet your goals. Be sure to revisit this plan every so often—say every year—to make sure you're still in agreement.

Following these steps has helped couples with a wide variety of financial differences come up with workable solutions. For example, Linda loved stylish clothes and working out at the health club near her office. Devon considered both of those frivolous wastes of money. He far preferred to spend his money on lunches out with friends and two skiing vacations every year. To Linda, *his* pleasures were overly indulgent. After they each filled out the form, they could see exactly how much money they had. They talked about their finances as a couple and arrived at a temporary compromise budget. Neither of them wanted to give up on their favorite pleasures, so they decided that they would open three savings accounts, one for each of them plus a joint account. They agreed to put a portion of each paycheck into their joint account to save for their children's education and other major expenses down the road. Then they individually would save for gym memberships and ski trips. They decided that in six months they would talk over this arrangement again to determine whether their new budgeting system was working for both of them.

Tina and Gene had a different dilemma. Their oldest son Brian was just two years away from college. Although they had saved enough for him to attend the local community college, Tina wanted to send him to the more rigorous (and more expensive) state university, which offered far more science courses. Brian had always been an exceptional student. His dream of becoming an aerospace engineer seemed like a realistic goal. But to pay the higher tuition this would entail, Gene would have to postpone his dream of buying a cabin in the mountains. Although Gene cared deeply about his son's education, he also worried that if they didn't buy a home now, they'd get priced out of the market and would never realize his life-long dream. Gene wanted Tina to go back to work full time so they could afford the college tuition and the country home. But Tina was resisting because her very elderly mother lived with them and depended on Tina for her daily care. Gene and Tina were at this point having almost daily fights over the issue. Gene thought it was time for Tina's sister to take over her mother's care. But Tina's sister worked full time and said she wasn't able to do that. The other option was to put her mother in a nursing home, but Tina was dead set against such a decision.

When Tina and Gene filled out the budgeting form, a simple solution did not present itself. But the process of looking through their expenditures together transformed the emotional climate between them dramatically. Rather than arguing about the issues, they felt like a team again. They made lists of the various pieces of information they needed to find out about student loans and scholarships. In the end, Gene accepted that he would have to postpone his dream for a few more years. Tina did go back to work, but only on a part time basis. Gene was able to shift his work hours so that he could be home with his mother-in-law while Tina was away. And Brian was able to take out enough student loans to allow him to go to the state university.

The problems and solutions encountered by these couples are unlikely to match yours. The point is that whatever your disagreement over finances, you'll defuse the tension by working as a team to devise a plan you both can accept, even if it doesn't give you everything you want right now.

SEX

The task: *Fundamental appreciation and acceptance of each other.*

No other area of a couple's life offers more potential for embarrassment, hurt, and rejection than sex. No wonder couples find it such a challenge to communicate about the topic clearly. Often they "vague out," making it difficult to decipher what they're actually trying to tell each other. Here's a classic example from a couple we taped in our lab:

SHE: Think about your feelings two and a half and three years ago, and how we dealt with the problem and how we felt. I mean, think. It was much more a problem then in my eyes than it is now.

HE: I think we're more secure together now than we were then. I don't know. I would say the actual problem we haven't dealt with anymore, any differently since then, I don't believe. I don't know if we've really changed.

SHE: Do you feel any differently about it, though?

HE: How do you feel?

SHE: Well, I guess I feel that the problem two and a half and three years ago, I viewed it as something that could ruin our marriage. I was real worried about us not making it. I don't really worry about that anymore.

HE: I never considered it a threat to our marriage. I know you did, but I never did.

SHE: Okay. And maybe I'm feeling more secure now, is why I don't.

The "problem" this couple is discussing is that he has always wanted sex more frequently than she does. In this snippet of conversation she is trying to get him to agree that it's not a problem anymore. She wants his reassurance. He thinks the problem still exists, but he avoids telling her that directly.

So often when a husband and wife talk to each other about their sexual needs, their conversations are like this—indirect, imprecise,

COPING WITH TYPICAL SOLVABLE PROBLEMS *201*

inconclusive. Frequently both partners are in a hurry to end the conversation, hopeful that they will miraculously understand each other's desires without much talk. They rarely say things like "I love it when you stroke my breasts for a long time the way you did last night," or "I really need you every day," or "Mornings are my favorite times for making love," and so on. The problem is that the less clear you are about what you do and don't want, the less likely you are to get it. Sex can be such a fun way to share with each other and deepen your sense of intimacy. But when communication is fraught with tension, then frustration and hurt feelings too often result.

Solution Learn to talk to each other about sex in a way that lets you both feel safe. That means learning the right way to ask for what you want, and the appropriate way to react to your spouse's requests. Because most people feel so vulnerable about whether they are attractive to their spouse and a "good" lover, the key to talking about sex is to be gentle. A lovemaking session that starts with one partner criticizing the other is going to end faster than a "quickie." The goal of sex is to be closer, to have more fun, to feel satisfied, and to feel valued and accepted in this very tender area of your marriage. Nothing is guaranteed to make your spouse want to touch you less than if you say, "You never touch me." It's better to say, "I loved when we kissed last weekend on the big couch. I'd love more of that, it makes me feel so good." Likewise, instead of "Don't touch me there," you'll get a better response if you say, "It feels extra good when you touch me *here.*" When you talk to your partner about sex, your attitude should always be that you are making a very good thing even better. Even if you aren't satisfied with your current sex life, you need to accentuate the positive.

If you are on the receiving end of your partner's request, try very hard not to see it as an implied criticism of your attractiveness, sexual virility, lovemaking skill, or innermost being. Try to have the same attitude as a professional cook. A chef isn't insulted if a customer isn't in the mood for polenta tonight or has an aversion to squid. Instead he or she makes accommodations that will satisfy the customer's palate.

This doesn't mean that you have to agree to all of your partner's requests. It is up to both of you to decide what you feel okay and safe doing and what you don't. Sexuality is incredibly malleable, so it is really possible to make accommodations to each other's desires that will be pleasurable to both of you. For example, Mike wanted to have sex several times a week, but Lynne thought once or twice was enough. As a result, Mike felt frustrated and rejected. Over time he became more insistent that they increase the frequency. He'd bring home books and all sorts of erotica in an effort to turn Lynne on. But this just made Lynne feel pressured, which backfired. As Mike's frustration grew, Lynne's desire dwindled.

By the time they came to our workshop, Lynne and Mike had no idea how they could work out this issue. We suggested that the person with the least interest (currently Lynne) needs to feel in control. We shifted the focus from sex to sensuality. Lynne loved massages, so we suggested she go to the bookstore and select a book on massage that appealed to her. We suggested that she be in charge of the couple's sensual experience. She directed their evenings. While there was no sex per se, there was a lot of holding and touching. Gradually, Lynne's sexual desire heightened, and they began to have sex more frequently—about once a week.

Often expectations get in the way of an optimum love life. Not all sex has to be of the same quality or intensity. Sometimes it will feel like you've touched each other to the core of your souls. Other times it will just be pleasant. Sometimes sex is slow, sometimes it's brief. Variety can and ought to exist in a sexual relationship. But there do have to be times when sex is an expression of love. Obviously, the more often this occurs, the better.

The best way to enrich your love life is to learn about each other's likes and take the time to remember and memorize these things, and to use this knowledge in the way your fingers and lips touch each other. Make sure that this knowledge is really available to you when you are turned on sexually, and make this knowledge live in your body and in your sensitivity to your partner's bodily reactions. This will mean tuning into nonverbal behaviors of your partner as you are beginning to make love. But try to develop the idea that words are also acceptable as ways of communicating even during lovemaking.

A major characteristic of couples who have a happy sex life is that they see lovemaking as an expression of intimacy but they don't take any differences in their needs or desires personally.

Your sexual life will be further enhanced if you feel safe enough to share your sexual fantasies with each other and even act them out together. This is a very delicate area. Although fantasies are the home of imagination, variety, and adventure in a marriage, very few couples are able to share their fantasies and then find some way of honoring them within their sex life. If you are able to share your fantasies, the result will be great intimacy, romance, and excitement.

Try to cultivate the idea that within the boundaries of your marriage, all wishes, images, fantasies, and desires are acceptable. Nothing is intrinsically bad or disgusting. You can say no to your partner's request, but don't disparage it. Expressing a fantasy requires a great deal of trust, so take care to be tender when you hear of a fantasy your partner has. If it's not one of your own, but it's not a turn-off, then agree to it. Don't take it personally if your spouse wants you to pretend to be a stranger, a nurse, or a pirate. Just consider it play. The idea, the desire, the fantasy is usually not understood at all by the person expressing it. No one knows why particular fantasies are erotic to certain people, they just are.

There are some open manhole covers in the area of sex that you should know about. The greatest of these is a lack of basic knowledge about sex. It leads people to base their expectations for their own performance from informal and unreliable sources, mostly those heard from friends during adolescence. The result is often that we judge ourselves quite harshly and feel that we are not very good in bed. For example, many men think that they have to always be able to get an erection whenever the situation calls for it. If it doesn't happen, it is common for great self-doubt to set in. These and many other expectations are things we carry around with us without being very aware of them.

Another problem with the lack of basic knowledge is that we presume we know about one another's anatomy and sexual physiology when we have never learned about these things anywhere. We wouldn't think to run a new, complex, modern appliance without at least glancing at the manual. But in the area of sexuality, we do. Fortunately in this day and age manuals and books about sexuality are readily available in bookstores. Just don't assume that you already know about sex without reading about it. Purchase whatever appeals to you. I highly recommend the classic *The Joy of Sex,* edited by Alex Comfort (Pocket Books, 1972), Lonnie Barbach's *For Each Other* (New American Library, 1984), and Bernie Zilbergeld's *The New Male Sexuality* (Bantam, 1992).

HOUSEWORK

The task: *Creating a sense of fairness and teamwork.*

Joanne was fed up. For months she had been asking Greg not to throw his dirty laundry on the bedroom floor. For months he kept forgetting, just like he kept forgetting to vacuum the carpet and wash the dishes every night, even though he agreed that these were his jobs. Both of them worked full time, but Joanne usually got home first and would end up picking up after Greg. As she ran the vacuum or rinsed the dirty dishes that were still in the sink, she would be seething. When he got home, she'd give him the silent treatment or make sarcastic remarks about being the maid. He'd insist that the problem was that she was a terrible nag. "Maybe if you'd leave me alone about it, I'd be more likely to do it," he'd tell her.

Greg didn't realize how damaging his attitude toward housework was to his marriage until the day he arrived home to the sound of banging from the bedroom. He walked in to find his wife, still in her business suit, nailing his dirty boxer shorts to the oak floor. "They've been there for three days," she told him. "So I figured you wanted to make them a permanent part of the decor."

Joanne and Greg eventually divorced, so I'm not suggesting that the solution to housekeeping conflicts can be found at the nearest hardware store. The point is that men often don't realize how deeply women care about keeping their home in order. There are certainly exceptions to the gender differences in this area, but as a general rule, in the *Odd Couple* spectrum of cleanliness, women skew more toward the fastidious Felix and men toward slovenly Oscar.

When a husband doesn't do his agreed-upon share of the housework, the wife usually feels disrespected and unsupported. Inevitably this leads to resentment and a less satisfying marriage. Many husbands just don't understand why housework is such a big deal to their wives. They may not be slackers on purpose. But many were raised in traditional homes where their father did no housework at all. A husband may pay lip service to the notion that times have changed and that it isn't fair for his wife to work a second shift when she gets home while he pops open a beer. But old ways die hard. On some level many men still consider housework to be a woman's job. When the husband helps, he feels he should be applauded—but instead his wife keeps demanding he do more, which makes him defensive and likely to do less.

A major cause of this unfortunate dynamic is that Greg, like most men, tends to overestimate the amount of housework he does. This has been documented by British sociologist Ann Oakley. I know this is true in my own home. When I complain that I'm doing all of the housework, my wife says, "Good!" because she knows that means I'm actually doing half.

Solution By now the key to resolving this issue should be clear: Men have to do more housework! Sometimes men shirk their responsibility in this department due to a sheer lack of motivation. Let's face it—no one wants to trudge out the recycling bags in the snow. So maybe this little fact will spark a husband's enthusiasm for domestic chores: *Women find a man's willingness to do housework extremely erotic.* When the husband does his share to maintain the home, both he and his wife report a more satisfying sex life than in marriages where the wife believes her husband is not doing his share. The benefits to these marriages extend beyond the bedroom. In these relationships the women also have significantly lower heart rates during marital arguments, which means they are less likely to begin a discussion harshly and so avoid triggering that whole downward spiral of conflict involving the four horsemen and flooding that leads to divorce.

I'm not suggesting that every husband must do a straight 50 percent of the housework if he wants to save his marriage and see his sex life improve. The key is not the actual amount he does but his wife's subjective view of whether it's enough. For one couple this could indeed mean an even split of chores. But in another marriage the wife may be just as satisfied if he takes care of some chores she hates—like cleaning the bathroom or vacuuming—or even if he agrees to budget for a weekly housekeeper to lighten both their loads.

The best way to figure out how much housework a husband needs to do is for the couple to talk over the following list. By itemizing exactly who does what, you'll finally have an objective basis for determining who *should* do what.

Use the list to describe to each other first your perception of how things are currently handled and then how you would like them to be. This list extends beyond actual cleaning to other domestic chores—like family finances and various aspects of child care—that can also be causes of conflict if the distribution of labor is seen as unfair.

You may find that certain patterns emerge. As I said, men often believe that they are doing a larger share of domestic chores than is actually the case. In many marriages the husband does more of the "brute strength" tasks like washing the car or mowing the lawn, or the abstract jobs like financial planning that don't have to be done on a daily basis or on a strict timetable. The wife carries more than her share of the mindless, daily drudge work—like cleaning and picking up—which leaves her resentful.

Who Does What List

Running errands	Now:	Ideal:
Taking clothes to the cleaners	Now:	Ideal:
Washing windows	Now:	Ideal:
Planning the food menu	Now:	Ideal
Going grocery shopping	Now:	Ideal:
Cooking dinner	Now:	Ideal:
Setting the table	Now:	Ideal:
Cleanup after dinner	Now:	Ideal:
Cleaning the kitchen	Now:	Ideal:
Cleaning the bathrooms	Now:	Ideal:
Putting out clean towels	Now:	Ideal:
Keeping counters clean	Now:	Ideal:
General tidying up	Now:	Ideal:
Getting the car serviced	Now:	Ideal:
Putting gas in the car	Now:	Ideal:
Sorting incoming mail	Now:	Ideal:
Paying the bills	Now:	Ideal:
Balancing the checkbook	Now:	Ideal:
Writing letters	Now:	Ideal:
Taking phone messages	Now:	Ideal:
Returning phone calls or e-mail	Now	Ideal:
Saving money	Now:	Ideal:
Taking out garbage and trash	Now:	Ideal:

Recycling	Now:	Ideal:
Doing the laundry	Now:	Ideal:
Folding the laundry	Now:	Ideal:
Ironing	Now:	Ideal:
Putting the clean clothes away	Now:	Ideal:
Sweeping kitchen and eating areas	Now:	Ideal:
Vacuuming	Now:	Ideal:
Washing and waxing floors	Now:	Ideal:
Changing lightbulbs	Now:	Ideal:
Repair of appliances	Now:	Ideal:
Making the beds	Now:	Ideal:
Defrosting and cleaning refrigerator	Now:	Ideal:
Shopping for clothing	Now:	Ideal:
Planning travel	Now:	Ideal:
Home repair	Now:	Ideal:
Remodeling	Now:	Ideal:
Home maintenance	Now:	Ideal:
Buying furniture	Now:	Ideal:
Redecorating home	Now:	Ideal:
Buying items for the home	Now:	Ideal:
Buying new appliances	Now:	Ideal:
Sewing and mending	Now:	Ideal:
Straightening kitchen cabinets	Now:	Ideal:
Yard and garden work	Now:	Ideal:

Lawn, tree, and shrubbery maintenance	Now:	Ideal:
Errands to the bank	Now:	Ideal:
Houseplant care	Now:	Ideal:
Straightening and rearranging closets	Now:	Ideal:
Getting house ready for guests	Now:	Ideal:
Party preparations	Now:	Ideal:
Buying children gifts	Now:	Ideal:
Taking children to school	Now:	Ideal:
Picking children up from school	Now:	Ideal:
Child care after school	Now:	Ideal:
Child meals and lunches	Now:	Ideal:
Pediatrician	Now:	Ideal:
Child homework	Now:	Ideal:
Child baths	Now:	Ideal:
Child discipline	Now:	Ideal:
Bedtime with kids	Now:	Ideal:
Dealing with a sick child	Now:	Ideal:
Handling child crises	Now:	Ideal:
Dealing with a child's emotions	Now:	Ideal:
Teacher conferences	Now:	Ideal:
Dealing with the schools	Now:	Ideal:
Special children's events	Now:	Ideal:
Child birthday and other parties	Now:	Ideal:
Child's lessons	Now:	Ideal:

Child's play dates	Now:	Ideal:
Shopping for children's stuff	Now:	Ideal:
Buying presents	Now:	Ideal:
Keeping in touch with kin	Now:	Ideal:
Preparing for holidays	Now:	Ideal:
Planning vacations	Now:	Ideal:
Planning getaways	Now:	Ideal:
Planning romantic dates	Now:	Ideal:
Planning quiet evenings at home	Now:	Ideal:
Planning weekends	Now:	Ideal:
Initiating lovemaking	Now:	Ideal:
Planning dinner out	Now:	Ideal:
Family outings, drives, picnics	Now:	Ideal:
Financial planning	Now:	Ideal:
Major purchases (cars, etc.)	Now:	Ideal:
Managing investments	Now:	Ideal:
Talking about the relationship	Now:	Ideal:
Get-togethers with friends	Now:	Ideal:
Keeping in touch with friends	Now:	Ideal:
Doing the taxes	Now:	Ideal:
Legal matters (e.g., wills)	Now:	Ideal:
Coordinating family's medical care	Now:	Ideal:
Drugs and other health areas	Now:	Ideal:
Exercise and fitness	Now:	Ideal:
Recreational outings	Now:	Ideal:

Now you should have a clear sense of which tasks you currently share and which fall into each partner's domain. Depending on what you consider ideal, it may be time to redivide domestic tasks so that the load is more equitable. Remember, the quantity of the husband's housework is not necessarily a determining factor in the housework = sex equation. But two other variables are. The first is whether the husband does his chores without his wife having to ask (nag). A husband who does this earns enormous points in the emotional bank account. The other factor is whether he is flexible in his duties in response to her needs. For example, if he sees that she's especially tired one night, does he volunteer to wash the dishes even though it's her turn? This conveys that all-important honor and respect for her. Helping his wife in this way will turn her on more than any "adults only" video.

BECOMING PARENTS

The task: *Expanding your sense of "we-ness" to include your children.*

"A child is a grenade. When you have a baby, you set off an explosion in your marriage, and when the dust settles, your marriage is different from what it was. Not better, necessarily; not worse, necessarily; but different." So wrote Nora Ephron in *Heartburn,* her *roman à clef* about the breakup of her previous marriage. Virtually every study that has looked at how people make the transition from couplehood to parenthood confirms her view. A baby sets off seismic changes in a marriage. Unfortunately, most of the time those changes are for the worse. In the year after the first baby arrives, 70 percent of wives experience a precipitous plummet in their marital satisfaction. (For the husband, the dissatisfaction usually kicks in later, as a reaction to his wife's unhappiness.) There are wide-ranging reasons for this deep disgruntlement—lack of sleep, feeling overwhelmed and unappreciated, the awesome responsibility of caring for such a helpless little creature, juggling mothering with a job, economic stress, and lack of time to oneself, among other things.

The big mystery is not why 67 percent of new mothers feel so miserable, but why the other 33 percent just seem to sail through the transition to motherhood unscathed. (In fact, some of these mothers say their marriage has never been better.) Thanks to the 130 couples we've followed from their newlywed stage to as long as eight years afterward, I now know the secret to keeping a marriage happy and stable even after the "grenade" explodes. What separates these blissful mothers from the rest has nothing to do with whether their baby is colicky or a good sleeper, whether they are nursing or bottle-feeding, working or staying home. Rather, it has everything to do with whether the husband experiences the transformation to parenthood along with his wife or gets left behind.

Having a baby almost inevitably causes a metamorphosis in the new mother. She has never felt a love as deep and selfless as the one she feels for her child. Almost always a new mother experiences nothing less than a profound reorientation of meaning in her life. She discovers she is willing to make enormous sacrifices for her child. She feels awe and wonder at the intensity of her feelings for this fragile little being. The experience is so life-altering that if her husband doesn't go through it with her, it is understandable that distance would develop between them. While the wife is embracing a new sense of "we-ness" that includes their child, the husband may still be pining for the old "us." So he can't help but resent how little time she seems to have for him now, how tired she always is, how often she's preoccupied with feeding the baby. He resents that they can't ride their bikes to the beach anymore because the baby is too small to sit up in a back carrier. He loves his child, but he wants his wife back. What's a husband to do?

The answer to his dilemma is simple: He can't get his wife back—he has to follow her into the new realm she has entered. Only then can their marriage continue to grow. In marriages where the husband is able to do this, he doesn't resent his child. He no longer feels like only a husband, but like a father, too. He feels pride, tenderness, and protectiveness toward his offspring.

How can a couple ensure that the husband is transformed along with his wife? First, the couple need to ignore some popular bad advice. Many well-meaning experts recommend that you consider marriage and family a balancing act, as if your lives are a seesaw with the baby on one end and your marriage on the other. Couples are counseled to spend some time away from the baby and focus on their marriage and outside interests: talk about your relationship, your job, her job, the weather, anything but the baby at home. But marriage and family are not diametrically opposed. Rather, they are of one cloth. Yes, the couple should spend time away from the baby occasionally. But if they are making this transition well together, they will find that they can't stop talking about the baby, nor do they want to. They might not even get through that first meal without calling home—at least twice. Too often, such couples are made to feel as if they have done something wrong because they have made their own relationship seemingly secondary to their new roles as parents. The result is that they feel all the more stressed and confused. But in fact, they have done something very right. The important thing here is that they are in it together. To the extent that both husband and wife make this philosophical shift, the parent-child relationship *and* the marriage thrive.

Here are some more tips to help couples stay connected as they evolve into parents.

Focus on your marital friendship. Before the baby comes, make sure that you really know each other and your respective worlds intimately. The more of a team you are now, the easier the transition will be. If a husband knows his wife, he will be in better tune with her as she begins her journey to motherhood.

Don't exclude Dad from baby care. Sometimes, in her exuberance, a new mother comes off as a know-it-all to her husband. While she pays lip service to the idea that they should share the baby's care, she casts herself into a supervisory role, constantly directing—if not ordering—the new father and even chastising him if he doesn't do things exactly her way: "Don't hold her like that,"

"You didn't burp him enough." "The bath water's too cold." In the face of this barrage, some husbands are more than happy to withdraw, to cede the role of expert to their wives (after all, their own fathers never knew anything about babies, either) and accept their own incompetence. The sad result is that they do less and less and therefore become less and less accomplished and confident in caring for their own child. Inevitably, they begin to feel more excluded.

The solution is simple. The new mother needs to back off. She needs to realize that there's more than one way to burp a baby. If she doesn't like her husband's way, she should remember that the baby is his child too and will benefit from experiencing more than one parenting style. A few baths in tepid water are a small price for an infant—and a marriage—to pay for the father's ongoing commitment to his family. If the mother feels her husband's approach is really unsafe, she should direct him to their pediatrician, Dr. Spock's tome, or some other edifying baby-care guide. Some small, well-timed doses of gentle advice-giving are fine (don't forget to use a softened startup), but lectures and criticism will backfire.

Feeding time can be especially difficult for the new dad. Penis envy may well be a Freudian myth, but breast envy is alive and well in almost every home where the wife is nursing an infant. Fathers can't help but feel jealous when they see that beautiful bond developing between their wife and baby. It's as if the two have formed a charmed circle that he just can't enter. In response to this need, some baby-care catalogs actually offer devices that allow men a close approximation of the nursing experience. There is, for example, an attachment that you can strap onto your chest that delivers warm milk to the baby through plastic breasts! But most couples don't need to resort to extra equipment to help the man feel included. Instead, they can find a role for the husband in the ritual of breastfeeding. For example, it can be the husband's job to carry the baby to the mother at feeding time. He can also be the official "burper." He could also make it his custom to sit quietly with his wife and child during feeding times, gently stroking the baby's head, for example, or singing to his baby.

Let Dad be baby's playmate. Some men have admitted to me that they don't feel much connection with their baby until the child gets older and can walk, talk, and play. Unfortunately, by then their distance from family life has created fissures in their marriage. The reason men may take longer to "bond" with their children is that, as countless studies have confirmed, women tend to be more nurturing toward children while men are more playful. And since most men assume you can't really play with a helpless baby, they don't feel engaged by their child for much of the crucial first year.

But dads who spend time with their young babies will discover that they are not "blobs" who do nothing but cry, nurse, poop, and sleep. Even newborns can be great playmates. Babies begin to smile at a mere three weeks. Even earlier than that they can track movements with their eyes. Soon they are chortling, kicking their legs in delight. In short, the father who gets to know his babies by bathing, diapering, and feeding them will inevitably find that they love to play with him and that he has a special role in their lives.

Carve out time for the two of you. Part of the transition to parenthood entails placing a priority (albeit usually second place) on the marriage itself. So you should use a baby-sitter, a relative, or friend to get some time alone with each other. But remember, you haven't failed if you end up spending a lot of your "dates" discussing the baby—you've succeeded. As the baby grows into a toddler and then becomes school-aged, you'll find that your conversations when you're alone together won't always gravitate toward your child and your role as parents.

Be sensitive to Dad's needs. Even if he is a good team player and is making the philosophical shift toward parenthood along with his wife, the man is still going to feel somewhat deprived by the baby's overwhelming and seemingly endless need for her. Even if, intellectually, he understands that the baby's needs supplant his own in priority, he's going to miss his wife. The more his wife acknowledges what he has given up and lets him know how central he still is to her life, the more understanding and supportive he will be able to be. If she never has any time for just the marriage, he will have a tendency to withdraw from the relationship.

Give Mom a break. For all the daily wonders a mother experiences during the newborn stage, she is also likely to be exhausted. It will help their marriage if her husband will modify his work hours so he can come home earlier and on the weekends take over for her now and then so that she can get a needed break to sleep, see a friend, or a movie, or do whatever else she needs to feel part of the world again.

Couples who follow this advice will discover that parenthood doesn't drag down their relationship but elevates it to a new level of closeness, understanding, and love for each other.

In this chapter I've tried to give you practical advice to help you solve some common marital problems. But sometimes, no matter how diligently you try to end a conflict, it just can't be done. If that's the case, you are dealing with a perpetual problem. Avoiding or breaking out of gridlock over such a problem is one of the chief challenges all couples face. My next principle will show you just how to save—or protect—your marriage from your irreconcilable differences.

10
Principle 6:
Overcome Gridlock

*Y*ou want to have children, he doesn't. She wants you to attend church with her, you're an atheist. He's a homebody, you're ready for a party every night. If you feel hopelessly gridlocked over a problem that just can't be solved, it can be cold comfort to know that other couples handle similar conflicts with aplomb, treating them the way they would a bad back or allergies. When you're gridlocked, trying to view your differences as a kind of psychological trick knee that you can learn to cope with may seem impossible. But you *can* do it.

The goal in ending gridlock is not to solve the problem, but rather to move from gridlock to dialogue. The gridlocked conflict will probably always be a perpetual issue in your marriage, but one day you will be able to talk about it without hurting each other. You will learn to live with the problem.

To navigate your way out of gridlock, you have to first understand its cause. Whether the issue is momentous, like which of your religions to pass on to your children, or ridiculous, like which way to fold dinner napkins, gridlock is a sign that you have dreams for your life that aren't being addressed or respected by each other. By dreams I mean the hopes, aspirations, and wishes that are part of your identity and give purpose and meaning to your life.

Dreams can operate at many different levels. Some are very practical (such as wanting to achieve a certain amount of savings), but others are profound. Often these deeper dreams remain hidden while the more mundane dreams piggyback on top of them and are easier to see. For example, underneath the dream to make lots of money may be a deep need for security.

WHAT DREAMS ARE MADE OF

Often our deepest dreams are rooted in childhood. You may long to re-create some of your warmest memories of family life from your youth—such as having dinner together every night without interruptions from the TV or telephone. Or, you may feel the psychological need to distance yourself from painful childhood memories by not duplicating the same activities. For example, you may resist having family dinners if the evening meal in your childhood home was often the scene of hostility between your parents that left you with indigestion.

Here is a list of some common "deep" dreams expressed by couples I've worked with.

1. A sense of freedom
2. The experience of peace
3. Unity with nature
4. Exploring who I am
5. Adventure
6. A spiritual journey
7. Justice
8. Honor
9. Unity with my past
10. Healing
11. Knowing my family

12. Becoming all I can be
13. Having a sense of power
14. Dealing with growing older
15. Exploring a creative side of myself
16. Becoming more powerful
17. Getting over past hurts
18. Becoming more competent
19. Asking God for forgiveness
20. Exploring an old part of myself I have lost
21. Getting over a personal hang-up
22. Having a sense of order
23. Being able to be productive
24. A place and a time to just "be"
25. Being able to truly relax
26. Reflecting on my life
27. Getting my priorities in order
28. Finishing something important
29. Exploring the physical side of myself
30. Being able to compete and win
31. Travel
32. Quietness
33. Atonement
34. Building something important
35. Ending a chapter of my life—saying good-bye to something

All of these dreams are beautiful. None of them are inherently bad for a marriage. But they can cause problems if they are hidden or not respected by your spouse. When this occurs, you may either have open battles over the issue, or it may go underground and be expressed symbolically. In the latter case, the couple may think they are at loggerheads over whether to go out to dinner every Sunday night, but the bottom-line issue has to do with something much deeper than a restaurant meal. Sunday night holds a special place in both of their hearts, stemming from their childhoods. Her dream is to eat out because her family did that every Sunday, a treat that made her feel special. But for her husband, a restaurant meal was always much less of a treat than having his very busy mother cook for the family—something she only did on Sundays. So the question of a restaurant versus a home meal is really symbolic of what makes each of them feel loved.

WHEN DREAMS ARE RESPECTED

Why do some couples cope so gracefully with these sorts of issues while others get bogged down? The difference is that the happy couple understands that helping each other realize their dreams is one of the goals of marriage. "We want to know what the other person wants in their life," says Justine, referring to herself and her husband, Michael. But she could just as well be talking for all emotionally intelligent couples. In happy marriages partners incorporate each other's goals into their concept of what their marriage is about. These goals can be as concrete as wanting to live in a certain kind of house or to get a certain academic degree. But they can also be intangible, such as wanting to feel safe or wanting to view life as a grand adventure.

Shelley wants to go to college. Malcolm's hefty paycheck allows her to do that. But he wants to quit his high-pressure marketing job because his dream is to be his own boss and build boats. In a happy marriage neither spouse insists or attempts to manipulate the other into giving up their dream. They work it out as a team. They fully take into account each other's wishes and desires.

Maybe Malcolm decides to keep at the grind till Shelley finishes school. Maybe Shelley studies part time or suspends her studies for an agreed-upon length of time. Maybe practicality demands that one or both of their dreams be put on hold for a while. Whatever they decide to do isn't really the issue. The point is that their concept of their marriage incorporates supporting both of these dreams. The way they go about making such decisions—with mutual respect for and acknowledgment of each other's aspirations—is part of what makes their marriage meaningful to them.

A Horse Named Daphne

When either spouse doesn't fully appreciate the importance of supporting his or her partner's dreams, gridlock is almost inevitable. That was the root cause of the severe marital problems between Ed and Luanne, a Seattle couple who were interviewed in my Love Lab for *Dateline NBC*. When Ed and Luanne were in the lab together, you could see that their fondness and affection were still there. But they were experiencing enormous stress over Daphne, Luanne's nine-year-old horse, which she often competed with in horse shows.

Before they were married, Ed was very taken with Daphne. But now that he was confronted with the monthly bills for her care and maintenance, she became a source of tension between him and his wife. He wanted Luanne to sell the horse so that they could save money. The more he and Luanne argued over selling Daphne the more he feared, deep down, that she cared for the horse more than she did for him and their marriage.

The couple talked out this problem in three fifteen-minute sessions, snippets of which were aired on the show. In between those sessions my team and I coached them, using the sorts of techniques you'll find in this chapter. Luanne was told not to give up on her dream *and* to make sure that Ed understood that he came first in her heart. I helped Ed understand that helping Luanne realize her dream to compete in horse shows with Daphne was part of his role as her spouse. He also needed to accept Luanne's influence when it came to making financial decisions. By the end of the three sessions Ed and Luanne had made a major leap forward in their marriage. When Ed told her he would support her decision to keep Daphne, her wide smile lit up the screen.

Today, two and a half years later, Ed and Luanne are happily married. Luanne has sold Daphne (though she still visits her) in order to lease a younger horse. She continues to compete in horse shows and Ed continues to support her right to do so.

WHEN DREAMS ARE HIDDEN

For Ed and Luanne it was apparent that a dream was the root cause of their conflict. The challenge was to respect the dream and each other's needs. But for many couples the dream that is at the core of the conflict is not so obvious. Only by uncovering this dream can the couple get out of gridlock.

Take the case of Katherine and Jeff. They were happily married until Katherine became pregnant. Suddenly, it seemed to Jeff, her Catholic faith took on a much more central role in her life. He himself was an agnostic. When he found out that she had been talking with her father about having the baby baptized, he was livid. He did not want his child to have any kind of formal religious instruction.

By the time Katherine and Jeff discussed this conflict in my lab, they had clearly become gridlocked. I could tell that their marriage was in serious danger because they were emotionally distant from each other. Even while discussing the highly personal issues of faith and family, they didn't raise their voices, cry, smile, or touch each other. They were able to talk intellectually about their difference of opinion, but they were emotionally disengaged. And since their problem was really an emotional one—concerning their feelings about families, parenthood, and religion—no amount of careful intellectual analysis would be able to resolve it.

At their next session, I suggested that instead of trying to solve the issue, they should just listen to each other talk about what religion symbolized to them. This was the only way to get to the hidden dreams that were fueling the conflict. Katherine went first. She described how her beliefs had carried her through very hard times. Her parents went through a rancorous divorce. For ten years her father had no contact with the family. Her mother became so depressed that Katherine couldn't depend on her. She felt completely unloved and alone until she turned to the Church, which embraced her. Not only did she feel a kinship with her fellow worshipers but she felt comforted by prayer. When all the chips were down, feeling God's love brought her deep comfort. Katherine started crying as she remembered those hard times and the solace she found in religion.

Jeff explained that he had been an agnostic his entire life. In contrast to Katherine's dysfunctional family, his was very strong and loving. When he went through hard times, he always turned to his parents. He wanted his child to feel the same trust in him and Katherine. He feared that if their son was "indoctrinated" into the Church, this would interfere with that bond; the child would be trained to turn to God instead of his parents.

Jeff and Katherine had opposing dreams: He envisioned them as a happy family that would supply all the love and support their children needed. He saw religion as a threat to their deep connection. Katherine viewed religion as a vital support system that she wanted to ensure was there for her children.

Once these dreams were discussed openly, the mood in the room changed dramatically. Jeff told Katherine that he loved her. It finally sank in to him that her desire to baptize their baby came out of her deep love for their child—for *his* child. He realized it made "perfect sense" that out of this love she would want to protect the baby from ever feeling the pain she had experienced. This helped him reconnect with his own deep feelings for Katherine, which had gotten buried under all of the bitterness and anger.

In the first session no emotion had passed between the couple. But this time you could see the compassion on Jeff's face as he listened to his wife recount her childhood. When she cried, he handed her tissues and encouraged her to keep talking. Katherine listened just as intently to his side of the story.

Now that the real issues were out in the open, they were able to talk about how they could raise their son in a way that honored both their visions. Jeff told her he wouldn't oppose the baptism. He himself would always be agnostic, but it was okay with him if the child received rudimentary training in Catholicism. However, he still opposed intensive religious study, because he feared the Church might impose ideas on the child. Katherine was able to accept this compromise.

Deep issues like these are unlikely to be declawed in just one session. But Jeff and Katherine made an important first step. They turned toward each other and acknowledged with respect each other's dreams for their child. They agreed to seek further counseling to build on the success of the lab session. Will this issue ever go away or be resolved in their marriage? Probably not. But they have begun to learn to live with it peacefully.

If you've reached gridlock on any issue in your marriage, big or small, the first step is to identify which dream or dreams are fueling the conflict. One good indicator that you're wrestling with a hidden dream is that you see your spouse as being the sole source of the marital problem. If you find yourself saying, for example, that the problem is simply that *he* is a slob or *she* is just irresponsible or overly demanding, that's a sign of a hidden dream. It may indicate that you don't see your part in creating the conflict because it has been hidden from view.

Uncovering a hidden dream is a challenge. The dream is unlikely to emerge until you feel that your marriage is a safe place to talk about it. That's why it's important to begin by working on my first three principles, outlined in Chapters 3, 4, and 5, in order to strengthen your friendship with your mate.

Keep working on your unresolvable conflicts. Couples who are demanding of their marriage are more likely to have deeply satisfying unions than those who lower their expectations.

You may find that when you first begin to recognize and acknowledge your dreams, the problem between you and your spouse seems to get worse rather than better. Be patient. Acknowledging and advocating for your dreams in a marriage is not easy. The very nature of gridlock means that your dream and your spouse's appear to be in opposition, so you've both become deeply entrenched in your positions and fear accepting each other's influence and yielding.

Once you're ready to overcome gridlock, here's how to proceed.

Step 1: Become a Dream Detective

Often, deeply personal dreams go unspoken or underground after marriage because we assume they must in order to make the relationship work. It's common for both partners not to feel entitled to their complaints. They may see their own desires as "childish" or "impractical." But such labels don't change the fact that the dream is something you long for, and if the marriage doesn't honor it, conflict will almost inevitably ensue. In other words, when you adjust to marriage by burying a dream, it just resurfaces in disguised form—as a gridlocked conflict.

Exercise 1: Detecting Dreams

This exercise will give you plenty of practice in uncovering hidden dreams without, at first, focusing on your own marriage. Below are six examples of common gridlocked conflicts. Read each one, and think about what dreams may be hidden inside each partner's perspective. Make up a brief story, or narrative, that explains the husband's dream and his position, then do the same for the wife. In each case imagine that this is your position and that it is very hard for you to yield. Think of what your position means to you and where this dream may come from in your past. Imagining other people's dreams will help you unlock the door to those causing gridlock in your own marriage.

This is a creative exercise that has no right or wrong answers. To get you started, we've included the suggested dreams and stories for the first two couples. For the rest of the couples, you'll find this material on page 229. Try not to look at our stories about these couples' dreams until you've come up with your own. You'll get far more out of this exercise if you do it yourself.

Couple 1

HUSBAND: I think my wife is too neat and tidy. I find myself constantly trying to find things after she has cleaned up. I think she is being inconsiderate and overly controlling, and I'm tired of it.

My Dreams Within This Conflict Might Be:

My parents were very strict disciplinarians. They saw any disagreement with them as insubordination. As a result I became somewhat of a rebel. I freely admit that I have a problem with authority, and that's why I decided to build my own business. My dream is to have a home where I can be myself, and that means not following any rigid set of rules. I want my kids to challenge authority and think for themselves, not simply learn to be obedient. I myself want to be free in my home, including being sloppy at times.

WIFE: I like a certain amount of order and neatness in our home. I find myself constantly cleaning up my husband's messes. I think he is being inconsiderate, and I am tired of this.

My Dreams Within This Conflict Might Be:

I grew up in a totally chaotic home. There was nothing I could count on as a child. I never knew who was driving me to school or picking me up. My mom would sometimes forget to pick me up, and I hated her for that sometimes. Then I would get home, and there would often be no dinner and no clean clothes. It fell on my shoulders to create all the order and sense of responsibility for my younger sibs. I resented having to do all that. My dream is to provide a much healthier family environment for my kids and family. To me order means predictability, security, and peacefulness. I want that for my kids. When the house is a mess, it takes me back to the chaos of my youth.

Couple 2

HUSBAND: My wife is very emotional and claims that I am far too unemotional. This difference between us makes me feel that she is overreactive and out of control at times, perhaps overly sensitive. I think that being rational is usually the best approach to strong emotional situations, not getting more emotional. My wife claims that I am hard to read and too distant.

My Dreams Within This Conflict Might Be:

I grew up in a family where everyone was a debater. We loved to argue with one another. My dad always asked a question, challenged me, and then took a contrary position to mine. Then the debate was on. It was no holds barred, and we all loved it. But getting emotional was illegal in this debating contest. Once someone got emotional, the argument was over. So staying in emotional control was highly prized in my family. It still is. So maybe I should be more emotional, but it's not in my makeup. My dream is to be strong. I think of being emotional as a weakness.

WIFE: I am a very emotional person and my husband is far too unemotional. This difference between us makes me feel that my partner is cold and "fake" at times, not really present. Many times I have no idea what he is feeling. I am frustrated by this difference between us.

My Dreams Within This Conflict Might Be:

I am just an emotional person and that's all there is to it. I think that's what life is all about, feeling things, being in contact, responding. That's what "responsible" ought to mean, "response-able," or able to respond. That's the highest value for me. I respond to everything around me, to great art, to architecture, to children, to puppies, to competition in athletics, to sad movies, to everything. To be emotional just means being alive. This is the way I was raised, and I'm glad. My dream is to share my emotions with the person I love. If I can't the marriage is doomed to seem dead, fake, and lonely.

Couple 3

HUSBAND: My wife is overly jealous, especially at parties. I think that social occasions are a time to meet new people, which I find very interesting. But my wife gets clingy and shy. She claims that I flirt with other women at parties, but this isn't true at all. I find the accusation insulting, and it makes me angry. I don't know how to reassure my wife, and I'm tired of not being trusted.

My Dreams Within This Conflict Might Be:

WIFE: At parties and other places my husband looks at other women and acts flirtatious. I find this upsetting and demeaning. I have brought this up repeatedly but cannot get him to stop.

My Dreams Within This Conflict Might Be:

Couple 4

WIFE: My husband likes to have sex much more often than I do. I don't know what to do when he keeps approaching me for sexual intimacy. I don't know how to say no in a gentle way. This pattern makes me feel like an ogre. I don't know how to deal with this.

My Dreams Within This Conflict Might Be:

HUSBAND: I like to have sex much more often than my wife. I keep getting my feelings hurt when she turns me down. This pattern makes me feel unattractive and unwanted. I don't know how to deal with this.

My Dreams Within This Conflict Might Be:

Couple 5

WIFE: I think that my husband is far too stingy when it comes to money and doesn't believe in spending enough on just enjoying life and having fun. I also resent not having more personal freedom and control when it comes to money.

My Dreams Within This Conflict Might Be:

HUSBAND: I think that my wife is impractical when it comes to money and spends far too thoughtlessly and selfishly.

My Dreams Within This Conflict Might Be:

Couple 6

WIFE: My husband likes to stay in much closer touch with our families than I do. To me family connections are great sources of stress and disappointment. I have broken away from my family, and I want much greater distance.

My Dreams Within This Conflict Might Be:

HUSBAND: I like to stay in much closer touch with my family than my wife does. To me family connections are very important. She wants greater independence from our families than I do.

My Dreams Within This Conflict Might Be:

Sample Dreams

Couple 3

HUSBAND: *I really do not flirt, nor do I have any interest in anyone but my spouse. It's just that parties are my only way of really satisfying my gregarious and wild side. I really don't want to be responsible for anyone else when I go to a party. My dream is to feel the freedom to explore.*

WIFE: *I have always wanted to be able to feel that I was "enough" for someone special in my life. That is my dream: to feel truly attractive and desirable to my partner. I want my partner to be interested in me, in knowing me and finding out what I think, wanting to know what I am like inside. I would find it incredibly romantic if I could go to a party with my husband and he didn't even notice that there was anyone else there, had eyes only for me, and was totally satisfied spending hours in rapt conversation and dancing with just me.*

Couple 4

WIFE: *I was sexually mistreated long ago. I had no control over this, and it was quite horrible, but it did happen. I know my partner is not to blame for many of the feelings I now have. But I feel that sex can be okay only if it is on my terms. In my marriage there has been a lot of healing and gentleness, but I probably will never get over these feelings of having gone through a real trauma. My dream is to have sexual closeness on my terms only.*

HUSBAND: *My dream is to have my partner initiate sexual encounters with me and somehow be "swept away" by passion, I guess to really be totally attracted to me. I know I am not especially much to look at, but on some days I am not too bad. I periodically want my partner to feel that I am simply irresistible.*

Couple 5

WIFE: *Life is too short to just save for the future all the time. I know that a certain amount of that is necessary, but I want to have some sense that I am not living just for tomorrow. I don't want to feel that life is passing me by. And that's what I often feel, that I am not special enough to "waste" money on. I want to feel special and very alive. Where this comes from is, I suppose, always having to scrimp when I was poor. But now I make a good income, and I don't have to live like that anymore.*

HUSBAND: *I want to enjoy life, but within limits. To me the problem with the world is greed. People never seem to be able to have enough "stuff" or get enough money. Just look at Americans on vacation, with all their things, campers, motorcycles, boats, cars. I don't want to want things. I want to be satisfied with just a small amount of things and a small amount of money. I honestly don't need very much to be happy. So I see myself as kind of like a monk, who has a purpose in life, and I do have that. A monk can be satisfied with very little, contented, counting all the blessings in life, and there are so many. So I believe in saving and spending very little. To me that's how one should lead a moral life. Where does this come from? I think it comes from my father, who also was very frugal. Thanks to him our family always did well, and when he died, my mom was well provided for. I respect what he accomplished.*

Couple 6

WIFE: *It took me a great deal of effort to get away from a very dysfunctional family. My parents were very cold and distant. My sister wound up in a mental hospital, and my brother became a drug addict. I was the only one who escaped. I escaped by becoming very distant from my family and becoming very close to my friends. Friendships have always meant a lot to me and continue to be very important. But I am wary of being close to my husband's family. I see a lot of dysfunctional patterns, and they scare me. My dream is for us to form our own family traditions and maintain our own independence.*

HUSBAND: *To me a feeling of an extended family has always been very important. I can recall many a Sunday when my mother would have twenty or thirty family members visit. The coffee and pastries would keep coming all afternoon, and there would be lots of good stories, and card playing, and lots of laughter. Then there would be great food for dinner. Even during the hard times, my mother was always able to stretch the soup and it stayed thick and hearty. My dream is to have this family feeling of community, closeness, and great comfort in my own family.*

STEP 2: WORK ON A GRIDLOCKED MARITAL ISSUE

Now that you have had some practice uncovering dreams, try it with your own marriage. Choose a particular gridlocked conflict to work on. Then write an explanation of your position. Don't criticize or blame your spouse. Use the statements made by the couples above as your guide—notice that they don't bad-mouth each other. Instead, they focus on what each partner needs, wants, and is feeling about the situation. Next, write the story of the hidden dreams that underlie your position. Explain where these dreams come from and why they are so meaningful to you.

Once you both understand which dreams are fueling the gridlock, it's time to talk about them. Each person gets fifteen minutes as the speaker and fifteen minutes as the listener. Do not try to solve this problem. Attempting to do that now is likely to backfire. Your goal is simply to understand *why* each of you feels so strongly about this issue.

Speaker's job: Talk honestly about your position and what it means to you. Describe the dream that's fueling it. Explain where the dream comes from and what it symbolizes. Be clear and honest about what you want and why it is so important. Talk as if you were explaining your dream to a good friend or neutral third party. Don't try to censor or downplay your feelings about your dream in order to avoid hurting or arguing with your spouse. If you find this difficult, review the advice in Chapter 8 about softening the startup. Some of the same approaches hold: namely, to make "I" statements and to talk only about *your* feelings and *your* needs. This is not the time to criticize or argue with your partner. How you feel about your spouse in relationship to this dream is a satellite issue that should not be addressed right now.

Listener's job: Suspend judgment. Listen the way a friend would listen. Don't take your spouse's dream personally even though it clashes with one of yours. Don't spend your time thinking up rebuttals or ways to solve the problem. Your role now is just to hear the dream and to encourage your spouse to explore it. Here are some supportive questions to ask. You don't have to use these verbatim—put the thought and spirit behind them into your own words.

- "Tell me the story of that. I'd like to understand what it means to you."
- "What do you believe about this issue?"
- "What do you feel about it?"
- "What do you want? What do you need?"
- "What do these things **mean** to you?"

Don't:

GEORGIA: I've always dreamed of going on a mountain-climbing expedition to Mount Everest.

NATHAN: First of all, we can't possibly afford something like that. Besides, I can't think of anything more stressful than mountain climbing. I get vertigo standing on a table.

GEORGIA: Forget it.

Do:

GEORGIA: I've always dreamed of going on a mountain-climbing expedition to Mount Everest.

NATHAN: Tell me more about what it means to you to climb a mountain. What would it do for you?

GEORGIA: I think I would feel exhilarated, like I was at the top of the world. As a child I was always told that I was weak and couldn't do anything. My parents were always saying "careful, careful." I think climbing a mountain would be the most liberating thing I could do. I'd feel such a sense of accomplishment.

If you can, tell your partner that you support his or her dream. That doesn't necessarily mean that you believe the dream can or should be realized. There are three different levels of honoring your partner's dreams—all of which are beneficial to your marriage. The first is to express understanding of the dream and be interested in learning more about it even though you don't share it. For example, Nathan could support Georgia's decision to take a course in mountain climbing and listen with enthusiasm when she talks about it. The second level would be to offer financial support for her dream. This would mean helping Georgia finance a mountain-climbing trip. The third level would be to become a part of the dream, to come to enjoy mountain climbing himself.

Acknowledging and respecting each other's deepest, most personal hopes and dreams is the key to saving and enriching your marriage.

You may find that you're able to "go all the way" with some of your partner's dreams while with others you can't get past the first level of understanding and interest. That's okay. The bottom line in getting past gridlock is not necessarily to become a part of each other's dreams (although your marriage will be more enriched to the extent that you can) but to honor these dreams. After all, you don't want the kind of marriage in which you triumph at the expense of crushing your partner.

STEP 3: SOOTHE EACH OTHER

Discussing dreams that are in opposition can be stressful. Since you'll accomplish nothing if either of you becomes flooded, take a break for some soothing before you attempt to slog through the gridlock. See the exercises in Chapter 8 ("Soothe Yourself and Each other," p. 176).

STEP 4: END THE GRIDLOCK

Now it's time to begin the ongoing task of making peace with this issue, accepting the differences between you, and establishing some kind of initial compromise that will help you continue to discuss the problem amicably. Understand that your purpose is not to solve the conflict—it will probably never go away completely. Instead, the goal is to "declaw" the issue, to try to remove the hurt so the problem stops being a source of great pain.

The way you start this process is by using the circle exercise ("Finding Common Ground") on page 182. You define the minimal core areas that you cannot yield on. To do this you need to look deep into your heart and try to separate the issue into two categories. In one put those aspects of the issue that you absolutely cannot give on without violating your basic needs or core values. In the second category put all aspects of the issue where you can be flexible, because they are not so "hot" for you. Try to make the second category as large as possible, and the first category as small as possible.

Share your two lists with your spouse. Working together, and using the skills you learned in Chapter 8, come up with a temporary compromise. Try it for about two months and then review where you stand. Don't expect this to solve the problem, only to help you both live with it more peacefully.

For example, Sally believes in living for the moment—she tends to be spontaneous and loose with her money. Gus's main goal in life is to feel secure. He moves slowly and carefully toward decisions and is very frugal. These differences lead them to clash when Sally insists that they buy a mountain cabin. Gus immediately says no— they can't afford it. Sally feels confident that they can.

For a year they gridlock over this issue. Whenever they try to discuss it, they become embroiled in a shouting match. Gus lets Sally know he considers her an irresponsible dreamer who always wants to squander the money he works so hard to earn. Sally accuses Gus of wanting to squash all the fun and joy out of her life.

To overcome the gridlock, Gus and Sally first have to explore the symbolic meaning of their positions on the cabin. In their first conversation to try to work on this issue, Sally says that her dreams are to pursue pleasure, to be able to truly relax, and to feel unity with nature, all of which she can realize by having a cabin. Although she also fears that Gus wants to turn her into a drone who's living just for tomorrow, she doesn't say this to him now. (She's said it frequently in the past.) Instead, she focuses on what she desires, not her anger and fears connected to Gus.

When it's Gus's turn to talk, he tells her that saving money has a lot of symbolic meaning for him. He longs to feel financially secure because he fears being destitute in his old age. He remembers seeing his grandparents suffering because they were so poor. His grandfather ended up in a state-run nursing home that Gus believes took away his dignity. One of his big goals in life is not to feel humiliated when he is old. Gus is also furious at Sally because he believes she is reckless and has a childish need for immediate gratification, which is a threat to his well-being and the life he's trying to build for both of them. However, he doesn't hurl those accusations at her this time. Instead, he sticks to explaining and describing his dream of financial security and its roots in his childhood.

Once Sally and Gus have discussed the symbolic meaning of their positions, a transformation takes place. Rather than seeing each other's dreams as threats, they see them for what they are: deep desires held by someone they love. Although their dreams are still in opposition, they are now motivated to find some common ground, to find a way to respect and perhaps even accommodate both of them. Here's how they do this:

1. *They define the* minimal *core areas that they cannot yield on.* Sally says she *must* have a cabin. Gus says he *must* save $30,000 in order to feel financially secure.

2. *They define their areas of flexibility.* Sally says she can settle for a small cabin on just a couple of acres, rather than the larger retreat she had envisioned. She can also be flexible on the *timing* of acquiring a cabin. She would like to buy one right now, but can wait a few years as long as she feels Gus supports the decision and they work toward it together. Gus says he can be flexible about how quickly he must save his $30,000 as long as he knows that they are consistently working toward that goal by saving a specific amount from each of their paychecks.

3. *They devise a temporary compromise that honors both of their dreams.* They will buy a small cabin, but not for another three years. Meanwhile, they will devote half of their savings to a down payment and half to a mutual fund. In a couple of months they will review this plan and decide if it's working.

Sally and Gus realize that their underlying perpetual problem will never go away. Sally is always going to be the visionary, having ideas for things like cabins and great trips, and Gus is going to worry about their financial security, their retirement fund, and so on. But by learning how to cope with their differences, they can avoid gridlock on any specific conflicts their fundamental differences trigger.

Here are a few other examples, using some of the couples from the "Detecting Dreams" exercise above, that show how you can learn to live with your differences through this process. While none of these conflicts are likely to mirror yours exactly, they should give you an idea of how couples with entrenched differences of opinion can overcome gridlock.

Couple 1

Gridlocked problem: Housecleaning—she wants him to be neater, he wants her to leave him alone about it.

The dream(s) within the conflict:
Hers: A sense of order and security at home
His: A sense of freedom in his own home

Nonnegotiable areas:
Hers: She can't abide dirty dishes left out in the kitchen or a dirty bathroom.
His: He can't abide having to clean up his papers right after he's finished with them.

Areas of flexibility: She can live with some clutter as long as there isn't any dirt. He can cope with cleaning dishes and bathrooms as long as he doesn't have to straighten up all the time.

Temporary compromise: They will both take responsibility for keeping bathrooms and kitchens clean. She will not bug him about his clutter more than once a week. But if he doesn't deal with it by then, she will pile it up and put it all on the floor of his home office.

Ongoing conflict: She will always hate clutter, he will always hate orderliness.

Couple 2

Gridlocked problem: Very different comfort levels with expressing emotions

The dream(s) within the conflict:
Hers: Being emotional is part of her self-identity and part of what gives meaning to her life.
His: He sees being emotional as a weakness.

Nonnegotiable areas:
Hers: She cannot stop reacting with great passion to life.
His: He cannot become a highly emotional person just to please her.

Areas of flexibility: They both accept that their spouse cannot change a basic personality trait.

Temporary compromise: They will be respectful of each other's difference in this area. He will be receptive to her need to talk about and share feelings. She will accept when he cannot do this.

Ongoing conflict: They will continue to have very different approaches to expressing emotion.

Couple 3

Gridlocked problem: He enjoys spending time with other people at parties, while she wants him to stay with her.

The dream(s) within the conflict:

His: To feel free and be able to explore by meeting new people at social events

Hers: To be the center of his attention

Nonnegotiable areas:

His: He must have the freedom to enjoy himself and meet new people.

Hers: She cannot abide her husband dancing with other women or touching them, even in a friendly way.

Areas of flexibility:

His: He doesn't have to be completely separate from his wife at parties.

Hers: She can tolerate her husband talking with other women for a few minutes.

Temporary compromise: They will stay together at parties for about half the time. The other half he can go off and mingle by himself. But he will not dance with or touch other women—and if she tells him she's upset by his behavior, he'll stop.

Ongoing conflict: He will always want to socialize, she will always wish he would pay attention to just her.

Now see if you can outline your own problem in the same way. First write a clear statement of what the problem is and which dream(s) of each of yours is fueling it. Then note which areas are nonnegotiable for each of you and which you are able to be flexible about. Finally, write out a temporary compromise that you agree to try for a brief period of time. It will be helpful if you also write a brief description of your ongoing conflict to confirm that you both understand it remains unresolved but can be lived with.

Step 5: Say Thank You

It may take more than one session to overcome gridlock on issues that have been deeply troubling to your marriage. These sessions can be stressful, no matter how diligently you attempt to accept each other's viewpoint without judgment.

This exercise lets you finish on a positive note. The goal here is to try to re-create the spirit of thanksgiving, in which you count your blessings and look inward to express gratitude for all you have. This may be particularly difficult to do after talking about gridlocked marital conflict, but that's all the more reason to try.

Exercise 2: Say Thank You

Select from the following list three things you really appreciate about your spouse. (Of course, you can add items not on the list.) Then tell your spouse what these three things are. This can be as simple as a statement like "I really like the way you are sensitive to my moods."

Your energy
Your strength
The way you are commanding
The way you let me direct things
How sensitive you are to me
How you support me and respond to my moods
Your ability to read me
The way you are when we make decisions
The way you let me be myself
Your skin
Your face
Your warmth
Your enthusiasm
Your hair
The way you touch me
How safe I feel with you

Your tenderness
Your imagination
Your eyes
The way I trust you
Your passion
How well you know me
Your gracefulness
The way you move
The way you kiss me
Your affection
Your playfulness
Your humor
How you look in clothes
Your loyalty to me
Your competence as a spouse
Your competence as a parent
What you are like as a friend
Your sense of style

Follow these five steps, and you'll be able to move out of grid-lock on your perpetual problems. Be patient with the process and each other. By their very nature, these problems are tenacious. To loosen their grip on your marriage will take commitment and faith on both your parts. You'll know you're making progress when the issue in question feels less loaded to you both—when you can discuss it with your sense of humor intact, and it no longer looms so large that it crowds out the love and joy in your relationship.

11

Principle 7:
Create Shared Meaning

We used to have a yuppie marriage," says Helen. "By that I mean it was very superficial. We got along okay and really loved each other, but I didn't feel that connected to Kevin. It was like we were roommates who made love." Helen, who calls herself a "devout feminist," had always prided herself on her independence. At first she thought it was great that she and Kevin had their own lives—their own careers, interests, and friends. But the longer they were married, and especially after they had children, the more she felt something was lacking. She didn't want to give up her strong sense of individual identity, but she wanted more from her marriage. After attending our workshop, she realized what it was: She wanted to feel more like she and Kevin were a family.

If your marriage adheres to my first six principles, there's a good chance that your relationship is stable and happy. But if you find yourself asking, "Is that all there is?" your situation may be similar to Helen and Kevin's. What may be missing is a deeper sense of shared meaning. Marriage isn't just about raising kids, splitting chores, and making love. It can also have a spiritual dimension that has to do with creating an inner life together—a culture rich with symbols and rituals, and an appreciation for your roles and goals that link you, that lead you to understand what it means to be a part of the family you have become.

Usually when we think of culture, we think in terms of large ethnic groups or even countries where particular customs and cuisine prevail. But a culture can also be created by just two people who have agreed to share their lives. In essence, each couple and each family create its own microculture. And like other cultures these small units have their customs (like Sunday dinner out), rituals (like a champagne toast after the birth of each baby), and myths—the stories the couple tell themselves (whether true, false, or embellished) that explain their sense of what their marriage is like, what it means to be part of their group.

Paula and Doug viewed themselves as the "runts" of their respective families. Both were considered the least intelligent, attractive, or likely to succeed of their siblings. But as it turned out, all of their brothers and sisters ended up unmarried or divorced, while Paula and Doug formed a happy, stable marriage, held steady jobs, and raised great kids in a nice home. Part of their marriage's culture, the story they tell themselves about themselves, is what a great team they make, how feisty they are, how they thumbed their noses at all the naysayers and succeeded against the odds.

Developing a culture doesn't mean a couple sees eye to eye on every aspect of their life's philosophy. Instead there is a meshing. They find a way of honoring each other's dreams even if they don't always share them. The culture that they develop together incorporates both of their dreams. And it is flexible enough to change as husband and wife grow and develop. When a marriage has this shared sense of meaning, conflict is much less intense and perpetual problems are unlikely to lead to gridlock.

It is certainly possible to have a stable marriage without sharing a deep sense of what is meaningful about your lives together. Your marriage can "work" even if your dreams aren't in sync. The last chapter showed you just how to navigate your way around perpetual problems so that you can live with them rather than ending up gridlocked. It is important to accept that you each will probably have some dreams that the other doesn't share but can respect. You may, for example, adhere to different religions but have enough respect for each other's spiritual journey to bridge the differences in your faiths.

But it is also true that a rewarding marriage is about more than sidestepping conflict. The more you can agree about the fundamentals in life, the richer, more meaningful, and in a sense easier your marriage is likely to be. You certainly can't force yourselves to have the same deeply held views. But some coming together on these issues is likely to occur naturally if you are open to each other's perspectives. *A crucial goal of any marriage, therefore, is to create an atmosphere that encourages each person to talk honestly about his or her convictions.* The more you speak candidly and respectfully with each other, the more likely there is to be a blending of your sense of meaning.

At our workshop Helen and Kevin were able to focus on the spiritual side of their lives together by talking over some of the questions you'll find later in this chapter. For the first time they spoke earnestly about their own families, their family histories, values, and symbols. When they returned home, Helen took out her family's old photo album and showed Kevin pictures of her great-grandparents who had come to America from Ireland. She told him the story she had heard countless times about her great-grandparents' marriage—how they had become engaged before her great-grandfather left for America. He then remained true and devoted to her great-grandmother during the four long years it took to save up enough money to bring her over, too. The message of this story, she had come to understand, was that loyalty is one of the backbones of marriage and family life. Until now she had never expressed that to Kevin so directly.

He himself reminisced about some of his own family's tales—especially about his grandmother who single-handedly ran a general store in rural Kansas and almost went broke because she was always giving away free food to poor neighbors during the Depression. The townspeople all knew that she reserved a certain amount of her goods for the town's needy families, who would come by every Monday night at closing time. "My dad always said that we Monahans tend to be generous to the point of being foolish," he told Helen. "But he always said it in a way that let you know he was very proud that we were like that." Kevin told Helen how that perspective had infused his own adulthood—from his insistence that they make large charitable contributions to the size of the Christmas tips he gave out.

That conversation marked a turning point in Kevin and Helen's marriage. From then on they talked frequently about values like loyalty and generosity that had been instilled in them by hearing family stories as children. Over time, as they heard each other's family stories and passed them on to their children, each other's stories became *their* stories, too—the stories of the new family that they had created. Helen accepted and incorporated the stories and values of the Monahans that were important to Kevin into her own life, and he did the same for her heritage.

As I said, the more shared meaning you can find, the deeper, richer, and more rewarding your relationship will be. Along the way you'll also be strengthening your marital friendship—as emphasized in my first three principles of a happy marriage. This in turn will make it even easier to cope with any conflicts that crop up. That's the beauty of the Seven Principles. They form a feedback loop that ensures that as you work on each principle, it becomes easier to work on the others.

Shared Meaning Questionnaire

To get a sense of how well you and your partner create a sense of shared meaning in your lives together, answer the following questions.

Your Rituals of Connection

I. We see eye to eye about the rituals that involve family dinnertimes in our home. **T F**

2. Holiday meals (like Thanksgiving, Christmas, Passover) are very special and happy times for us (or we both hate them). **T F**

3. End-of-the-day reunions in our home are generally special times. **T F**

4. We see eye to eye about the role of TV in our home. **T F**

5. Bedtimes are generally good times for being close. **T F**

6. During the weekends we do a lot of things together that we enjoy and value. **T F**

7. We have the same values about entertaining in our home (having friends over, parties, and so on). **T F**

8. We both value, or both dislike, special celebrations (like birthdays, anniversaries, family reunions). **T F**

9. When I become sick, I feel taken care of and loved by my spouse. **T F**

10. I really look forward to and enjoy our vacations and the travel we do together. **T F**

11. Spending our morning time together is special to us. **T F**

12. When we do errands together, we generally have a good time. **T F**

13. We have ways of becoming renewed and refreshed when we are burned out or fatigued. **T F**

Scoring: Give yourself one point for each "true" answer. If you score below three, your marriage could stand some improvement in this area. Be sure to work together on Exercise 1, which follows this questionnaire.

Your Roles

14. We share many similar values in our roles as husband and wife. **T F**

15. We share many similar values in our roles as mother and father. **T F**

16. We have many similar views about what it means to be a good friend to others. **T F**

17. My partner and I have compatible views about the role of work in one's life. **T F**

18. My partner and I have similar philosophies about balancing work and family life. **T F**

19. My partner supports what I would see as my basic mission in my life. **T F**

20. My partner shares my views on the importance of family and kin (sisters, brothers, moms, dads) in our life together. **T F**

Scoring: Give yourself one point for each "true" answer. If you score below three, your marriage could stand some improvement in this area. Be sure to work together on Exercise 2, which follows this questionnaire.

Your Goals

21. We share many of the same goals in our life together. **T F**
22. If I were to look back on my life in very old age, I think I would see that our paths had meshed very well. **T F**
23. My partner values my accomplishments. **T F**
24. My partner honors the personal goals I have that are unrelated to our marriage. **T F**
25. We share many of the same goals for others who are important to us (children, kin, friends, and community). **T F**
26. We have very similar financial goals. **T F**
27. We tend to have compatible worries about potential financial disasters. **T F**
28. Our hopes and aspirations, as individuals and together, for our children, for our life in general, and for our old age are quite compatible. **T F**
29. Our life dreams tend to be similar or compatible. **T F**
30. Even when different, we have been able to find a way to honor our life dreams. **T F**

Scoring: Give yourself one point for each "true" answer. If you score below three, your marriage could stand some improvement in this area. Be sure to work together on Exercise 3, which follows this questionnaire.

Your Symbols

31. We see eye to eye about what home means. **T F**
32. Our philosophies of what love ought to be are quite compatible. **T F**
33. We have similar values about the importance of peacefulness in our lives. **T F**

34. We have similar values about the meaning of family. **T F**

35. We have similar views about the role of sex in our lives. **T F**

36. We have similar views about the role of love and affection in our lives. **T F**

37. We have similar values about the meaning of being married. **T F**

38. We have similar values about the importance and meaning of money in our lives. **T F**

39. We have similar values about the importance of education in our lives. **T F**

40. We have similar values about the importance of fun and play in our lives. **T F**

41. We have similar values about the significance of adventure. **T F**

42. We have similar values about trust. **T F**

43. We have similar values about personal freedom. **T F**

44. We have similar values about autonomy and independence. **T F**

45. We have similar values about sharing power in our marriage. **T F**

46. We have similar values about being interdependent, being a "we." **T F**

47. We have similar values about the meaning of having possessions, of owning things (like cars, nice clothes, books, music, a house, and land). **T F**

48. We have similar values about the meaning of nature and of our relationship to the seasons. **T F**

49. We are both sentimental and tend to reminisce about things in our past. **T F**

50. We have similar views about what we want in retirement and old age. **T F**

Scoring: Give yourself one point for each "true" answer. If you score below three, your marriage could stand some improvement in this area. Be sure to work together on Exercise 4, which follows this questionnaire.

The exercises below are really just a list of questions for you both to answer and discuss. They are divided into the four categories that usually form the bases of shared meaning between husband and wife: rituals, roles, goals, and symbols. These questionnaires are not designed to be completed in an evening or even a month.

Consider them starting-off points for many future discussions and fireside chats.

To make the best use of these questions, focus on them one at a time. You can even write your thoughts about the question in your notebook. Then read each other's entries and discuss the question face to face.

Talk about your differences on this issue as well as your areas of common ground, areas that you can build upon. Find ways to honor both of your values, philosophies, and dreams. Although in many areas you may have separate needs, find ways to be supportive of each other's. Where you differ fundamentally, find ways of being respectful, of honoring the differences between you. (If this leads to an argument, work through the exercises in the chapters concerning Principles 4, 5, and 6 even if you've already done so.) Write out, if you like, your own family constitution, what you agree on about meaning and shared philosophy of life.

FAMILY RITUALS

It is a sad fact that less than a third of U.S. families eat dinner together regularly, and more than half of those that do have the television on during dinner. This effectively ends conversation during dinner. Creating informal rituals when you can connect emotionally is critical in a marriage.

Midnight Mass on Christmas Eve, lighting Kwaanza candles or the menorah, Thanksgiving at Grandma's, family reunions: Most of us were raised in families in which some rituals were considered important. By making them a part of your married life (or coming up with your own new ones together), they become your rituals as well and further your identity as a family.

Jesse came from a very close-knit extended family on his father's side—the Feldmans. From the time he was a little boy, the photographer at all of their family weddings was asked to spend a few minutes rounding up all fifty or so Feldmans for the Feldman Photo. Every member of his father's family, along with their spouses and children, would gather together, the bride and groom seated in the middle.

As a youngster, Jesse would roll his eyes and think posing for the photo was a big joke. But when he fell in love with and married Amanda, the ritual of the Feldman Photo took on a new meaning for him. Suddenly *he* was the groom sitting on the chair surrounded by his family. Now every time he looks at the Feldman Photo in his own wedding album, he feels a sense of pride and connection, knowing that Amanda has really joined his family. This feeling has been reinforced over the years, every time he attends another Feldman wedding and he and Amanda pose along with the rest of the clan.

Rituals don't necessarily have to derive from your respective childhoods and family histories. You can create your own. New rituals might come from a sense of what your family *lacked*. If you wished your family had gone on outings together on the weekends, you may want to incorporate that into your weekly routine. Or if you wish a bigger deal had been made out of the spiritual side of Christmas, you may decide to attend Midnight Mass together every year.

Sometimes rituals that don't seem quite so momentous can be important for a family. Nick and Halley, for example, always celebrate family birthdays by baking a cake together. This ritual started when their son, who was then a toddler, was allergic to eggs, so they were unable to buy birthday cakes at the bakery. Over the years their son got over his allergy, but the family ritual remained because it had become meaningful to them. It gave them a chance to come together and celebrate their family and the birthday in a very quiet, homey way.

Exercise 1: Rituals

In the following exercise, create your own family ritual of connection by talking about what you want. Discuss what these rituals (or lack of rituals) were like for you growing up, what the best times and the disasters were like for you. Then "script" your ritual so you will know who is expected to do what, and when. Make these rituals something you do regularly and can look forward to.

1. How do we or should we eat together at dinner? What is the meaning of dinnertime? What was dinnertime like in each of our families growing up?
2. How should we part at the beginning of each day? What was this like in our families growing up? How should our reunions be?
3. How should bedtime be? What was it like in our families growing up? How do we want this time to be?
4. What is the meaning of weekends? What were they like in our families growing up? What should they be like now?
5. What are our rituals about vacations? What were they like in our families growing up? What should they mean now?
6. Pick a meaningful holiday. What is the true meaning of this holiday to us? How should it be celebrated this year? How was it celebrated in each of our families growing up?
7. How do we each get refreshed and renewed? What is the meaning of these rituals?
8. What rituals do we have when someone is sick? What was this like in our families growing up? How should it be in our family?

Sociologist William Doherty emphasized the importance of rituals of connection in families. He and his wife, Leah, created the tradition of after-dinner coffee in which their children played or did homework while he and his wife had coffee and talked. They all cleaned up after dinner, then Bill made coffee and brought it out to Leah in the living room. It was a time of peace and connection. You can continue building in family rituals of connection you would cherish by creating the following:

• A weekly date for the two of you, away from children.
• Celebrations of triumph—ways of celebrating almost any minor or major achievement and creating a culture of pride and praise in your marriage.
• Rituals surrounding bad luck, setbacks, fatigue, or exhaustion. How can you support, heal, and renew yourselves?

• Community rituals for entertaining friends, caring for other people in your community, or opening your home to others you care about.

• Rituals surrounding lovemaking and talking about it. These are important events that get left till the very end of the day when everyone is exhausted. Couples often think that lovemaking should be spontaneous and don't want to plan for it. But if you think about when sex was at its best, usually it's during courtship. Those romantic dates were planned, down to what to wear, what perfume or cologne to use, where to go, the music and wine after dinner, and so on. So you need to plan for romance and sex. A ritual that makes you feel emotionally safe in talking about what is good and what needs improvement in lovemaking can be very helpful.

• Rituals for keeping in touch with relatives and friends. Family events and reunions can be planned.

• Birthdays and special events that recur. Examples are holidays of importance to you, religious celebration cycles, and anniversaries.

There are also important rites of passage that can be discussed, such as confirmations, bat mitzvahs, graduations, and weddings.

YOUR ROLES IN LIFE

Our sense of our place in the world is based to a great extent on the various roles we play—we are spouses, children, perhaps parents, and workers of one kind or another. From the standpoint of marriage, our perspective on our own roles and our mate's can either add to the meaningfulness and harmony between us or create tension.

Your marriage will feel deeper to the degree that your expectations of each other—what you feel your wife's or husband's place in your family ought to be—are similar. We're not talking here about seemingly superficial issues like who washes the dishes; we're talking about deeper feelings about what you expect of yourself and your spouse. For example, both Ian and Hilary believed that a husband should be a protector and provider and the wife more of a nurturer. Chloe and Evan believed in an egalitarian marriage in which the spouses supported each other emotionally and financially. Because in both of these marriages husband and wife had a similar philosophy about their roles, their marriages worked. Of course, were Ian married to Chloe and Hilary to Evan, there'd be more cause for friction.

Having similar views about parenting—for example, the values you consider important to pass on to your children—also adds to a marriage's meaning. So do questions about the kind of interaction you should now have with your parents and siblings. (Do you consider them part of your family, or outsiders you keep your distance from?) Even your views of what it means to work—and the meaning you attach to your own work—can deepen your sense of connection with your spouse. In other words, to the extent that you feel similarly about these issues, your marriage will be strengthened.

None of this means that you should (or, for that matter, *could*) see eye to eye on every philosophical or spiritual aspect of life. For example, couples who are in the same line of work may draw different meanings from it. Johnny is passionate about being a scientist. His work as a geologist forms a significant part of his identity and colors how he sees the world. He feels personally inspired by the scientific approach with its emphasis on objectivity and analysis, and he takes great pride in being a geologist. If you ask him what he is, he will say he is a geologist first. His wife, Molly, is also a geologist, but she doesn't identify quite so deeply with her profession. She sees herself as a woman first, rather than as a scientist. But this poses no difficulty in their marriage. They connect deeply in so many other areas of their lives together that this difference is never a sticking point.

Exercise 2: Roles

The more you can talk to each other frankly about your deeply held views about your roles in life, the more likely you are to reach a consensus that makes sense and comes naturally to your family. Musing over these questions separately and then together can help.

1. How do you feel about your role as a husband or wife? What does this role mean to you in your life? How did your father or mother view this role? How are you similar and different? How would you like to change this role?

2. How do you feel about your role as a father or mother? What does this role mean to you in your life? How did your father or mother view this role? How are you similar and different? How would you like to change this role?

3. How do you feel about your role as a son or daughter? What does this role mean to you in your life? How did your father or mother view this role? How are you similar and different? How would you like to change this role?

4. How do you feel about your role as a worker (your occupation)? What does this role mean to you in your life? How did your father or mother view this role? How are you similar and different? How would you like to change this role?

5. How do you feel about your role as a friend to others? What does this role mean to you in your life? How did your father or mother view this role? How are you similar and different? How would you like to change this role?

6. How do you feel about your role in your community? What does this role mean to you in your life? How did your father or mother view this role? How are you similar and different? How would you like to change this role?

7. How do you balance these roles in your life?

PERSONAL GOALS

Part of what makes life meaningful are the goals we strive to achieve. While we all have some very practical goals—like earning a certain income—we also have deeper, more spiritual goals. For one

person, the goal may be to find peace and healing after a tumul-
tuous, abusive childhood. For another it may be to raise children
who are good-hearted and generous. Many times we don't talk
about our deepest goals. Sometimes we haven't even asked ourselves these questions. But when we start, it gives us the opportunity to explore something that can have a profound impact on
ourselves and our marriage.

Not only will you increase the intimacy of your marriage by sharing your deepest goals with your spouse, but to the extent that you
work together to achieve shared goals, they can be a path toward
making your union even richer. For example, both Emilie and Alex
were committed to doing volunteer work for their church. Once
their kids were grown, they decided they wanted to leave a spiritual
legacy to their community. So he joined the board of directors of
the religious school, and she started an adult education program at
the church for people who wanted to become reacquainted with
their faith. "I would have done this on my own," says Emilie. "But
feeling in partnership with Alex about the importance of giving
something back to my community and my church has made it an
even more rewarding experience. I feel renewed not just in my faith
but in my marriage as well."

Exercise 3: Goals

To explore with your spouse the meaning of goals in your individual lives
and your marriage, ask yourselves the following questions.

1. Write a "mission statement" of what your mission in life is. Write your
   own obituary. What would you like it to say?
2. What goals do you have in life, for yourself, for your spouse, for your
   children? What do you want to accomplish in the next five to ten
   years?
3. What is one life dream that you want to fulfill before you die?
4. We often fill our time with things that demand our immediate
   attention—putting out fires, so to speak. But what are the truly impor-

tant things in your life that are great sources of energy and pleasure that you really need to block out time for, the important things that keep getting postponed or crowded out?

5. What is the role of spirituality in your lives? What was this role in your families growing up? How should this be in your family?

Shared Symbols

Another sign of shared meaning in a marriage is that your lives are surrounded by things that represent the values and beliefs you share. Often, these "things" are literally objects. Religious icons like a crucifix or mezuzah are the most obvious symbols of faith a couple may display in their home. But there are other, more personalized ones as well. For Jenna and Michael, their dining room table held special significance. They had saved up for many years to have it custom made by a local carpenter who was an expert carver. Every time they opened it up for family celebrations, its beauty and strength spoke to them of the beauty and stability of their own marriage. Another family kept a little statuette of a baby angel on the mantel in memory of their first baby, who was stillborn. The angel commemorated the baby but also represented their own resilience and deep love and support for each other, which had gotten them through this tragedy and allowed them to go on to have a large, happy family.

Some symbols are abstract but no less significant to a marriage. Family stories, for example, can be symbolic of a whole set of values. In that sense, Helen's story about her great-grandparents who kept their love alive even when separated by an ocean symbolized the family's deep sense of loyalty. Every time that story was retold (and almost by definition, family stories do get told over and over again through the years), it was symbolic of the great value they place on loyalty. Her husband Kevin's story of his great-grandmother's general store and her gracious generosity toward the poor was also a metaphor for another deeply held family value—that money is not as important as being connected to your community. Even a home itself can be of great symbolic meaning to a couple. They may view it not only as the place they eat and sleep but as the spiritual center of their lives together—the place where they consummate their love, where their children were conceived and grew, and so on.

Exercise 4: Symbols

The following questions will help you talk to each other about the significance of symbols in your marriage.

1. What symbols (such as photos or objects) show who our family is in the world, what we value about being _____ (supply your last names)?
2. Family stories are also symbols—they often stand for and teach a whole set of values. What are some stories about your family that go way back in history, stories you are proud of and want to be a part of the tradition your family continues?
3. What does a home mean to you? What qualities must it have for you? What was a home like in your families growing up?
4. What in your life is symbolic of your philosophy of how to lead a meaningful, good life? For example, giving to charity, or wearing a crucifix, or lighting a candle for dead ancestors may be symbolic of your sense of meaning. Do you feel that you are failing to do this to the degree you'd like?

Feeling a sense of unity with your spouse on most of the deep, burning issues is unlikely to occur overnight. Exploring these issues together is really an ongoing, lifelong process. The goal shouldn't be to agree on every aspect of what is profoundly meaningful to you, but to have a marriage where you are both open to each other's most dearly held beliefs. The more you create a marriage where these convictions can be readily divulged, the more joyous will be the journey through life that you share.

Afterword:
What Now?

No book (or therapist) can solve all of your marital problems. But by incorporating these Seven Principles into your marriage, you really can change the course of your relationship. Even making just a small and gentle change in the trajectory of your marriage can have a dramatic, positive effect over time. The catch, of course, is that you have to build on the change and keep it going. Improving your marriage is a kind of journey. Like all journeys it begins by suspending disbelief, taking one small step, and then seeing where you are and taking the next step. If you get stuck or take a few missteps, reread portions of this book with an eye toward charting where your marriage is now. Then you'll be able to figure how to help it along in the right direction.

Once you feel your marriage is "on course," here are some ideas to help you maintain momentum.

THE MAGIC FIVE HOURS

When we followed up on couples who attended our Seattle workshops, we wondered what would distinguish those couples whose marriages continued to improve from those whose marriages did not. Would we find that the successful group had dramatically overhauled their lives? Far from it. To our surprise, we discovered that they were devoting only an extra five hours a week to their marriage. Although each couple had their own style of spending these extra five hours, some clear patterns emerged. In general, what these couples were doing was giving their marriage a concentrated refresher course in the Seven Principles. The approach works so phenomenally well that I've come to call it the Magic Five Hours. Here's how you can do it, too:

Partings. Make sure that before you say good-bye in the morning you've learned about one thing that is happening in your spouse's life that day—from lunch with the boss to a doctor's appointment to a scheduled phone call with an old friend.
Time: 2 minutes a day × 5 working days
Total: 10 minutes

Reunions. Be sure to engage in a stress-reducing conversation at the end of each workday (see page 87).
Time: 20 minutes a day × 5 days
Total: 1 hour 40 minutes

Admiration and appreciation. Find some way every day to communicate genuine affection and appreciation toward your spouse.
Time: 5 minutes a day × 7 days
Total: 35 minutes

Affection. Kiss, hold, grab, and touch each other during the time you're together. Make sure to kiss each other before going to sleep. Think of that kiss as a way to let go of any minor irritations that have built up over the day. In other words, lace your kiss with forgiveness and tenderness for your partner.

Time: 5 minutes a day × 7 days
Total: 35 minutes

Weekly date. This can be a relaxing, low-pressure way to stay connected. Ask each other questions that let you update your love maps and turn toward each other. (Of course, you can also use these dates to talk out a marital issue or work through an argument you had that week, if necessary.) Think of questions to ask your spouse (like "Are you still thinking about redecorating the bedroom?" "Where should we take our next vacation?" or "How are you feeling about your boss these days?").

Time: 2 hours once a week
Total: 2 hours
Grand Total: Five hours!

As you can see, the amount of time involved in incorporating these changes into your relationship is quite minimal. Yet these five hours will help enormously in keeping your marriage on track.

**Remember, working briefly on your marriage
every day will do more for your health and longevity
than working out at a health club.**

THE MARITAL POOP DETECTOR

Some marriage "experts" claim that a significant cause of unhappiness in marriage is that husbands and wives just have overblown expectations of each other. By lowering these expectations, the argument goes, you become less likely to feel disappointment. But Donald Baucom, Ph.D., of the University of North Carolina has debunked this idea thoroughly by studying couples' standards and expectations of each other. He has found that people with the highest expectations for their marriage usually wind up with the highest-quality marriages. This suggests that by holding your relationship to high standards, you are far more likely to achieve the kind of marriage you want than you are by looking the other way and letting things slide.

Our research on newlyweds confirms what Baucom found. The couples we studied who adjusted to high levels of negativity (irritability, emotional distance) in their marriage ended up *less* happy or satisfied years later. Those who *refused* to put up with lots of negativity—who insisted on gently confronting each other when, say, contempt or defensiveness threatened to become pervasive, wound up happy and satisfied years later.

These findings suggest that every marriage ought to be equipped with a built-in early warning system that lets you know when your marital quality is in danger of deteriorating. I call this system the Marital Poop Detector because it's really a way of saying something just doesn't smell right!

Someone once said that to men the five most frightening words in the English language are "Let's talk about our relationship." Truth is, those words can be just as frightening to plenty of women. The best way to conquer this fear is to talk about issues in your relationship while they are still minor, before they build up steam and become combustible. A Marital Poop Detector lets you do that.

Usually one member of a couple tends to take the lead in sniffing out trouble. More often than not it is the wife. When her husband gets cranky or withdrawn, she calls him on it and finds out what's wrong. But there's no reason why you *both* can't perform this function in your marriage.

Here is a list of questions to ask yourself once a week. It will guide you in assessing how your relationship is faring. Just remember to discuss these things using a softened startup and without being critical of your spouse. The best approach is to say something like "Hey, I really feel out of touch with you. What's going on?" (Be careful not to address any issues right before bedtime. This could interfere with your sleep.)

Instructions: Use this questionnaire to assess how things went in your marriage today (or lately), and whether you want to bring up any issues. Check as many as you think apply. If you checked more than four, think about talking things over *gently* with your partner, within the next three days.

1. I have been acting irritable.
2. I have been feeling emotionally distant.
3. There has been a lot of tension between us.
4. I find myself wanting to be somewhere else.
5. I have been feeling lonely.
6. My partner has seemed emotionally unavailable to me.
7. I have been angry.
8. We have been out of touch with each other.
9. My partner has little idea of what I am thinking.
10. We have been under a great deal of stress, and it has taken its toll on us.
11. I wish we were closer right now.
12. I have wanted to be alone a lot.
13. My partner has been acting irritable.
14. My partner has been acting emotionally distant.
15. My partner's attention seems to be somewhere else.
16. I have been emotionally unavailable to my partner.
17. My partner has been angry.
18. I have little idea of what my partner is thinking.
19. My partner has wanted to be alone a lot.
20. We really need to talk.
21. We haven't been communicating very well.
22. We have been fighting more than usual.
23. Lately small issues escalate.
24. We have been hurting each other's feelings.
25. There hasn't been very much fun or joy in our lives.

FORGIVE YOURSELF

After working through the Seven Principles, it is probably very clear to you that there is no such thing as constructive criticism. All criticism is painful. Unlike complaints—specific requests for change—criticism doesn't make a marriage better. It inevitably makes it worse. What causes a spouse to be chronically critical? We have discovered that there are two sources. The first is an emotionally unresponsive partner. Put simply, if Natalie keeps complaining to Jonah about leaving his newspapers on the bathroom floor and he just ignores her, eventually she is likely to start criticizing him—calling him a slob instead of politely reminding him about recycling. This change in Natalie's approach is understandable, but it is hardly helpful to her marriage since her criticism will make Jonah even less responsive. The only way out of this cycle is for both of them to change—which won't be easy. It takes courage to be less critical of an unresponsive mate, and it takes courage to turn toward a partner who's always harping on your flaws. But both changes are necessary to end the cycle.

The other source of criticism in marriage comes from within. It is connected to self-doubt that has developed over the course of one's life, particularly during childhood. In other words, it begins as criticism of oneself. Aaron cannot really appreciate or enjoy his own accomplishments. When he has a setback in his business, he feels deep down that he is worthless. When his business is successful, he doesn't allow himself to be proud. There's a voice inside him that says this is not good enough. He continually searches for approval but cannot enjoy it or even accept it when it is offered.

What happens to Aaron when he marries Courtney? Since he has trained his mind to see what is wrong, what is missing, and not to appreciate what is there, it's difficult for him to rejoice in what's right with Courtney or their marriage. So instead of appreciating Courtney's wonderful qualities, including her sweetness, her devotion, and the deep emotional support she offers him when he is in danger of losing a major client, he focuses on what he considers her flaws—that she is highly emotional, somewhat awkward socially, and not as meticulously clean around the house as he'd like.

The story of Aaron and Courtney is what's wrong 85 percent of the time in most marriages. If you consider yourself inadequate, you are always on the lookout for what is not there in yourself and your partner. And, let's face it: Anyone you marry will be lacking in certain desirable qualities. The problem is that we tend to focus on what's missing in our mate and overlook the fine qualities that *are* there—we take those for granted.

If you recognize yourself in the description of the self-critic, the best thing you can do for yourself and your marriage is to work on accepting yourself with all of your flaws. As I look back on my own life so far, I realize the immense difference it has made in my role as a husband and a father for me to forgive myself for all of my imperfections.

One route toward this forgiveness may be your personal spiritual beliefs. My religion, Judaism, has helped me to cherish and nourish what is good and strong in myself and in my relationship. In Judaism prayer is primarily used either for thanksgiving or to praise. Yet the religion claims that God does not require endless praise, flattery, or thanks. So what is the purpose of these prayers? They are not meant for God's benefit but to help the person who is praying. These prayers are designed to help us appreciate the works of God, this beautiful world we have inherited, and to notice and be thankful for the blessings we continually receive. Whatever your religion, there is a message in here for your marriage: Expressions of thanksgiving and praise are the antidotes to the poison of criticism and its deadly cousin, contempt. The following exercise will start you on this path.

An Exercise in Thanksgiving

Step 1. For one week try to be aware of your tendency to criticize, to see what is missing, to focus on what is not there and comment on it. Try instead to focus on what is right. Notice what you have and what others contribute. Search for things to praise. Begin with simple things. Praise the world. Appreciate your own breathing, the sunrise, the beauty of a rainstorm, the wonder in your child's eyes. Utter some silent words of thanksgiving (to no one in particular) for these small wonders in your day. This will begin to change your focus on the negative.

Step 2. Give at least one genuine, heartfelt praise to your spouse each day for an entire week. Notice the effects of this exercise on your partner and yourself. If you are able, extend the exercise one more day. Then add another day. Extend the exercise to others—for example, to your children. When you meet someone new, look for what is special about this person. Appreciate these qualities. Remember, this all has to be genuine and heartfelt. Don't be phony. Notice these positive qualities. Enjoy them. Try to tell people what you notice and genuinely appreciate about them. Just find one thing for each person. Ignore the shortcomings.

As you stretch the period of thanksgiving one day beyond a week, and then another day, and then another, you'll receive a great gift: You will begin to forgive yourself. Grace and forgiveness will enter your world. This is what the spiritual "Amazing Grace" is all about. You begin to enjoy your own accomplishments, rather than consider them inadequate.

One of the most meaningful gifts a parent can give a child is to admit his or her own mistake, to say, "I was wrong here" or "I'm sorry." This is so powerful because it also gives the child permission to make a mistake, to admit having messed up and still be okay. It builds in the forgiveness of self. In the same way, saying "I'm sorry" and meaning it to your spouse is a very significant event. The more you can imbue your relationship with the spirit of thanksgiving and the graceful presence of praise, the more meaningful and fulfilling your lives together will be.

Index

About the Authors

JOHN GOTTMAN, a leading research scientist on marriage and family, is the Mifflin Professor of Psychology at the University of Washington and Codirector of the Seattle Marital and Family Institute. He graduated magna cum laude from Fairleigh Dickinson University with a B.S. in mathematics-physics. He obtained his M.S. in mathematics-psychology at the Massachusetts Institute of Technology, and his Ph.D. in clinical psychology from the University of Wisconsin. Dr. Gottman is the author of more than one hundred professional journal articles and several books, as well as the recipient of numerous prestigious awards for his extensive contributions to marriage and family research. As codirector of the Seattle Marital and Family Institute, Dr. Gottman conducts several intensive weekend workshops per year for clinicians and for couples, based on his scientific research on how long-term happy and stable marriages work. Contact the Institute at their toll-free number, (888) 523-9042, or on the web at www.Gottman.com.

NAN SILVER is a Contributing Editor of *Parents* magazine. She is a former Editor-in-Chief of *Health* magazine and coauthor, with Dr. Gottman, of *Why Marriages Succeed or Fail*. She lives in Montclair, New Jersey, with her husband and children.

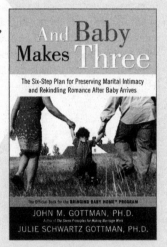

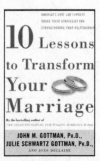